Student's Guide
for *Writing*
College Papers

STUDENT'S GUIDE
for Writing College Papers

Kate L. Turabian

Third Edition

The University of Chicago Press
Chicago and London

The University of Chicago Press, Chicago 60637
The University of Chicago Press, Ltd., London

Published 1963. Third Edition 1976
Printed in the United States of America
80 79 78 77 76 10 9 8 7 6 5 4 3 2 1

Library of Congress Cataloging in Publication Data

Turabian, Kate L.
    Student's guide for writing college papers.

    Bibliography: p.
    Includes index.
    1.   Report writing.   I.   Title.
LB2369.T82   1977   808'.042   76–435
ISBN 0–226–81622–2
ISBN 0–226–81623–0 pbk.

Contents

Contents

Contents

Prefatory Note

This third edition of the *Student's Guide* includes sections on numbers and punctuation, which did not appear in earlier editions, and a greatly expanded List of Reference Works.

The enormous development in every area of our culture has prompted a large amount of writing, not least the writing of reference works in every field. A specialist in bibliography, Donald F. Bond, Professor Emeritus of English, University of Chicago, has selected the works included in this *Guide,* giving priority to those he considers most likely to be useful to students who are writing their first college papers. Also helpful are the annotations accompanying the items in the list and the brief discussions of the uses of various types of reference works (e.g., subject indexes, biographical aids, dictionaries and encyclopedias, gazetteers and handbooks).

1 Introduction

1:1   This book is to help you in your research project, from the choosing of the topic to the writing of the paper in its final form.

1:2   The greater number of undergraduate research papers are library studies—"a close searching" (to quote Webster's first definition of "research") of written materials, which involves not only a studious inquiry into the subject but also a critical examination, assessment, and interpretation of the materials found. A smaller number of papers make considerably less use of library sources, relying mainly upon laboratory investigations or upon investigations among people "in the field." All of them make use in some measure of the techniques which it is the purpose of this guide to explore.

1:3   Although research as the college student knows it is not the same kind of enterprise as that of the chemists, physicists, and biologists to whom we owe the partial conquest of disease and an ever widening knowledge of the universe, it affords some valuable training—training that the "pure" researcher as well as the student can use to advantage. For both must set forth the results of their investigations in written reports that are correctly, clearly, and forcefully expressed, well organized and properly documented.

1:4   If it is not carried on efficiently, the research project can be time-consuming and tedious. This guide is designed to relieve you of some of the tedium, to show you short cuts, to keep you from getting bogged down, to help you add to your knowledge.

1:5   The research paper, which is ordinarily assigned after some months of rigorous training in freshman English composition and in the art of written communication, is intended to show the student's ability to express ideas—both his own and others' —clearly, correctly, and effectively. It is intended to show also the student's competence in areas less thoroughly explored in the course: his ability to discover and make use of all the resources of a library in gathering materials on a given subject, as well as his ingenuity in finding other sources yielding additional information. And, still further, it is intended to show the student's skill in selecting from the material available those facts and ideas that are immediately pertinent to his topic, in organizing and documenting his information properly, and in presenting it clearly, logically, effectively, and correctly with respect to grammar, spelling, and punctuation.

1:6   A good deal of writing is called for throughout the college curriculum, and the skills acquired in producing the first research paper will be increasingly valuable as the student moves to more advanced and specialized courses. In extra-curricular activities scarcely less than in academic work, the student will make use of some parts of the research techniques in a variety of ways: to report a committee's findings or to apply for a scholarship or fellowship, a student loan, or a job. After college the methods used in writing the research paper will continue to serve men and women in business, in the professions, and in the civic and social activities they will pursue. Fact-finding, with its analysis and reporting, is so important an aspect of our present-day civilization that every educated person must be prepared to undertake it.

2 Choosing a Topic

WHAT TO CONSIDER

2:1   Choose for your research paper a topic in which you are interested or, better perhaps, one in which you think you could develop an interest. Something encountered in study or reading that piqued your curiosity at a time when there was no opportunity to pursue the subject might well be a good choice. There is something of the detective in all of us. If nothing appealing comes to mind, you may find an idea worth considering in the following list:

Current live issues

National or international events

Political, educational, religious, artistic, or humanitarian movements, organizations, or persons connected with them

Art forms: architecture, pictures, sculpture, ceramics, theater, dance, music, literature

Figures in the world of politics, business, agriculture, sports, arts, sciences, professions, religions

Processing of goods for food, clothing, shelter, transport

Plant or animal breeding and nurture

Your city, town, or region: its history, institutions, economy, outstanding persons

Your school, college, or university: its history, notable achievements or persons; student social life, organizations, sports

An experience in the life of a forebear

Your own experiences in travel, vacations

Your hobbies or special interests

2:2   You should avoid a topic calling for a background of knowledge that you do not have. There are, for example, many fascinating subjects based on recent developments in the biological and the physical sciences, but to treat them satisfactorily presupposes a considerable grounding in chemistry, physics, and mathematics.

2:3   Although the satisfactory handling of a controversial topic requires the utmost discrimination in analyzing and appraising the evidence, it can be stimulating and rewarding in high degree. You may have your own answers regarding such matters as political campaign finance reform, the energy crisis, compulsory school busing, public transportation, and subscription television; and more often than not your answers may derive from little more than personal tastes, prejudices, or loyalties. Following your own preferences, you may write a paper which seeks to support your point of view. In examining the sources for such a study, in sifting and analyzing the evidence, the greatest alertness is needed to prevent your preconceived ideas and prejudices from blinding you to the intended meanings of the writers, to keep you from rationalizations favorable to your stand. Setting aside your prejudices, you may undertake a more fruitful study in which you strive to get at the truth through a strictly impartial, responsible, and thorough examination of the sources and a careful assessment of all the evidence, reporting the findings both for and against the proposition. In such a report you and your readers can find logical bases for sound judgment and well-grounded conclusions.

2:4   The topic must of course be one upon which you are able to get enough material, and that sufficiently varied, to ensure thorough coverage. A paper based wholly upon the summary of three or four encyclopedia articles does not fulfill the purposes of the research project. To be satisfactory, your topic should be one upon which you can locate pertinent information and interesting detail in books and articles as well as in encyclopedias. Moreover, you should make it a part of your aim to gain some experience in the use of primary sources.* Try to get at least some of your facts from original

---

* *Primary sources* consist of manuscript materials such as state archives or parish registers, and letters, diaries, wills, and other manu-

sources, and make your own evaluations, draw your own conclusions, instead of taking them ready-made from writings based upon the original research of others. The satisfaction is certain to be well worth the effort. For example, a paper on low-cost housing for retired persons could be founded upon such primary sources as personal interviews with possible tenants, with welfare workers, public officials, and real estate operators, combined with secondary sources in the form of published discussions and statistics. In the paper on "Liberty and Equality," here reproduced as Appendix A, the writer made use of one primary source, the Constitution of the United States. A valuable feature of the Controlled-Materials method (see footnote, p. 6) is its provision of primary source materials.

HOW TO NARROW THE TOPIC

2:5   In general, students tend to think first of subjects too large to be treated satisfactorily in the length of paper assigned. This does not mean necessarily that the subject should be discarded but rather that ways to narrow it should be considered. If you try to cover too much ground, the treatment is bound to be superficial. To limit a topic by omitting essential data will not do. Whatever the subject, a thorough examination of the evidence and a full and interesting presentation are required. Narrow your topic, therefore, in some such way as the following.

2:6   Let us suppose that you have chosen as your general subject the American Indian. Realizing that it would have to be

---

scripts found in library collections, in private homes, or elsewhere; an author's own works, published or not; original notes on surveys, investigations, or interviews; and accounts by first recorders of an event as given in contemporary newspaper articles. *Secondary sources* include all encyclopedias and other reference works, histories, and biographies, and any article or book which deals with the work of others. To be specific: if you were writing on Emily Dickinson's work, your primary sources would be her poems, perhaps her letters and those of her family and friends, and any contemporary reviews you might find; your secondary sources would be some of the many articles and books already published about her life and work. The distinction between primary and secondary sources is really that of first-hand and second-hand reports.

narrowed, you noted as a first step the following progression from the general to the specific:

> The American Indian
> The North American Indian
> The Sioux Indians
> Chief Little Crow

But none of the topics could be handled in all its aspects within the limits of the assignment. It would be necessary to choose (*a*) a particular aspect, or (*b*) a particular period of time, or (*c*) an event, or (*d*) some combination of two of these. Thus under (*a*) you might consider the position of women and girls among the Sioux, or their food customs, or their clothing and personal adornment. Under (*b*) you might treat of Indian-white relations in the late colonial period; under (*c*) the part played by the Sioux in a particular battle; and under (*d*) the effect on Indian education of the Indian Reorganization Act of 1934.

2:7   If your choice of a topic is restricted to one from a list provided in your course, the task of selection is greatly simplified.* But if you are free to choose your own topic—always with the final approval of the instructor—you will save time and effort later on by spending a few hours first in considering a subject that is within your ability, in reading some general articles on it, and in compiling a preliminary bibliography.

2:8   But first you should know more about the library, since its resources are the indispensable tool for your research, and success depends greatly upon your efficient use of that tool.

* Many colleges use the Controlled-Materials method in teaching the research paper project. For this, there are now available a number of books, each on a general subject, which provide collections of primary source materials and list subtopics suitable for preliminary research articles and others for full-scale research papers.

3   Collecting Material

USING THE LIBRARY

3:1   Up to the assignment of a research paper, you may not have "discovered" the library in all its aspects. Now you will want to familiarize yourself with its manifold resources and learn to use them efficiently. In some colleges and universities a guided tour of the library is part of the orientation program for freshmen or is given during the freshman English course prior to the assignment of the research paper. Often a printed guide to the library is provided. If you have not had the advantage of one or both of these offerings, you will do well to take a tour of your own and to make a guidebook, including a ground plan or a floor plan, however simple.

3:2   Libraries are organized for the most part on much the same general plan, although they show individual differences, of course. The main divisions found in every college library are: reference section, card catalog, stacks, reserve section, loan desk, and information desk. Most colleges and universities also have special collections, which include rare books and manuscripts as well as materials for specialized research, and specialized departmental libraries. Some or all of these are frequently housed in buildings apart from the main library.

3:3   Library holdings in general are classified as reference materials and call materials. The first include works so much consulted that they need to be readily accessible at all times. These are encyclopedias, both general and special, bibliographies, biographical collections, dictionaries, guides, handbooks, yearbooks, atlases, and indexes. Call materials include

7

roughly the remaining resources of the library. Reference works are placed on open shelves in one or more reading rooms and are available to anyone. Call materials are kept in the stacks (which normally are not open to undergraduates) and are available to students on their presentation to the loan (or circulation) desk of call slips.

THE INFORMATION DESK

3:4   Your tour should begin at the information desk. There you may find material for distribution that has not interested you before now. You will need to know where to find magazines and newspapers. Libraries follow varying practices in their handling of periodicals (i.e., magazines, scholarly journals, newspapers). You may learn that some of these materials are available on microfilm and that a viewing machine, which enlarges the microfilm, is provided for library users. You may want to learn the conditions for using the interlibrary loan service, through which your library can borrow for you materials which it does not have. You will want to know what special collections and special libraries there are and their locations. You will need to know whether there is one central card catalog listing all the holdings of the library or whether there are separate catalogs for some collections and, if the latter, where they are to be found. And, since the arrangement of catalog cards is not uniform for all libraries, you must understand the filing scheme of the card catalog before you can use it efficiently. Here are questions you should ask about the filing system, recording the answers in your personal guidebook.

Are abbreviations alphabetized as though written in full? That is, *Dr.* filed as Doctor; *Ft.* filed as Fort; *St.* filed as Saint; *U.S.* filed as United States, etc.?

Are names beginning with *M'*, *Mc*, and *Mac* alphabetized as they stand or as though each were spelled *Mac?*

What scheme of alphabetization is used for names with prefixes such as *de, von, le, la?*

Are Germanic words containing vowels with an umlaut alphabetized as they appear with the umlaut or as though *ä* were *ae, ö* were *oe,* and *ü* were *ue?*

Is alphabetization word-by-word or letter-by-letter? That is, do all the entries beginning with the *word* "new" follow each other in alphabetic sequence before words of which the *first syllable* is "new-" (word-by-word); or are individual words disregarded and a strict alphabetic order maintained through a second or even a third word (letter-by-letter)? Under the word-by-word scheme "New York" would precede "Newark"; under the letter-by-letter scheme, the opposite order would obtain.

How are anonymous works cataloged?

How are the works of authors writing under pseudonyms cataloged?

What other filing rules are there?

3:5   Further questions pertinent to your own situation may occur to you. The information desk can undoubtedly refer you to other sources for answers it cannot supply.

THE REFERENCE ROOM

3:6   Spend some time in the reference room, noting the various kinds of materials and where each kind is located. Notice whether there is a card catalog of the room's contents. At the librarian's desk you can learn what rules and regulations govern the use of the room and its resources. In some reference rooms the newest books, and possibly some others, are available only upon application to the librarian and must be signed for. One regulation is universal: reference works must never be removed from the reference room, even for the shortest period, since they are meant to be accessible at all times. Also, since accessibility depends upon the exact placement of the books, most libraries guard against misplacement by asking readers not to return books to the shelves.

General Reference Works

3:7   In beginning to gather notes for a research paper you will first want to obtain a general view of the topic you have chosen and to assemble for your paper a list of useful books and articles which deal with your subject or with some particular aspect of it. In other words, the first step is twofold: to obtain a good background of information on your subject (or of the larger field of which it is a part) and to assemble a reading list or "bibliography" which will be of use when you come to organize and document your paper. As you read, make a note of such references which you think will be useful and enter each on a separate "bibliography card." These will provide a solid basis for the research which you will undertake in organizing and writing your paper.

3:8   Appendix B (pp. 183–244) contains a list of the more important reference works in all fields of knowledge. They have been chosen for their general usefulness and for the likelihood that most, if not all, can be found in every college library. To learn about other works that might be helpful in research, consult either of the two standard bibliographical guides, by A. J. Walford and Constance M. Winchell, listed on page 185. Both supply full information on reference works of all kinds and in various languages. These reference works are classified and described—some at considerable length—and most are evaluated as well. The Walford *Guide* is more up to date, since its third edition is now in progress. The most recent edition of the Winchell *Guide* appeared in 1967, but three supplements have since been published and a complete revision (the ninth edition) is in preparation. The two *Guide*s will be of great help in following up any aspect of your research.

3:9   You may find as you begin your investigation that a bibliography has already been published on your subject. The best way to find out if this is the case is to consult the standard "bibliography of bibliographies" by Theodore Besterman (p. 185). This is arranged alphabetically by subjects, but the index volume should also be consulted. Note that Besterman includes only bibliographies which have been separately published as such. Of course, most histories and general treatises on any subject are likely to contain bibliographies (usually at the end of the book), and many scholarly articles published in periodicals will provide bibliographical footnotes. To find out about these you should look at the *Bibliographic Index,* the standard current bibliography of bibliographies. Published monthly, it will enable you to become aware of the latest and most up-to-date references in any area of research.

3:10   As you begin working with reference books, you must realize that their efficient use requires a thorough understanding of the way they are put together—their scheme of headings and subheadings, of cross-references, and of alphabetization, the meaning of abbreviations and symbols. Explanation of all such matters and other guides to the use of the book usually appear in the front matter of the volume, and they should be read in their entirety. Then, by comparing the information with entries in the main part of the work, you will soon understand the "system."

3:11   Learn the importance of the date of publication of a work. If your topic lies in a field of rapidly expanding knowledge or treats of a person or an event only recently become "news," the date alone may determine whether a work will be of value to you. Look at the title page, either the face or the reverse, for the date of publication, which sometimes is expressed only in the copyright date. To gain some idea of the scope, limitations, and special features of the work, go over the preface and the table of contents. Look at the appendix, if there is one; and, finally, examine the index with some care, noting its general pattern and whether smaller subjects are brought together under large headings, such as a country. Only after such a careful examination will you be able to make the best possible use of a work of reference.

3:12   *Encyclopedias.* For introductory information on a topic, the general encyclopedias are usually consulted first. They treat of a great number of subjects throughout the whole circle of human knowledge. And, although many of the articles are contributed by specialists, they are written primarily for the layman and therefore employ a minimum of technical terms. Moreover, besides giving an overview of the subject, many articles are valuable for their "bibliographies," which mention other works on the subject and make cross-references to other articles.* These give the student a starter for his own bibliography.

---

* A bibliography is "a list or catalog of writings . . . relating to a particular subject, period, or author."—*Webster's Third New International Dictionary* . . . (Springfield, Mass.: G. & C. Merriam Co., 1961).

3:13   The general encyclopedias best known in the United States are the *Encyclopaedia Britannica* and the *Encyclopedia Americana.* Less well known but considered thoroughly reliable are three others: *Chambers's Encyclopaedia, Collier's Encyclopedia,* and the *Columbia Encyclopedia.*

3:14   The *Encyclopaedia Britannica* has long enjoyed a reputation as the most useful encyclopedia in the English language. First published in three volumes, "by a society of gentlemen in Scotland" (Edinburgh, 1771), it has included contributions from many distinguished scholars, notably in the seventh edition (1839–42), the ninth (1875–89), and the eleventh (1910–11). Long and comprehensive articles, especially in the ninth and eleventh editions, continue to be highly regarded by scholars and are still of considerable value to students in the humanities. The most recent edition, the fifteenth (1974), organized on an entirely new plan, presents the latest findings in the sciences and up-to-date evaluations of knowledge in the humanities—all written in language which can be understood by the layman in any field. The introductory volume (*Propaedia*) affords a comprehensive view of all areas of learning and their relationships to each other in the "circle of knowledge." The encyclopedia itself is in two sections: a *Micropaedia* (10 volumes) containing shorter articles for ready reference with summaries of the longer articles and cross-references; and a *Macropaedia* (19 volumes) which contains lengthy scholarly articles providing "knowledge in depth." Used properly, the new *Britannica* has immense value for any research project.

3:15   The *Encyclopedia Americana,* which began publication early in the twentieth century, has for the most part shorter articles and consequently is valuable for quick reference on almost any subject. It is continuously revised, so that one should be sure to consult a recent printing. It is particularly noteworthy for its information on American towns and cities and for clear and accurate explanation of technical and scientific matters.

3:16   *Chambers's Encyclopaedia,* originally published by the well-known Edinburgh firm of Chambers in the mid-nineteenth century, has undergone several complete revisions, notably in 1950 and 1967. The latest edition contains shorter articles, mainly by British contributors, and apparently aims at a wider audience than did the earlier editions.

3:17   *Collier's Encyclopedia,* a comparative newcomer in the field, seems to be designed for readers at the college level and hence is excellent for obtaining a quick and up-to-date view of a research subject, written in clear and concise language. Unlike the arrangement in other encyclopedias, the bibliographies for all the articles in *Collier's* are placed together in the final volume.

3:18   The *Columbia Encyclopedia,* since it compresses information in all fields into a single volume, does not provide extensive coverage for any subject but has very good and up-to-date articles and an extraordinarily vast amount of information in such relatively small compass.

3:19   Most of the larger encyclopedias are kept up to date by annual supplements, which include calendars listing the principal events, discoveries, and persons in the news of the preceding year as well as articles on every significant aspect of life throughout the globe. The dates of events listed in these supplements afford useful clues to articles on such events in newspapers and magazines. The volumes are well indexed.

3:20   *Subject Indexes to Books and Periodicals.* Encyclopedias, it will be seen, since they are unlimited in scope, are of immense value at the beginning of research in any field. The same is true of the Subject Indexes, to books and to periodicals, listed in Appendix B. Not restricted to any field, they open the way to research on any subject, whether in the humanities or the sciences. Two of the great libraries in the world, the British Museum Library (now called the British Library) and the Library of Congress, contain millions of books; their catalogs have been published, but arranged alphabetically by authors. Fortunately subject indexes to both collections have been published, so that one can readily find abundant references to any subject under investigation (see p. 186 under "British Museum" and p. 188 under "U.S. Library of Congress"). These subject indexes not only give information on books of the past but also are kept up to date by supplements at regular intervals. For even more up-to-date references there are important subject indexes to recently published books: the *American Book Publishing Record,* the *British National Bibliography,* and the *Cumulative Book Index* (see pp. 186–87). The first two, published weekly and cumulated monthly, contain titles of new books arranged by subject according to the Dewey decimal system. The third, "a world list of books in the English language," provides a threefold index, by author, title, and subject. All three subject indexes will be found in most college libraries and are of the greatest value, no matter what subject is under investigation. Finally, do not forget that the main card catalog in your library, although it is arranged primarily by authors, has many subject entries also which will be an important source in constructing your own bibliography (see below under "Using the Catalog," pp. 25–26).

3:21   In addition to these subject indexes to books, there are a number of important indexes to articles in periodicals. These too are unrestricted in subject matter and will be useful in the investigation of any topic, whether in the sciences or humanities. They are an indispensable tool, for if your research is to be complete, it must cover periodical literature as well as books. Especially if your topic is one of current interest or is in a rapidly changing field, you are likely to find the greatest amount of detail, the latest thought, and the most recent discoveries set forth in periodicals.

3:22   Some students are not aware that articles, short stories, and essays in newspapers and magazines are not listed in the card catalog either under their titles or under the authors' names unless they appear also as *separate publications.* Similarly, short stories in a collection are not individually cataloged, their titles appearing in general only on the catalog card giving the title of the collection. The title is frequently that of one of the stories.

3:23   Magazines and newspapers are represented in the catalog under their individual names (*Time, Harper's, Elementary School Journal, New York Times,* etc.), together with notations of when publication began, whether it continues or has ceased, and pertinent information about the publisher.

3:24   Articles, short stories, plays, essays, speeches, sermons, and poems which are published only in collections must be located through the periodical indexes, of which there are a considerable number in the reference rooms of most libraries. Each issue of an index lists in its preliminary pages the periodicals it covers.

3:25   Probably the most generally useful is the *Readers' Guide to Periodical Literature,* published twice a month from September to June, and once each in July and August. Annually all entries for the preceding year are brought together under their proper headings and published in a volume called a "cumulation." Beginning in 1900 the *Readers' Guide* indexes articles in approximately one hundred magazines of general interest and wide circulation, including some scientific periodicals since 1953. Indexing is under author and subject and occasionally also under title.

3:26   A first look at the *Readers' Guide* may be confusing, but the explanations in the front matter of each issue and a little careful study of a few pages will reveal the basic scheme of headings, subheadings, and cross-references and the significance of the various typefaces (styles and sizes of printers' letters, figures, and symbols) used. Notice the kinds of subjects that are brought together under the name of a country, for example. Examine the various headings and subheadings under "United States," for instance.

3:27   The sample entry below is for John Vliet Lindsay, former mayor of New York City, and locates five articles in periodicals: three *by* Mayor Lindsay and two *about* him.

1. LINDSAY, JOHN VLIET
2. Law & order. Life 65:32–3 S 27 '68
3. Memo to: convention delegates, from: Mayor John V. Lindsay, New York; subject: Vietnam. Look 32:61 Ag 20 '68
4. We can lick the problems of the ghetto, if we care; interview, ed. by J. N. Miller. por Read Digest 93:105–10 Ag '68

   about
5. How about Lindsay? Nation 206:524–5 Ap 22 '68
6. Lindsay of New York. L. L. King. Harper 237–44+ Ag '68

Item 1 is the person's name. Item 2 refers to an article by him that is entitled "Law and Order," which was published in *Life,* volume 65, pages 32–33, dated 27 September 1968. Item 3 refers to a memorandum to convention delegates (the Republican National Convention) from Mayor Lindsay on the subject of Vietnam, appearing in *Look,* volume 32, page 61, under date of 20 August 1968. Item 4 is concerned with an interview given by Mayor Lindsay and reported by J. N. Miller in the *Reader's Digest,* volume 93, pages 105–10, under date of August 1968. The abbreviation "por" indicates that the article included a portrait. Item 5 refers to an article *about* Mayor Lindsay entitled "How about Lindsay?" that appeared in the *Nation,* volume 206, 22 April 1968, pages 524–25. Finally, Item 6 refers to an article entitled "Lindsay of New York," by L. L. King, appearing in *Harper's* of August 1968, pages 237–44, and continued, as indicated by the plus symbol, on later pages of the same issue.

3:28   The *Social Sciences and Humanities Index,* begun in 1907, was first published as a supplement to the *Readers' Guide,* indexing scholarly journals and many foreign titles not included in the *Readers' Guide.* Volume 1, covering the period 1907–15, was published in 1916. From 1955 to January 1965, it was entitled *International Index to Periodicals: A Guide to Periodical Literature in the Social Sciences and the Humanities.* Since March 1965 it has borne its present title and no longer indexes foreign journals and scientific periodicals.

3:29   *Poole's Index to Periodical Literature,* published from 1802 to 1906, indexes, mainly by subject, articles in American and English periodicals. Titles of articles are given only when they offer no clue to the subject, and authors' names appear only when there is an article *about* an author or his work. For locating source materials in periodicals of the nineteenth century, *Poole's Index* is indispensable.

3:30   The *Short Story Index,* with its supplements, lists entries under author, title, and subject.

3:31   The *Essay and General Literature Index,* published semi-annually, indexes by author, subject, and occasionally by distinctive title, essays and articles in collections of essays and in collections of miscellaneous works, biography, criticism, and book reviews.

3:32   Besides the aforementioned general indexes there is a multitude of special indexes for specific countries and for specific subjects. To mention a few: the *Applied Science and Technology Index,* the *Education Index,* the *Business Periodicals Index,* the *Public Affairs Information Service Bulletin,* the *Speech Index, The Art Index, The Music Index,* and *Granger's Index to Poetry and Recitations.* Many more can be found by using the library's card catalog, looking under "Index to" and "Index of."

3:33   Indexes are published by four great newspapers: *The Times* (London), the *New York Times,* the *Christian Science Monitor,* and the *Wall Street Journal.* Since news of general interest appears in all large newspapers on the same day, the indexes of the four just mentioned serve in some sense for all.

3:34   *Biographical Aids.* For almost any topic, you are likely to need information about persons connected with it, and for this you should turn to one or more of the works dealing especially with biographical information.

3:35   *Who's Who in America,* issued every other year, gives information about noteworthy living persons in America; and *Who's Who,* issued every year, does the same for living persons in Great Britain and the Commonwealth, and for some well-known international figures as well. There are, besides, *The International Who's Who,* and a "who's who" publication for almost every country, for many regions and cities, and for the arts, sciences, and professions. These are readily found under "Who's who" in the card catalog. *The Directory of American Scholars* publishes biographical sketches of scholars mainly in history and the humanities, and *American Men of Science* does the same for scientists. *Current Biography,* issued monthly, publishes each year some four hundred biographies of contemporary figures in the world news. Not only does this publication provide biographical data concerning persons too recently become prominent to be mentioned in the current *Who's Who,* but the data are much more detailed than those given in *Who's Who.*

3:36   For celebrities no longer living, the renowned *Dictionary of American Biography* and *Dictionary of National Biography* contain biographies, respectively, of men and women of America and of Great Britain and the Commonwealth. In using these monumental works, students should be aware that not all the volumes of each series were published in the same year and that this is true of their supplements as well. Since the works are alphabetically arranged, their publication at various dates means that the biography of a person whose name begins with *A* who died after the *A* volume had been completed does not appear until the publication of the next supplement.

3:37   The various encyclopedias and handbooks also contain some biographical sketches of celebrities, both those living and those not living.

Specialized Reference Works

3:38   All the reference works so far discussed—bibliographical guides, encyclopedias, subject indexes to books and to periodicals, and biographical aids—are works of general information and, like Francis Bacon, take "all knowledge" for their province. No matter what subject is under investigation, the foregoing works will, in varying degree, provide a solid basis for a research paper.

3:39   In addition to these, there are specialized bibliographies and encyclopedias and handbooks which provide indispensable information in their particular fields—whether in broad areas such as the humanities, the social sciences, history, or the biological and physical sciences—or in more specialized subjects such as music, political science, American history, botany, or astronomy. The specialized encyclopedia, in several volumes, is able to cover more aspects of its subject and at greater length than is possible in the general encyclopedia.

3:40   It should be noted, on the one hand, that a specialized encyclopedia may not be called such. *Grove's Dictionary of Music and Musicians* (p. 213), for example, is actually in all but name an encyclopedia. On the other hand, a one-volume "encyclopedia," such as Leonard Feather's *Encyclo-*

pedia of Jazz in the Sixties (p. 213) on an extremely specialized subject, might as appropriately be called a "dictionary"
—or a "handbook" or a "companion." The old word for such
a work was "vade mecum" (go with me); "companion" is
now perhaps the most popular name. The *Oxford Companion
to the Theatre* (p. 206), for instance, a large volume of over
a thousand pages, with 176 plates and a classified bibliography
of over forty pages, is, in effect, as its publishers claim a
"one-volume encyclopaedia of world theatre." As you look
through the list of references in Appendix B, therefore, you
will encounter many important works which, though not so
called, are in fact specialized encyclopedias.

3:41   Among the multivolume specialized encyclopedias, a few call
for special attention. *The International Encyclopedia of the
Social Sciences* (p. 227), designed to complement rather than
to supplant the earlier work (1930–35), reflects the rapid
growth that has occurred in this field since the earlier work
appeared. Reliance is placed more and more on the social
sciences today, not only by administrators and professionals
in disciplines outside those traditionally seen as belonging
to it, but by society in general. The social sciences ramify now
very widely into other fields of knowledge, and the new *Encyclopedia* includes material on geography (exclusive of physical geography), history, law, and statistics, in addition to
anthropology, economics, political science, psychiatry, psychology, and sociology.

3:42   Two full-length encyclopedias in the field of religion have
been published recently. The *New Catholic Encyclopedia*
(1967) not only provides information on the dogmas of the
church but also treats such recent matters as the Second
Vatican Council, with biographies of noted Catholics and
accounts of other religions. The *Encyclopedia Judaica* (1971–
72) is the latest authoritative encyclopedia covering all aspects of Jewish history, life, and thought, prepared by a distinguished staff of scholars. An older but still valuable
encyclopedia of religion is Hastings's *Encyclopaedia of Religion
and Ethics,* which covers not only all religions and ethical
systems but also many related topics in folklore, mythology,
psychology, and other fields.

3:43   The *Encyclopedia of Philosophy,* published in 1967, is note-worthy in that it is the first major philosophical reference work to appear in more than fifty years. Its seven volumes cover all aspects of philosophy as well as areas in science and religion which have had an impact on philosophic thought. The articles are provided with very good and extensive bibliographies. Volume 8 is an index to the whole work.

3:44   *The Encyclopedia of World Art,* published in fifteen volumes, 1959–68, is a magnificent survey which includes, according to the preface, "architecture, sculpture, painting, and every other man-made object that regardless of its purpose or technique enters the field of esthetic judgment because of its form or decoration." It was published simultaneously in Italy (in Italian) and in the United States. There are of course a wealth of handsome illustrations accompanying the text. Volume 15 is the Index.

3:45   The best and most recent encyclopedic survey of all the literatures of the world is *Cassell's Encyclopaedia of World Literature,* a replacement of the earlier work published in 1953, containing articles on literary genres and movements, surveys of various literatures, and an extensive section dealing with biographies of authors in all ages and countries. A similar work, differently organized, is the four-volume *Penguin Companion to Literature,* concentrating mainly on biographies of authors but including also short sketches of literary movements (such as symbolism) and anonymous works (such as the *Niebelungenlied*). The coverage is extremely wide, and most of the articles are quite brief.

3:46   In the physical and biological sciences so many discoveries are constantly made and so many new theories advanced by scientists working in all parts of the world that a general encyclopedia of science needs constant revision. The most satisfactory of the multivolume encyclopedias is no doubt the *McGraw-Hill Encyclopedia of Science and Technology: An International Reference Work,* of which a third edition in fifteen volumes was published in 1971. But it needs frequent checking and updating through the use of even more recent reference works.

3:47   Among the specialized reference works in the various dis-

ciplines, attention should be paid to the one-volume handbooks, particularly to those of recent date, and to the bibliographies which cover your special subject of research. The
Oxford Companion to American Literature, for example, includes a wealth of material on authors, literary movements,
and many auxiliary subjects. The same is true of others in
this series—on English literature, on classical literature, on
art, and many more which you will find listed in Appendix B.
Among the many bibliographies listed in this appendix, the
New Cambridge Bibliography of English Literature should be
especially noted, since it is the indispensable work of reference
for the study of every aspect of English literature, from the
beginnings down to the middle of the present century. In
American literature the two best are the bibliographical volume in *The Literary History of the United States,* by Robert
E. Spiller and others, and the *Bibliographical Guide* of Clarence Gohdes.

THE CARD CATALOG

3:48   Having given attention to the library's reference materials,
you should turn to the call materials, and first to the card
catalog, which is the key to those materials. You undoubtedly
have learned that all the materials of a library are organized
under a system of classification which allows them to be
quickly and easily located by the persons who use the library.
And, although a thorough knowledge of the system is primarily the concern of librarians and attendants, some understanding of it can be very useful to you.

Classification Systems

3:49   One of two systems of classification, either the Dewey decimal system or the Library of Congress system, is used by most
American libraries.

3:50   The Dewey system of classification is based on figures used
decimally. The fields of knowledge are divided into nine main
classes, with general knowledge—such as that represented by
encyclopedias, handbooks, newspapers, and the like—forming
a tenth class, which precedes the others as the 000 class. Each
class is assigned one hundred numbers:

000–099	General Works	500–599	Pure Science
100–199	Philosophy	600–699	Technology
200–299	Religion	700–799	The Arts
300–399	Social Sciences	800–899	Literature
400–499	Language	900–999	History

Each main class is again divided into ten divisions, each division being assigned ten numbers. Take "History," for example, and note that numbers 900–909 are reserved for works of general history, as shown in the following:

900–909	History—General Works
910–919	Geography, Travels, Description
920–929	Biography
930–939	Ancient History
940–949	Europe
950–959	Asia
960–969	Africa
970–979	North America
980–989	South America
990–999	Other Parts of the World

Each division is further divided into ten sections. As an example take "North America":

970	North America—General Works
971	Canada
972	Mexico and the Caribbean
973	United States
974	Northeastern States
975	Southeastern States
976	South Central States
977	North Central States
978	Western States
979	Far Western States and Alaska

3:51   Thus each main class with a division and section is indicated by a three-digit number, after which is placed a decimal. Tracing number 973, for example, from the general field to the specific subject area, you see that the 9 stands for History, the 7 for North America, and the 3 for United States: the number 973, therefore, is the classification number for United States history. The subject field is further defined by arabic numerals following the decimal point. Numbers 1–9 following 973 cover periods of United States history; and each of these periods is again divided into nine specific fields of interest; and each of these specific fields may also be divided, and so on. Every additional number following the decimal indicates, then, a further subdivision of the general topic. Here we illustrate, in part, two levels:

973.1   Discovery and exploration to 1607
973.2   Colonial period, 1607–1775
973.3   Revolution and confederation, 1775–89
       and so on, through 973.9

Another breakdown of each period shows nine more specialized areas. For example:

973.31   Political and economic history in the period 1775–89 and so on, through 973.39

3:52   Next, to distinguish the many books in one classification from one another, and also to distinguish between books in the same classification written by one author, each work is assigned a book (or author) number. A table for determining author numbers was devised by C. A. Cutter at about the same time that Dewey was developing his classification system. Cutter's system, too, uses numbers decimally, assigning certain numerals to letters of the alphabet in alphabetical order. In its simplest form a book number consists of the initial of the author's surname plus certain numerals. When under a given classification there are two or more books by the same author, the book numbers differ only in the addition of letters which distinguish the books from each other. In the author number of a book that is about a person, the initial of the surname of that person replaces the author's initial preceding the numerals, and the author's initial follows them. Thus a book by Emily S. Hamblen entitled *On the Minor Prophecies of William Blake* carries the classification number 821.5 and the author number B633h.

3:53   The Library of Congress classification system, which was devised for the purpose of reclassifying the collections of the Library of Congress, is used by libraries with very large holdings.

3:54   This system divides the fields of knowledge into twenty main groups, assigning a letter to each, and combines arabic numerals and additional letters to separate the main groups into divisions and subdivisions in somewhat the same way as that used in the Dewey decimal system. Following is an outline of the main classes as set up in the Library of Congress system: *

A	General Works—Polygraphy	L	Education
		M	Music
B	Philosophy—Religion	N	Fine Arts
C	History—Auxiliary Sciences	P	Language and Literature
		Q	Science
D	History and Topography (except America)	R	Medicine
		S	Agriculture—Plant and Animal Husbandry
E–F	America		
G	Geography—Anthropology	T	Technology
		U	Military Science
H	Social Sciences	V	Naval Science
J	Political Science	Z	Bibliography and Library Science
K	Law		

Features of the Card Catalog

3:55   Most library catalogs are in the form of printed or typewritten cards, 3 inches by 5 inches, which are alphabetically arranged in drawers of filing cabinets. Guides to the contents of the drawers are provided by labels on the outside and by guide cards on the inside.

3:56   For each book or pamphlet there are at least three entries (individual cards, each covering a separate listing) in the catalog: (1) one card under the author's last name; (2) one under the first word (exclusive of *A, An,* or *The*) of the title; and (3) at least one under the subject. The many works that treat of more than one subject are represented by more than one "subject card." In addition, a work may be entered in the catalog under the name of a coauthor, an editor, a translator, and an illustrator.

* From The Library of Congress, Subject Cataloging Division, *Outline of the Library of Congress Classification,* rev. and enl. ed. of "Outline Scheme of Classes" (Washington, D.C.: U.S. Government Printing Office, 1975).

3:57   The "author card" is considered to be the main entry. This card may show the "author" to be an individual, an editor or a compiler, an institution, company, or committee. If the publication has none of these, the main entry is under the title of the publication, as, for example, the Bible, or *U.S. News and World Report.* All the cards made for a particular work carry identical printed information, but the name of the "author" is typewritten at the top of the "author card"; the title at the top of the "title card"; the subject at the top of the "subject card." Similarly, the name of a coauthor, editor, translator, or illustrator appears as the first line of a card which is filed under the name of such a collaborator.

3:58   Reproduced on page 27 is the main entry for a work by two editors rather than by one author. It is filed under the name of the senior editor—the one whose name appears first on the title page of the book. There are four other cards for this work: one filed under the name of the joint editor, one under the title, and two under subject, as indicated on the cards themselves (see items 15 and 17 in the explanation below the sample card).

Using the Catalog

3:59   You may have had little occasion to use subject headings in the catalog, and, to be able to rely on them, you must learn the principles of their arrangement.

3:60   Subject headings are on the projecting tabs of the guide cards. It will be worth your time to select one of the larger headings and go through the cards so that you may understand how the divisions are arranged. Within the main headings are found subdivisions, the first one covering works that deal with the subject in general. There follow, in alphabetic order, the remaining subdivisions; and the order within each subdivision is likewise alphabetic, according to the library's particular scheme of alphabetization, which you learned at the library information desk. The last card in each subdivision is often headed *"See also"* and lists other subject headings under which works relating to the topic can be found.

3:61   It is well to choose for examination a subject heading to which you might refer in collecting material for your research paper; or you might choose "Transportation," or "Indians," or a specific country. You should know that for every country there are, in addition to the subdivisions covering the several legislative bodies and the many governmental departments, bureaus, offices, commissions, and the like, subdivisions for all the concerns of the national life, such as agriculture, commerce and industry, finance, law, education, history, art, religion, family life, social life, and scores—sometimes hundreds —of others. The subsection "History," wherever found, is divided into chronological periods, with the entries within each period being alphabetically arranged.

3:62   When you have examined one of the more extensive divisions of the catalog, you might like to see what you could do with a particular topic. Some large libraries have separate subject catalogs in which almost any topic can be found; but, if yours does not appear, try topics that are related to it. If your subject is the "Pony Express," for example, and you find no such subject heading, try "Transportation," "Communication and Traffic," "Coaching," "Postal Service," and similar headings, all under "United States." Although you may find in any particular subdivision no works dealing exclusively with the Pony Express, you are pretty sure to find other subject headings worth investigating on the *"See also"* cards of the categories just mentioned.

3:63   Having in mind the general scheme of the card catalog, you should have no difficulty in finding works on your own topic. Guided by the subject headings on the catalog cards, take out three or four of the more promising works. Whether they actually are promising depends upon a number of factors, which ought to be considered before going further.

EVALUATING SOURCE MATERIALS

3:64   To distinguish positively between "good" and "bad" materials on which to base your paper is possible only to the expert in the field. Nevertheless, you have some means of testing that can be—indeed, should be—used.

3:65   You may rightly assume that the reference works mentioned

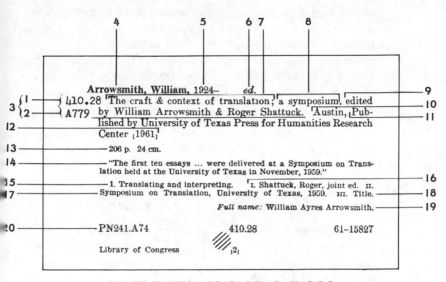

MAIN ENTRY IN CARD CATALOG

1. Class number. 2. Book or author number. 3. Call number. 4. "Author's" name (inverted). In this case the name of the senior editor replaces name of author, since the work was produced by editors rather than an author. 5. Birth date. The absence of a second date indicates that the editor was living when the card was made. 6. Indicates "Editor." 7. Main title of book. 8. Subtitle. 9. Names of editors. 10. Place of publication. 11. Publisher. 12. Date of publication. Enclosure of the date in brackets indicates that the date does not appear on the face of the title page and was found in some other place. 13. Collation (number of pages and measurement of the book). 14. Explanatory note. 15. Subject heading (that is, the subject fully treated). 16. Name of joint editor, under whose name there is a card in the catalog. 17. Another heading under which the work appears in the catalog. 18. Indicates title card in the catalog. 19. Full name of the senior editor. 20. Library of Congress call number. The other two numbers on the line with the Library of Congress number are of interest only to the staff of the library. Recent library catalog cards may also contain the International Standard Book Number (ISBN), which is useful to book buyers because it identifies the publisher and the book.

earlier in this chapter and those in the selected list appearing in Appendix B are "good" insofar as they meet your special requirements. Their statements of fact can be accepted as accurate, but among the several works the degree of coverage of a topic may vary considerably, and some of their opinions may conflict. It is not out of place here to warn students against the indiscriminate use of encyclopedias—those aimed at the primary or the secondary school level as well as those acquired at a supermarket. However useful for their purpose the first two may be, they are of no use for college research papers. And the information contained in the supermarket set may well be unreliable either because it is incomplete or inexact or out of date.

3:66   To the works found entirely by your own efforts through use of the card catalog and subject indexes, and possibly also to some recommended in the bibliographies appended to articles in the reference works, the following criteria should be applied.

3:67   First, consider the outward evidences of reliability.

3:68   Is the author a recognized authority in the field? If he is not known to you as such, does he have the necessary qualifications for writing as an authority on the particular topic? His professional or business status, his experience, and his academic degrees are some indications of his capabilities. If the title page, preface, or introduction does not show them, look up the author in *Who's Who* or in a similar publication. But note that the information should point to his competence in the specific topic. A brilliant financier may have no special qualifications—beyond the superior ability shown by his success as a financier—for writing authoritatively on behaviorism or on civil rights. A work for which there is no author's name given on the title page is a "poor risk."

3:69   Is the publisher known for his reliability? The best publishers—and students soon come to know which are the best—are jealous of their reputations. A work for which no publisher is shown should be looked upon with skepticism, and so also in most instances a work that is privately printed.

3:70   If the work is in a periodical, is the periodical one from which to expect authoritative information on the subject? A scholarly or technical journal in a particular field is likely to be a more trustworthy reporter on a topic in that field than either a popular periodical or a serious publication in a different field.

3:71   Is the date of publication such as to give significance to the reporting? The importance of the date varies with the topic. If the disclosure of the Pentagon Papers, the take-over of passenger train operation by Amtrak, the launching toward the moon of Apollo 14, or the trial of Lt. William L. Calley were your topic, it is doubtful that you would get any help from works published before 1971. If your topic were in a field where there is continuing rapid development, you would require the most up-to-date publications available. But, on the other hand, if your topic were Hinduism or the medieval miracle plays, or one treating of a person, a movement, or an event much in the public view some years ago, you might be as well served by older reference works as by later ones. Faced with the need to provide more space for topics in scientific fields, editors of the more recent editions of encyclopedias have shortened some articles in other fields. Look for the publication date of a book on the face of the title page below the name of the publisher. If it is not there, look for the copyright date on the reverse of the title page. The latest date shown there is that of the work before you. Especially for a reference work that has gone through many printings, such as a general encyclopedia, the dates shown need interpretation. Each succeeding copyright date denotes a printing with at least minor changes from the one preceding. As a matter of fact, the major encyclopedias have followed a policy of continuous revision for more than thirty years, adding new articles and revising many others with each new printing. The meaning of the words "revised" and "reprinted" appearing with a date should not be confused. Normally a reprinting merely duplicates an earlier edition.

3:72   Second, evaluate the material itself for its probable usefulness in treating your subject.

3:73   Does the work seem to deal directly with the topic or merely to touch the fringe? To judge this: read the preface for the author's statement of purpose and his evaluation of its achievement; examine the table of contents and the index for coverage; sample a few pages of text to see what grasp of his subject the writer shows.

3:74   Is the author's point of view objective and impartial? Does he present all sides of the matter and give due weight to each aspect, or does he try to prejudice the case by disparaging and sarcastic comment upon some aspects?

3:75 Is the language generally free of emotion-arousing words and expressions such as "moron," "blackguard," "hoodlum," "traitor," "fascist," "red," "dim-witted," "a pack of lies," "it is a well-known fact," "it has been substantially proved," "there can be no question of doubt"? When any of these appears, is its use supported by authoritative evidence? In general, the more violent the language used, the greater the number of unsupported "facts" stated, the less reliable the work is likely to be.

3:76 Are there more statements of fact than of opinion?

3:77 Are the opinions expressed the logical conclusions of the evidence presented?

3:78 Does the support for opinions come from known, reliable authorities?

3:79 When figures are given on population, wages and hours, crops, rainfall, and the like, are dates included?

3:80 Are statements substantiated whenever necessary by footnote references? Much can be determined about a writer's reliability by his care in acknowledging the sources of his information. If he asserts, for example, that just before the Civil War there was more abolitionist sentiment in the South than in the North, and brings forth no evidence to support his statement, his trustworthiness as a reporter may well be questioned. If his readers are to have confidence in him, an author must make it possible for them to verify his statements.

3:81 But when all the foregoing criteria have been applied, you may still be bothered by conflicting opinions among authors who seem to be equally reliable. And it may take the most painstaking efforts to resolve the difficulty, which you are bound to do as best you can by weighing and counting the evidence for each point of view and then "casting your vote." In this process, consideration of the dates of the writings is sometimes highly significant, the later work having had the benefit of recently acquired knowledge. And, too, reviews of the works may be of considerable help. They can be found through the *Book Review Index,* the *Book Review Digest,* and the *Technical Book Review Index.* The *Digest* gives excerpts of reviews, not merely their locations.

4 Planning the Paper

EXPLORATORY READING

4:1 Although you may have decided upon a tentative topic, until you know the available sources of information and do some exploratory reading, you cannot be sure that it is a suitable one as measured against the criteria set forth in chapter 2. In earlier thinking about the subject you undoubtedly considered several ways of limiting it by treatment of one or more aspects (see pars. 2:5–6). So, while it was necessary to start with one topic, you actually have alternatives in mind. It is the chief function of the exploratory reading either to indicate the suitability of one of the topics already considered or to suggest a new one. This reading need not—indeed, should not—take a great deal of time, but it must be done with such care that, when it is finished, you are satisfied that you have a suitable topic and that the work can go forward to completion within the limits of the assignment.

4:2 Notetaking at this point should consist only of locations of those materials that your preliminary investigation has shown to be useful.

MAKING A PRELIMINARY BIBLIOGRAPHY

4:3 Although no rule can be given that will cover all cases, normally the preliminary investigation of a topic consists of reading articles in general encyclopedias and their yearbooks—and in a specialized encyclopedia if there is one relating to your topic. As already mentioned, many encyclopedia articles give a selected bibliography at the end. Make a note of these works, look them up in the card catalog, and take out those that are available. They may mention still other works you will want to look into. Examine tables of contents and indexes to find sections that might be useful and skim through those sections. Next consult two or three subject indexes to find magazine and newspaper articles and give these attention.

4:4   For each work—book or article—with promising source material, make a separate 3 × 5-inch card, setting down (*a*) the bibliographical information, (*b*) the call number, (*c*) notations of page numbers and other necessary identification of sections to be reviewed, and (*d*) some indication of the relative value of the material (a rating scale of *A, B, C* might be used). *Be sure to do all this while the works are at hand.* Of course, you must never disfigure any library materials either by markings or by removal of pages or parts of pages. The penalties imposed by libraries do not offset the harm done to a student who finds himself seriously handicapped because of the temporary loss of needed material. If the bibliography cards are made out as directed while the works are at hand, call numbers need not be looked up a second time; the rating will be a guide to the order in which the works should be taken up; pertinent passages can be readily found; and completeness and accuracy of the bibliographic information will be assured.

4:5   These bibliography cards comprise the tentative bibliography —the preliminary readings which give evidence that you have a suitable topic. Now it is time to confer with your instructor and get approval of the project before proceeding further. But first you must learn the correct forms for bibliography cards.

FORMS FOR BIBLIOGRAPHY CARDS

4:6   Here we begin with a word of caution to students who think that they may copy at random the forms of bibliographic reference used in the various works consulted. There is, to be sure, more than one acceptable style of making footnote and bibliographic references. But an examination of the references in any given work will show that they follow a consistent style throughout. And so also must your research paper, whatever the approved style you may adopt. The style of documentation here recommended is that of the University of Chicago Press, as set forth in its *Manual of Style,* twelfth edition, revised (1969). The various forms may be explained and illustrated as follows:

Book

4:7   Three items of information are necessary to identify a book: (*a*) name of author, (*b*) title of the work, and (*c*) facts of publication. The items should always appear in that order on the bibliography cards, as also later in the bibliography accompanying the paper. The information should be taken from the title page of the work and be set down uniformly in the prescribed style.

Name of author or authors

4:8   Last name first, followed by a comma; first name or names, followed by a period. If initials are used in place of name (or name and initial), the period after the last initial serves also as the final period:

```
Baldwin, James Mark.     Crane, Ronald S.
```

4:9   If the work has two or three authors, the names are written as follows:

```
Baldwin, Ruth I., and Clark, John R.
Chamberlain, Joseph P.; Dowling, Noel T.;
          and Hayes, Paul R.
```

4:10   If there are more than three authors, use one of the following forms, and use it consistently:

```
      Halsey, William D., et al.
or: Halsey, William D., and others.
```

Name of editor or compiler in place of author

4:11   If the work is the product of an editor (or editors) or compiler rather than of an author, replace the name of an author with that of the editor or the compiler, using the following form:

```
Sandys, John E., ed.        Todd, Robert L.,
                              comp.
```

4:12   The names of two or more editors or compilers are set down in the same forms as those used for authors, with the abbreviation "eds." or "comps." following, as shown below:

```
Fadiman, Clifton, and Van Doren, Charles,
    eds.
```

4:13   But from your observation of scholarly bibliographies, you will notice that, for many edited or compiled works, the title of the work is the first item of information and that the name of the editor or compiler follows. "Ed." or "Comp." before the editor's or compiler's name stands for "Edited by" or "Compiled by." These are best spelled out in your bibliography:

```
The Reader's Companion to World Literature.
    Edited by Lillian H. Hornstein.
```

Name of institution, company, or committee in place of authors

4:14   The "author" may be an organization rather than a person. In such case, write the name of the organization first and follow with the name of the work:

```
American Council on Education.  American
    Junior Colleges.
```

Name of author and of translator

4:15   A book that is translated from another language shows on its title page the name of the translator as well as that of the author. The bibliography card should give both in the following form:

```
Cervantes, Miguel de. Don Quixote. Trans-
    lated by Samuel Putnam.
```

Name of author and of editor

4:16   A work of one author that has been edited by another—as is sometimes the case, particularly with works written a century or more ago—is recorded with the name of the original author given first, then the title of his work, followed by the name of the editor, in the same way as for a translator:

```
Jonson, Ben.  The Alchemist.  Edited by G. E.
    Bentley.
```

34

Title of book

4:17   Capitalize the first and last words and all nouns, pronouns, verbs, adjectives, adverbs, and subordinate conjunctions (*after, because, if, since, until,* and *when, where,* and *while*); underline and place a period at the end:

The Way of All Flesh.

4:18   Follow this same style in citing book titles, and other titles capitalized in the same way as book titles, any place in the paper.

4:19   Note that the style of capitalization indicated in paragraph 4:17 does not hold for papers in some of the sciences (see par. 7:131).

Facts of publication

4:20   Usually these consist of (*a*) city of publication, followed by a colon; (*b*) name of publisher, followed by a comma;* (*c*) date of publication, followed by a period.

New Haven, Conn.: Yale University Press, 1958.

4:21   For a work of which an edition other than the first is cited, or when there is more than one volume, the number (or name) of the edition and the total number of volumes is noted before the facts of publication. For example:

2d ed.   10 vols.   New York: Henry Holt & Co., 1906.

4:22   Occasionally, the edition information is qualified by such words as "revised" ("rev.") or "enlarged" ("enl."), or by both, and sometimes this is followed by the name of the person or persons who made the revision or the enlargement. Note the following example:

Thompson, Oscar.   International Cyclopedia of Music and Musicians.   5th ed.,

---

* Although in some fields the bibliographic practice is to omit the name of the publisher, we shall follow the more general practice of including it.

                              rev. and enl. by Nicholas Slonimsky.
                              New York: Dodd, Mead & Co., 1949.

Magazine Article

4:23   The items necessary to identify an article in a magazine are: (*a*) name of author, (*b*) title of article, (*c*) name of magazine, (*d*) volume number and date, or date alone, and (*e*) inclusive page numbers. Take the information from the magazine.

4:24   Do not be led astray by the greatly abbreviated form of reference used by periodical indexes; translate it for your documentation into the form here illustrated.

Name of author or authors

4:25   Write it in the same way as for a book.

Title of article

4:26   Capitalize as for a book. Follow the title with a period and place double quotation marks at beginning and end:

            "Douglas and the Chicago Mob."

Name of magazine

4:27   Capitalize as for a book title and underline the title:

            American Historical Review

Volume number and date

4:28   Popular magazines, even though they carry volume numbers, are best identified by date alone; scholarly journals, by volume and date.

4:29   Write the volume number in *arabic* numerals, regardless of whether the work referred to expresses the number in arabic or in roman numerals. Give month and year, enclosed in parentheses, after the volume number:

            54 (April 1949):

4:30   When the volume number is omitted and the date alone identifies the magazine, it appears without parentheses, either:

```
12 December 1962, (for a weekly)
        or:
December 1962,     (for a monthly)
```

Note that there is no comma between month and year.

Page numbers

4:31   Inclusive page numbers are desirable, but if the article begins in the front of the magazine and skips to the back, making inclusive page numbers meaningless, give just the first number. In citing inclusive numbers like the following, omit all but the last two digits of the second number, unless the first digit of the second number is higher than the first digit of the first number, in which case express both numbers in full. For example:

```
Right: 553-56
       558-612     Not: 558-12
```

(See also par. 6:67.)

Examples

4:32   Following are examples of bibliographic entries for articles, the first from a scholarly journal, the second from a popular magazine:

```
Davis, Granville D.   "Douglas and the
        Chicago Mob."  American Historical
        Review 54 (April 1949): 553-56.
Spender, Stephen.  "Is a New Literature
        Possible?"  Saturday Review, 22
        September 1962, pp. 16-19.
```

4:33   Notice in the foregoing examples some details of style:

(*a*) In the first example, there is no mark of punctuation separating magazine title and volume number. The punctuation mark required to separate volume and page numbers is a colon rather than a comma, and it is placed after, not before, the parentheses. This usage illustrates the rule that any mark of punctuation which would follow a word (or a number) if that word did not have a parenthetic element coming after it is placed after the parenthesis when there is one.

(*b*) When volume number is omitted and identification of the issue is by date alone, there is no parenthesis around the date. And if month and year date alone are given, no comma intervenes.

(*c*) The page numbers in the first example are not preceded by the abbreviation "pp." This is the approved style in a reference that gives both volume and page numbers. In the second example, where pages only are given, the abbreviation "pp." is used.

Newspaper Article

4:34   The title of the newspaper and the date of the issue are usually sufficient. The title of the article, or the author, or both, may be included if desired. For large metropolitan dailies, page numbers should be included; and when the paper is made up of several sections, with each section separately paginated, it is necessary to give both section number (or letter) and page number. Reference to a newspaper that does not include the name of the city should give the name in parentheses after the title (except such well-known newspapers as the *Wall Street Journal* or the *Christian Science Monitor*).

<u>Palo Alto</u> (California) <u>Times</u>, 7 October
        1974.
"Allies Foresee Difficult Time in Paris,"
        <u>Sacramento Bee</u>, 28 January 1969,
        p. 12.
"Amazing Amazon Region," <u>New York Times</u>,
        19 January 1969, sec. 4, p. Ell.
<u>Times</u> (London), 11 July 1967, p. 9.

Encyclopedia or Dictionary Article

4:35   The *edition* rather than volume and page numbers, together with the title of the article, should be cited. Since some general encyclopedias have for a considerable time omitted mention of the edition on their title pages, the year date is in some cases the sole identifying item. But when the number of the edition is mentioned, the citation should include it, and the year date, enclosed in parentheses, had best follow it. In an alphabetically arranged work, such as an encyclopedia or dictionary, an article is most readily found under the first word (exclusive of an initial article) of its title, or under the last name of a person. Place before the title the abbreviation "s.v." (*sub verbo*, "under the word"). In citing a signed article, include the name of the author. If the author's initials alone appear beneath the article, consult the list in the front matter of the work, where names corresponding to the initials are given. Citations of well-known reference works omit publisher's name and city.

Encyclopaedia Britannica, 11th ed. (1910–
    11), s.v. "Blake, William," by J. W.
    Comyns-Carr.
Encyclopedia Americana, 1963 ed., s.v.
    "Sitting Bull."
Webster's New Geographical Dictionary
    (1972), s.v. "Dominican Republic."
Grove's Dictionary of Music and Musicians,
    5th ed. (1954), s.v. "Harp Lute."

Sample Bibliography Card

4:36   Following is a sample bibliography card for a book. The call number is in the upper left-hand corner; the rating is indicated by an *A* in the upper right-hand corner.

SAMPLE BIBLIOGRAPHY CARD

OUTLINING

4:37   With the completion of the preliminary reading and tentative bibliography, it is time to think about a first outline. What you have at present is probably an accumulation of largely unrelated facts and ideas. They are of enough interest that you want to pursue them further and to pass them on to others, the readers of your paper. To pursue the subject further calls first for some stocktaking. What, actually, have you learned about the topic? Where do there seem to be gaps? To go on with your reading, it is necessary to know what you are looking for; to take notes efficiently, it is important to know what to take notes on; and, to make your material interesting and meaningful to others, you must present it according to some logical plan. The faith that a project "will somehow come out all right" without careful planning is not borne out by experience. The ability to construct a well-ordered outline, since it requires logical thought and a nice discrimination of values, is useful in many an undertaking besides the theme and the research paper.

4:38   Two objectives are to be considered first in making the outline: (*a*) finding out what information you already have on the subject and (*b*) seeing how this information may be arranged in a logical order. Two further objectives should be considered while the outline is taking shape: (*c*) selecting a controlling idea (the *thesis*) of your paper and (*d*) noting the points where your information is incomplete as well as those where it seems irrelevant. This last makes explicit the stocktaking implied in the first objective.

TAKING STOCK

4:39   To get anywhere, one first has to start. And a good way to start the outline is to jot down quickly and at random all the ideas you have about your topic, asking what there is of interest that you want to pass along to the reader. Let us say that you propose to write on "The Harp" and set down the following:

1. The harp is a stringed musical instrument of great antiquity

2. Probable origin in the hunter's bow
3. Prevalent throughout the ancient world
4. Delineations in ancient art
5. Examples found by archaeologists
6. Mentioned in the Bible
7. Greatly esteemed in Ireland
8. Styles of ancient instruments strongly reminiscent of the bow
9. Different positions held in playing
10. Development of the modern harp
11. Place as a solo instrument
12. Importance as an orchestral instrument

Looking over the list, you ask whether the "vital statistics" are covered, at least in embryo. Let us see.

What is it? See no. 1.
What does it look like? See nos. 4, 5, 8, and 10.
Where did it come from? See no. 2.
For what, and how, is it used? See nos. 9, 11, and 12.
How do we know about its early history? See nos. 3, 4, 5, 6, and 7.

4:40   You may rightly decide that you have a foundation on which to build, although thinking of what you know—how much or how little—about each of the topics listed, you realize that the stockpile must be built up in some places.

ORGANIZING YOUR MATERIAL

4:41   Now you should consider the organization of the material—in what arrangement and what order you will present it in writing. And another consideration, that of the controlling idea of the paper, should be kept in mind while the outline is taking shape.

4:42   *Arrangement* calls for separation of the material into categories.

4:43   You see the harp itself mentioned in numbers 1 and 10 and have no difficulty in recognizing that your subject falls naturally into two main parts. You decide to indicate them as: "I. The Ancient Harp" and "II. The Modern Harp."*

4:44 Next, using some logical basis of separation—chronological, spatial, logical, general-to-particular, particular-to-general, cause-to-effect, greater-to-lesser (to name but a few)—determine how the remaining material is to be grouped under I and II. *Chronological order* means that the ideas are presented in the order of their happening. For example, an event, a biographical sketch, or the steps in a process are normally set forth in chronological order. A natural or common-sense order, known as *logical order,* is one in which the presentation of each idea depends for its comprehension upon the reader's grasp of the idea preceding it. A simple example is a recipe for making fruitcake; another is found in the provisions of an agreement, such as a treaty. Complex ideas and complex objects—most objects, as a matter of fact—are described in logical order. *Spatial order* is frequently used in setting forth the design of a city, building, garden, picture, or statue; it is often employed as well in describing a journey, as the landscape unfolds before the eyes. The *general-to-particular order* begins with a broad, general statement and goes on to support it with specific examples. Thus, for example, the statement might be made that women are becoming an increasing force in politics, and this statement be corroborated by giving concrete examples of women's various volunteer services in politics, and of their elections to office. In the *particular-to-general order* the process is reversed by beginning with examples and ending with a general summing-up to show their significance. Such studies as those of an author's philosophy as evidenced by his treatment of a specific character or of his repeated use of a particular image as a symbol are often arranged in the order of *general-to-particular* or of *particular-to-general.* *Cause-to-effect order* may be employed in a variety of studies, such, for example, as delineations of experiments, programs, social conditions, styles of writing, and the like.

4:45 Normally, at least two categories—two levels—may be distinguished in the material remaining after the major divisions

---

* It should be noticed that the ideas, but not the expressions used, in the list of interest items will be carried over into the outline.

have been established. One level may fall naturally into a
chronological order, for example; and another just as simply
into a general-to-particular or cause-to-effect. Examining the
items on the harp with various kinds of order in mind, you
see that some express rather general ideas about it and that
others express particular ideas. You think of "Antiquity,"
"Origin," and "Styles" as the general ideas, with another idea,
that of "Use," implicit in numbers 11 and 12. Now you must
decide where each of them belongs, and in what order. The
first three seem obviously to belong under I, and "Use" seems
to apply both to I and to II. The order as found in the list
seems a natural one. To think about the harp's antiquity and
origin before discussing styles and use makes sense, although
a presentation in the reverse order could be worked out effectively. So far, the outline looks like this:

        I. The ancient harp
           A. Antiquity
           B. Origin
           C. Styles
           D. Use
       II. The modern harp
           A. Development
           B. Use

4:46   The remaining items to be placed are numbers 3, 4, 5, 6, 7,
and 9. You decided earlier that they are "particular" items
and therefore relate to the "general," that is, to "Antiquity,"
"Origin," "Style," and "Use." But, in trying to fit them in, you
run into difficulty, and it takes a bit of study to understand
why. Gradually it becomes clear that "Prevalent throughout the ancient world" overlaps "Antiquity" and should be
omitted. Then that "Mentioned in the Bible" and "Esteemed
in Ireland" appear to confine knowledge of the harp to but
two parts of the ancient world, whereas your reading has
shown that the instrument was known throughout that world.
The subsection needs expansion, and the subtopic should indicate the greater scope. Last, you realize that, since "Positions held in playing" is an aspect common both to the arched
harp and to the angular harp, it belongs at the level below
them rather than at the same level. To include it raises the

question of another level of subtopics elsewhere in the outline, and, since you are not now prepared to say what they
might be, the subtopic "Positions" should be left out. Now
relating the several "particulars" to their proper subdivisions
presents no problem. Their order of greater-to-lesser is logical
in the light of your knowledge of the materials.

4:47   In the completed tentative outline shown below, the order
of the main divisions (I and II) is chronological; that of the
first-level subdivisions (A, B, etc.) is logical, and that of
the second-level subdivisions (1, 2, 3, etc.) is greater-to-lesser.

THE HARP: ANCIENT AND MODERN

<u>Controlling idea</u>: The harp, esteemed for
some 5,000 years as a solo instrument and
as an accompaniment to the voice, has
been largely replaced by the piano and
violin, but has gained a firm place as
an orchestral instrument.
  I. The ancient harp
     A. Antiquity
        1. References in writings through-
           out the ancient world
        2. Delineations in ancient art
        3. Examples found by archaeologists
     B. Probable origin
     C. Styles of main types
        1. The arched harp
        2. The angular harp
     D. Use
        1. Solo and voice-accompanying
           instrument
        2. Orchestral instrument
 II. The modern harp
     A. Development
        1. The chromatic harp
        2. The pedal harp
     B. Use
        1. Orchestral instrument
        2. Solo instrument

CONVENTIONS OF OUTLINING

4:48   In considering the working outline as a rough scheme for the writing of the research paper, we have been concerned until now with showing relationships among the various items of information and of placing them in a logical order. But in its final form the outline usually is presented in advance to the instructor, and often it accompanies the paper in its completed form. It should, therefore, be set up in accordance with the conventions of outlining.

Notation

4:49   In the foregoing outline it will be seen that the relative values of the items are shown by a system of notation and indentation. There are a number of such systems from which to choose. The following is one that is widely used.

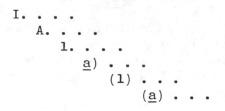

Parallelism

4:50   Furthermore, it will be seen that all entries of the same level of importance (as a matter of fact, sometimes *all* entries, as in our outline) are expressed in the same grammatical form. Thus if capital roman numeral I is a noun, II, III, and so forth, should be nouns; if capital A is an infinitive phrase, B, C, and so forth, should be infinitive phrases, and so on.

4:51   Outlines are of three kinds: the topic outline, the sentence outline, and the paragraph outline. In the topic outline every heading should be a noun or its equivalent (a gerund or an infinitive phrase). In the sentence outline every heading should be a sentence, although an acceptable alternative is one in which the main heading is a noun and every subheading a sentence. The third style is the paragraph outline, in which—except perhaps for the main headings being nouns—every heading is a paragraph. Because the greater substance of a piece of writing can be better indicated in a sentence or a paragraph outline than in the topic variety, the longer form has its place in circumstances where greater detail may be a decisive factor. A preliminary outline designed to show the instructor may well be expressed in sentence or even paragraph form, even though it is reduced to the concise, topic style for presentation with the finished paper. Parallelism in the sentence and the paragraph outline does not require that all headings be in the same, or very nearly the same, number of words.

4:52 There should be no single divisions in an outline, as in 1 under A in the following:

```
Wrong: I. The ancient harp
          A. Origin
             1. The hunter's bow
          B. Styles
```

When you are tempted to subordinate a single item under a topic, either you have not considered other items of similar importance or you have not realized that the entire discussion centered on that one idea—that it was in fact coordinate, not subordinate.

4:53 Compare the following example of a partial outline in which entries at the same level are not parallel in grammatical construction with the corrected version that follows. Notice how easily the conversions to correct forms can be made.

```
Wrong: I. The ancient harp [noun]
          A. It is a musical instrument of
                great antiquity [sentence]
             1. Read about it in the Bible
                   [sentence]
             2. References to it by writers
                   all over the world [noun]
             3. Pictured in ancient art
                   [incomplete sentence]
             4. Examples found by archaeol-
                   ogists [noun]
          B. Origin [noun]
```

Right: I. The ancient harp [noun]
    A. Antiquity [noun]
       1. References in the Bible
         [noun]
       2. References by writers from
         all over the world [noun]
       3. Delineations in ancient art
         [noun]
       4. Examples found by archaeol-
         ogists [noun]
    B. Origin [noun]

4:54   In organizing the facts and ideas gained in your early reading so as to construct a rough outline, you have come to a fairly definite understanding of the kinds of information that your further reading and your notetaking must supply. At the same time you should not feel too much bound by the preliminary outline, for, as wider reading increases your knowledge and develops your point of view, the relative values of the subtopics may change; you may even decide to drop some and to add others. The outline, then, will almost certainly be adjusted as you go along and will not reach its final form until the reading and notetaking are finished and there has been time for a discriminating appraisal.

NOTETAKING

MECHANICS

4:55   You may choose your own system for recording notes, so long as it *is a system*. Some students find notebooks satisfactory—some preferring the bound variety and others the loose-leaf. Still others prefer cards of uniform size and usually larger than the bibliography cards. Cards have the advantage of being easily shuffled, thus minimizing the mechanical difficulty of organizing the material for the writing of the paper. The difference in size makes it easy to distinguish between bibliography and note cards, and the larger card—4 by 6 inches is a good choice in most instances—is better adapted to notetaking than the smaller one.

4:56   The kinds of information set down on a note card should be the same for all cards, and the items should be uniformly placed. (*a*) A heading (or "slug") showing the subtopic, corresponding with the subtitle in the outline, to which the note refers. (*b*) The exact source of the information. (*c*) The note itself. The heading is usually placed at the top of the card, and enough space allowed either above or below to make a change. New information gained as the reading progresses often suggests revisions in the outline and, therefore, in some of the headings. The author's name, title of the work, and exact page (or volume and page) reference may be placed immediately following the note or in one corner of the card— but always in the same location on every card.* Make it an unalterable rule to put but one note on a card, or on one page of a notebook, using the reverse only for completing the note.

4:57   Shortcuts are legitimate on note cards where they are not on bibliography cards. Thus the source of a note may be indicated merely by the author's last name and the page number. But there are two exceptions to this: (*a*) If the bibliography includes two authors with the same last name, the reference in each case must show the appropriate initials or given name as well as the last name. (*b*) If the bibliography includes two or more works by the same author, the reference in each case must give the title of the appropriate work. This title may be abbreviated, however. For example, a work by Harold Bruce entitled *William Blake in This World* might be written simply "Bruce, *Blake*."

4:58   Abbreviations both of names and of words may be used in the notes themselves. Many papers mention the same name over and over again. In the notes, the initial of the last name would be enough to identify the person. Thus the notes for a paper on William Blake might refer to him consistently as "B."; but, of course, you would need to know what you were about and not use "B." also to refer to Blake's friend Thomas Butts. In the notes any scheme of abbreviation and condensation may be used, always provided that it can be accurately translated when needed. But it is well to remember that nothing cools more quickly than a note; what is clear when you

* See suggestions in paragraphs 4:57–58 for ways of abbreviating some of the items.

write it can be unclear when next you see it. The shortcuts
just mentioned must not be used in the final copy of the paper.

TYPES OF NOTES

4:59   There are four principal ways of using source materials in
notes, and all of them require individual acknowledgment of
the sources in footnotes.* The first is the summary; second, the
paraphrase; third, the direct quotation; fourth, the combined
summary or paraphrase with quotation. There is in addition
another way of employing the thoughts of others—a way of
which you may sometimes not be aware—the mentioning of
facts, ideas, and opinions as though they were your own, when
actually they have been "borrowed" from your reading. Thus
in a study of slum housing, you might state as a "fact" that
"one reason for the existence of substandard dwellings is their
low tax liability." Your readers would have the right to know
how you came by this fact. Of course it is true that much
factual material is common knowledge and needs no citing of
authority. Such, for example, are the dates of the signing of
the Declaration of Independence, the Battle of Gettysburg,
the defeat of the Spanish Armada, the births and deaths of
world-famous figures; the facts that Sir Isaac Newton formulated the law of gravitation and that light travels at a speed
of approximately 186,000 miles a second. But the fact just
quoted about substandard housing is not one which may be
accepted without question; it must be supported by reference
to recognized authority.

4:60   It must be understood at the outset, then, that there is the
same obligation to acknowledge the source of a fact or of a
borrowed idea as there is to acknowledge the source of a summary, a paraphrase, or a direct quotation. Failure to give
credit in your paper for the loans made by other writers is
plagiarism—a serious offense.

The Summary

4:61   In the summary, the substance of a larger account is given
entirely in your own words, employing fewer words than used

---

* Footnote form for the various kinds of source materials is discussed in "Footnote and Bibliographic Forms," with numerous illustrations (chap. 7).

in the original. To write a good summary, you must be able to use your own thought, and this requires mastery of the material. Consider the following passage and the accompanying summary note:

Original quotation

> The whole theory of war among the Sioux was different from that of the civilized white man. It resembled in many respects the feudal system of the middle ages. There was a certain wild chivalry, for example. A brave enemy was often spared rather than ruthlessly killed. The warriors looked upon war as an opportunity to win honor. There was always greater rivalry to do some deed of daring, than merely to inflict damage upon the enemy.—Paul I. Wellman, *Death on Horseback* (Philadelphia: J. B. Lippincott Company, 1974), p. 44.

> [Used by permission.]

Summary

```
War on the Plains
     The Sioux, like the warriors of the
Middle Ages, regarded war more as an oppor-
tunity of winning honor through deeds of
daring and chivalry than as a means of
punishing their enemies.--Wellman, p. 44.
```

The foregoing summary cuts the number of words in the original by more than 50 percent. Ordinarily, the longer the original passage, the greater the possible reduction in the summary.

4:62   Not everyone sees the same substance in a given passage. For example, a student writing on Sioux treatment of their prisoners might summarize the passage just quoted by saying simply that the Sioux often spared a brave enemy.

The Paraphrase

4:63   In the paraphrase, the meaning of a passage is expressed in approximately the same number of words, using your own phraseology. The following examples illustrate an illegitimate, and a legitimate, use of paraphrase. Compare first the following quotation with a plagiarized wording.

Original quotation

> Among the novel objects that attracted my attention during my stay in the United States, nothing struck me more forcibly than the general equality of condition among the people. I readily discovered the prodigious influence that this primary fact exercises on the whole course of society; it gives a peculiar direction to public opinion and a peculiar tenor to the laws; it imparts new maxims to the governing authorities and peculiar habits to the governed.—Alexis de Tocqueville, *Democracy in America,* 2 vols. (New York: Vintage Books, 1959), 1: 3.

Plagiarized version—illegitimate use of quotation

> Among the new things that attracted Tocqueville during his visit to the United States, nothing impressed him more than the equality of the people. He easily discovered the stupendous influence that this equality had on the whole course of society; lending a particular direction to the public opinion, special meaning to the laws, new principles to those who governed, and distinctive habits to the governed.

4:64   The foregoing unacknowledged paraphrase is an awkward attempt to disguise the expression of another writer. Although there are a number of substitutions of words, much of the original author's phrasing remains. One change—that of substituting "equality of the people" for "general equality of condition among the people"—is a serious misrepresentation of the author's meaning. The two expressions are by no means alternates. This paraphrase would not be considered satisfactory even if the source were properly acknowledged. Now compare the paraphrase on the note card on page 52, for which the source is duly acknowledged. Wisely, the student makes no effort to translate Tocqueville's expression "general equality of condition among the people." preferring the author's exact wording.

> *Influences of equality*
>
> Nothing of the new that he saw in the U.S. more impressed Tocqueville than the "general equality of condition among the people." This he saw reflected in every aspect of life, giving a distinctive stamp to public opinion, laws, and habits, and influencing alike both the governors and the governed.   Tocqueville 1:3

SAMPLE NOTE CARD
(Paraphrase)

4:65   It is expressly recommended that summaries and paraphrases be composed while the works are before you. Often the sentences that immediately precede or follow a passage to be summarized help to clarify your thought, making the summary easier to write than it would be later on. It is sheer waste of time to copy the passage and then to be obliged to restudy it when the book is not at hand.

The Direct Quotation

4:66   *Criteria of use.* In most undergraduate research papers, long direct quotation should be sparingly used.* Besides producing monotony, too much quotation reduces the student's opportunity for practice in composition, tends to destroy his individual style (or prevents him from developing such style), and gives the impression of his not really having mastered the material. Nevertheless, there are occasions when it is better to quote than to summarize or to paraphrase. Three may be

---

* Studies involving a critical discussion or an analysis of a text, a comparison of the treatment of a particular matter by two writers, and the like require much direct quotation. But such studies are rarely undertaken at the undergraduate level.

mentioned: (*a*) when it is felt that no other words could adequately express the meaning or could express it in so telling a fashion; (*b*) when the author's exact description of a mechanism or of a procedure would obviate the possibility of misinterpretation; (*c*) when the contrast of opposing ideas makes the precise wording of the author essential.

4:67   *Mechanics of quoting.* A quotation must be copied exactly as it appears in the original, with every mark of punctuation, every capital letter, every peculiarity of spelling preserved. The whole must then be enclosed in double quotation marks, with the following exception: When double quotation marks occur *within* the passage you are quoting, they must be changed to single quotation marks. (See also pars. 6:3–5, which mention the preferred style of giving long quotations.)

4:68   Occasionally you may want to omit from a quotation an expression that is felt to be nonessential to your purpose. Such an omission is indicated by an ellipsis mark consisting of three spaced periods (never by asterisks [stars]), in addition to any period marking the end of a sentence. Note the following:

```
Of the attitude of the Sioux toward war,
Wellman says:
"The whole theory of war among the Sioux
. . . resembled in many respects the feudal
system of the middle ages. . . . There was
always greater rivalry to do some deed of
daring, than merely to inflict damage upon
the enemy."
```

(Additional information concerning the use of ellipsis dots found in pars. 6:5, 6:7.)

4:69   Upon occasion, you may find it advisable to insert into a quotation a word or more of explanation or of correction. To assure the reader that the faulty logic, incorrect word, or incorrect spelling is in the original quotation, you may insert the Latin word *sic* after the error. Occasionally, too, you may wish to make a correction or to supply the antecedent in a passage that omits it. All such interpolations must be enclosed in square brackets—in ink if need be. Parentheses *may not be substituted.*

Antecedent supplied:

"But since these masters [Picasso, Braque, Matisse] appeared to be throwing away or rebelling against academic training, art teaching has itself been discredited."

Correction of fact:

"The recipient of the Nobel Peace Award for 1961 [1960] is Albert John Luthuli."

Incorrect spelling noted:

"When the fog lifted, they were delighted to see that the country was heavily timbered and emmence [sic] numbers of fowl flying about."

Do not overdo the use of *sic*. Quotations from a work of the sixteenth century, for example, or from obviously archaic or illiterate writing, should not be strewn with *sic*s.

4:70   For the sake of emphasis, you may underline in a quotation words that are not italicized in the original, but you must acknowledge responsibility for the addition by an interpolation in square brackets within the quotation, or by a parenthetical note following it, as shown in the following examples:

"This man described another large river beyond the Rocky Mountains, the <u>southern branch</u> [italics mine] of which he directed me to take."

"This man described another large river beyond the Rocky Mountains, the <u>southern branch</u> of which he directed me to take." (Italics mine.)

4:71   Note that when a final quotation mark and another form of punctuation come together, certain rules must be observed concerning which mark to put first (see "Multiple punctuation," pars. 6:181–84).

The Combined Paraphrase, or Summary, and Quotation

4:72   A fourth use of source materials combines paraphrase, or summary, with quoted matter:

> Even if a sudden attack by the Arab armies
> should be successful in achieving its ob-
> jective within a very short time, two
> things would inevitably follow: "Interven-
> tion by the United Nations. . . . The same
> principles by which Israeli aggression was
> denounced in 1956 would now be used against
> us." The Arabs would lose a great deal
> "internationally, but especially in Asia
> and Africa." Hisham Sharabi, <u>Palestine and
> Israel</u> (New York: Pegasus Press, 1969),
> p. 183.

Addition of Personal Remarks

4:73   There are circumstances when it may be advisable to add to a
note a remark of your own. Some sign should be used to
distinguish it from the note proper. A convenient scheme is to
prefix your initials to the remark; another is to place slashes
at either side, as in the following:

> / Important to compare this view with X's
> given in ------. /

5 Writing the Paper

5:1   The written word exists to be read. Your research paper must have an audience, and in your paper you will have a specific attitude toward that audience and a purpose in addressing them. These considerations of audience, attitude, and purpose must be determined before you begin to write.

5:2   Depending upon the topic and the audience, your attitude will be formal or informal, detached or sympathetic, serious or humorous. Your purpose may be only to present your materials factually, or it may be to win adherents to a cause, or to destroy a popular misconception. Your audience may be assumed to include your instructor and your fellow students in the class; it may be narrowed to a small group known to be especially interested in the particular topic; it may be widened to include the reading public in general, of which you hold yourself to be representative.

AUDIENCE AND ATTITUDE

5:3   If you write principally for the instructor, and the topic is one on which his views are known, you may seek to condemn or to support those views. If you address your classmates primarily, and the topic bears on a general consensus with which you do not agree, you may be as zealously persuasive as your facts will allow. If the audience consists of a group who are especially interested in the topic, you will probably address them rather informally as fellow enthusiasts and equals. If you write for that larger reading public mentioned above, your attitude may be determined chiefly by the topic and your individual response to it. For example, if you have no

56

more than intellectual interest in an investigation of slum housing, you will probably recount your findings in a formal, detached manner. Your whole purpose will be to give an accurate, complete, well-ordered report. On the other hand, if your humanity is outraged and you seek redress for those obliged to live in squalor, your report in all its factual accuracy and completeness will reflect your sympathetic interest and understanding. You will illustrate it with telling details and comparisons calculated to move your readers to remedial action.

PURPOSE AND TONE

5:4   Your purpose will be reflected both in your attitude toward the audience and in your attitude toward the material, and these will result in a certain tone. Remember that tone affects the reader and adopt one that is most likely to produce the effect you desire.

5:5   We should expect that the two reports on slum housing suggested above would differ sharply in tone. In the objective, purely factual account, the writer's attitude would be intellectual, the tone serious and formal. A somewhat formal vocabulary, a carefully logical order, matter-of-fact details, absence of humor—all would reflect the writer's main purpose of giving a clear, purely factual report. On the other hand, in the sympathetic presentation, the writer's attitude would be emotional, and his tone would be personal and informal. Although he would be careful to guard against any appearance of fanaticism prejudicial to his case, he would look for effectiveness in action verbs, strong adjectives and adverbs, repetition, forceful comparisons, and vivid details which would produce mental pictures and sensuous images. Thus by his tone the writer would hope to gain not only a sympathetic hearing but adherents to a humanitarian cause.

5:6   When you have decided upon your audience and your attitude and have clearly in mind the general purpose and tone of your paper, you should be prepared to write—to develop your topic.

WRITING THE FIRST DRAFT

5:7   Your outline, note cards, bibliography cards, handbook, and dictionary—and perhaps a thesaurus as well—should be placed on your desk or work table within easy reach. Separate the note cards and place together all those with the same heading; then arrange the several piles in the order in which you expect to use them. Alphabetize the bibliography cards and place them in a pile by themselves.

PARAGRAPH STRUCTURE

5:8   Remembering that good prose must have not only grammatical correctness but unity, coherence, and emphasis as well; and, further, that the paragraph may be thought of as the whole work in miniature, you will concentrate upon producing paragraphs that satisfy the acknowledged requirements. The paper must develop in their order all the headings of the outline, but there is no rule about the number of paragraphs to be used to cover a heading or, for that matter, about the number of headings that may be covered in a paragraph.

Unity

5:9   Essential to the unity of the paragraph is the controlling idea, the nucleus of the thought that the paragraph is to develop. In the hands of the less experienced writer, this controlling idea had better be expressed in the first sentence, although he should know that it may appear in the last sentence, at some convenient place within the paragraph, or even be implied. It may be expressed in a word, a phrase, or a clause. It must be an idea that can be covered in a paragraph; not one so broad and general that it would take a book to develop. Consider, for example, the two sentences following:

> Charles Dickens is a great writer.
>
> The writings of Charles Dickens had a profound influence on the reform of laws pertaining to public health.

In order to develop the first, a book would be needed. To cover the second, a paragraph could be made to do the job.

5:10   Let us suppose that you were developing the first section of the outline on "The Harp" and wrote this topic sentence: "The harp is a musical instrument that has been known from the beginning of recorded history." In the sentences following, you would support the idea of the antiquity of the harp with information from your reading to show that: (*a*) The harp is mentioned in the Bible and in other writings from the ancient world. (*b*) It is depicted on frescoes and bas-reliefs, tablets and seals, from widely scattered areas. (*c*) Examples uncovered by archaeologists are to be found in a number of museums.

5:11   For many paragraphs a good check of their unity is to make certain that the word "because" (or a substitute of one word or more having the same meaning as "because") could be placed logically at the beginning of every sentence that supports the controlling idea. For example:

```
The harp is a musical instrument that has
been known from the beginning of recorded
history. We know this

because: (1) it is mentioned in the Bible
             and in other writings from the
             ancient world;

because: (2) it is depicted on frescoes and
             bas-reliefs, tablets and seals,
             from widely scattered areas;

because: (3) examples uncovered by archaeol-
             ogists are to be found in a
             number of museums.
```

5:12   However, paragraphs often contain what we may call secondary sentences whose function is to round out the thought of the main sentences. To assure unity of the paragraph, the "because" test must be applied again in order to see that every secondary sentence supports the controlling idea of the main sentence whose thought-idea it is designed to develop. Here is an example of a well-unified paragraph:

```
The decision of the House-Senate Joint
Economic Committee to hold hearings early
next week on the state of the economy will
```

serve two useful purposes. First it will
bring into the open testimony on whether
a tax cut is needed to spark business activ-
ity. Secondly it will exhibit the gathering
storm over interest rates between Congress
and the Federal Reserve Board. The storm
is being stirred by administration efforts
to move the economy off the plateau,
while at the same time the Federal Reserve
Board seeks to avoid the monetary swamps
that excessively easy money policies might
entail.

The first sentence announces the topic of the paragraph:
". . . hearings on the state of the economy will serve two useful
purposes." The second and third sentences state that the hearings will be useful *because:* "First it will bring . . . testimony
on whether a tax cut is needed . . ."; *because:* "Secondly it will
exhibit the storm over interest rates. . . ." The fourth sentence
supports the third by explaining "the storm over interest
rates." Notice that the subject of this secondary sentence is
"storm" and that it furnishes an immediate link with the parent sentence.

5:13   So it may be seen that, with a topic sentence and main
sentences which clearly support the controlling idea, there is
a foundation on which to build, if building is desired. By
means of secondary sentences each main idea may be elab-
orated with specific details, illustrations, or personal observations, always provided that every secondary sentence does
clearly illuminate the main sentence with which it is used
and, further, that it preserves the meaning and purpose of the
paragraph as a whole as set forth by the controlling idea.

Coherence

5:14   Necessary to the coherence of the paragraph is order. If
your reader is to be able to follow and to understand the
points that are being made, he must be led along in an orderly
fashion. Arrangement of the material according to a specific
plan, such as enumerative, chronological, spatial, logical, cli-
mactic, general-to-particular, particular-to-general, or some

combination of two of these;* repetition of key words to keep
main ideas before the reader; provision of transitional expressions to lead from sentence to sentence; use of parallel construction to express ideas of like value—all are valuable aids
to coherence.

5:15   The material itself frequently suggests the order, and the
topic sentence often indicates both the controlling idea and
the order of its development. Notice how the topic sentence
of the example in paragraph 5:12 indicates the use of the
enumerative order to develop the controlling idea. "The
decision . . . to hold hearings . . . on the state of the economy
will serve two useful purposes." The description of a mechanism or of a process, in which the reader's understanding of
the whole depends upon a step-by-step delineation of parts
and their relationships, observes a logical order. The portrayal
of a life, career, event, or development is most often arranged
in chronological order.

5:16   The following paragraph is an excellent illustration of the
way in which a number of aids are used to secure coherence.
Notice, first, that the topic sentence serves the double purpose of announcing the controlling idea and of indicating
the chronological order of its development. Notice, next, that
although the transitions are handled differently from the
ways more commonly used, they carry forward unmistakably
the idea of one "major controversy" after another and at the
same time offer pleasing variety. Observe, then, how the use
of the same grammatical construction at the beginning of
each supporting sentence helps the thought to move along
freely. And feel, finally, the mounting intensity of the strong
action verbs, "led," "fought," and "plunged."

> The chief reason why studying Edwards is important
> to one who wishes to understand eighteenth-century New
> England is that he played a very prominent part in many
> of the major philosophical and theological controversies
> of the time. Between 1736 and 1746, he led one party in
> the heated debate over the religious upheaval known as
> the Great Awakening. In the middle of the century, he

---

* These various orders of arrangement have been discussed in some
detail in the section "Outlining," pars. 4:37–54.

fought staunchly for the Calvinistic theory of the freedom of the will. A little later, he was the recognized champion of the Calvinistic forces in the bitter conflict over the doctrine of the total depravity of man. Finally, he plunged into the controversy over the nature of virtue and put on the Calvinistic armor in defense of the doctrine of election.—Clarence H. Faust and Thomas H. Johnson, *Jonathan Edwards* (New York: American Book Co., 1935), p. xv.

5:17   In a report of research involving a trip, the order may well be a combination of the chronological and the spatial orders, as in the opening paragraphs of an article on Stonehenge. It was written by the inventor of high-speed flash equipment who visited the site for the express purpose of photographing it at sunrise of the summer solstice. The importance of a specific time in carrying out his purpose is shown in the writer's observations of the weather. These provide sensuous images that enrich the narrative and illustrate one way in which the writer's stated purpose may be made to function—to lend interest and thus to capture and hold the reader's attention.

> I chose the solstice—June 22—because many archeologists believe that Stonehenge was deliberately and precisely oriented toward that point on the horizon at which the midsummer sun rose in those far-distant prehistoric dawns.
>
> From London my son and I set out in a rented automobile for Stonehenge. Knowing English weather, I allowed several days' grace before the 22d. Clouds would not be our only photographic hazard. Over Salisbury Plain, even when the night sky is clear, a dense ground fog often forms. But we were lucky. The heavens were bare, and as we drove, we felt on our faces a north wind strong enough to dispel any mist. We made Salisbury about midnight and continued onward another ten miles until, caught in the car's headlights, the famous Heel Stone loomed from the darkness. Beyond rose the huge monoliths, dimly outlined against the sky. Here we would wait out the night in order to see and photograph the ruins at sunrise.—Harold E. Edgerton, "Stonehenge," *National Geographic* 117 (June 1960): 850–51.

Types of Paragraph Development

5:18 Along with the considerations of unity and coherence in paragraphs is another matter for thought—types of paragraph development. When the controlling idea has been stated in the topic sentence, you must decide whether to support it by use of details, or of examples, or of reasons, or of comparison or contrast, or by use of a combination of these.

5:19 Look closely at the topic sentence to see what the effect of the controlling idea is likely to be and what expectations it arouses in the reader. If a topic sentence reads, "The inventor's financial difficulties increased daily," the reader normally looks to the following sentences for details of how and why the inventor came to financial distress. The sentence might be further clarified by the use of examples. If a topic sentence states that "general education is appropriate to the generality of mankind," the reader naturally expects to be given reasons to support the truth of the statement. And if a paragraph begins with this sentence, "The methods of making pottery, like those of most other industries, passed through a rapid succession of changes in the eighteenth century,"* the reader's questions are answered in sentences that contrast older with newer methods.

SENTENCE STRUCTURE

Emphasis

5:20 After unity and coherence of paragraphs the third quality of good writing is emphasis. The way you express your ideas should indicate their relative importance. Emphasis may be acquired (*a*) through the types of sentences used, (*b*) through the arrangement of the parts of the sentences, (*c*) through the use of specific and concrete words rather than general and abstract ones, and (*d*) through repetition of important words and phrases.

Types of sentences

5:21 Choose the periodic sentence, in which the main clause is

* J. L. Hammond and Barbara Hammond, *The Rise of Modern Industry* (New York: Harcourt, Brace & Co., 1926), p. 167.

either placed at the end or completed at the end. Keeping the reader in suspense is a way of gaining effectiveness.

Loose: The administration's proposed increase in the debt ceiling may be thwarted by some members of Congress who feel strongly that the public debt is getting out of control.

Periodic: Some members of Congress who feel strongly that the public debt is getting out of control may thwart the administration's proposed increase in the debt ceiling.

5:22   Employ the balanced sentence, in which the same grammatical construction is made to express coordinate ideas.

Unbalanced: To urge construction in a location close to a good shopping area, the committee called on the president of the company; and because they also felt the importance of apartments with cross-ventilation, they set forth this requirement as well.

Balanced: To urge construction in a location close to a good shopping area, and to set forth the importance of apartments with cross-ventilation, the committee called on the president of the company.

5:23   Prefer the stronger active voice to the weaker passive voice.

Weak: The new schedule could not be kept by the students.

Emphatic: The students could not keep the new schedule.

Arranging sentences

5:24   Place the important words at the beginning or at the end of the sentence, allowing the less important ones to rest in the middle.

<u>Weak</u>:   The president of the company will not be sympathetic to the cause, in all probability.
[Here the least important part of the sentence occupies the most important position--the end.]

<u>Emphatic</u>:   In all probability, the president of the company will not be sympathetic to the cause.

5:25   Arrange the ideas in the order of climax.

<u>Weak</u>:   To earn one's bread is best; to go hungry is better than to beg.

<u>Emphatic</u>:   To go hungry is better than to beg; to earn one's bread is better than either.

5:26   Move words or phrases out of their natural order.

<u>Emphatic</u>:   Never in all his experience of climbing had he encountered a sudden storm of such violence.

<u>Emphatic</u>:   Above the lake a dark bank of clouds was building up fast; another storm threatened. To return by the shore road, then, I dared not.

To be effective, changing the normal word order must be done in places where it will not sound strained and unnatural.

Specific and concrete words

5:27   Instead of vague, abstract terms, choose informative, expressive, colorful words—action verbs and adjectives and adverbs producing sensuous images.

65

Ineffective: The traffic moved through the Place de la Concorde and on up to the Étoile.

Effective: The traffic whipped round the Place de la Concorde and swept up to the Étoile.

Effective: A beardless, boyish face, very fair, no features to speak of, nose peeling, little blue eyes, smiles and frowns chasing each other over that open countenance like sunshine and shadow on a wind-swept plain.— Joseph Conrad.

Repetition of words and phrases

5:28   Choose only words or phrases that are important in the sentence. Careless repetition results in wordiness and monotony.

Careless
repetition: The chairman, who made the report, has done considerable research, which has been reported in leading journals. His interest in juvenile delinquency made his report especially interesting to our group.

Effective
repetition: Returning to college after his war experience, he was determined to make the most of his opportunity, determined to prepare himself for congenial and lucrative employment, determined to see that his children should never know the deprivations he had suffered as a child.

Effective
repetition: He was a dismal man, with a
perpetual tear sparkling at the
end of his nose, who either
had been in trouble, or was in
trouble, or expected to be in
trouble--couldn't be happy unless something went wrong.--
Joseph Conrad.

Variety

5:29 To make your writing effective, vary the length and structure of your sentences. The same pattern, the same rhythm,
produce a monotony that can make the reading tiresome. In
general, students tend to begin all their sentences with nouns
or pronouns and to write a great many short sentences. The
monotonous, choppy effect produced by a succession of short
sentences all starting with the subject can be avoided by an
occasional change from simple to compound sentences and
from the normal order of the subject, predicate, and complement to other arrangements (see pars. 5:24–26). Following are some of the ways to get pleasing variety:

5:30 Place the direct object of a verb before the subject.

Effective: Bitterness and hostility I had
foreseen, but open violence
I had not expected.

5:31 Open with an adjective or with an adverb or an adverbial
clause.

Effective: Undamaged by its centuries-long
burial in the dry, hot sands
of the desert, it was a handsome instrument that had been
found the preceding year by
a young English archaeologist.

Effective: Just as our car turned into the
square, it began to cough and
jerk ominously.

5:32   Open with a prepositional or a participial phrase.

<u>Effective</u>:   Through the fog we could see
only the tops of the tallest
buildings.

<u>Effective</u>:   Being convinced of the man's
sincerity, I hesitated to ques-
tion him further.

5:33   Open with a coordinating conjunction, such as *and, or, nor,*
or *but.*

<u>Effective</u>:   But there is no doubt that coal
is coming back. It will not
be without problems inherent in
its nature, however, and it
will not be a panacea for all
the energy problems.

5:34   Separate subject and predicate by words or phrases, but take
care that the separation results in a clear and pleasing sentence, not an awkward one.

<u>Awkward</u>:   Her report was clear and well
organized, and it was received
with enthusiasm.

<u>Effective</u>:   Her report, clear and well
organized, was received with
enthusiasm.

5:35   Change a series of short, simple sentences to a compound
or to a compound-complex sentence.

<u>Monotonous</u>:   I asked the welfare agency for
the name of a long-time resi-
dent. They directed me to a Mrs.
Morris. It appeared that she had
lived in the neighborhood for
more than fifty years.

<u>Effective</u>:   My request of the welfare
agency for the name of a long-
time resident led me to a Mrs.
Morris, who, it appeared, had

> lived in the neighborhood for
> more than fifty years.

5:36   Give variety to the pattern of your sentences by occasionally composing a sentence that is a question, exclamation, or exhortation.

<u>Effective</u>:   Should we not, then, work for
political candidates whose
platforms are built on peace
issues?

<u>Effective</u>:   Away with clichés! Away with
the status quo!

DICTION

The Right Word

5:37   The right words are an important element in the success of any written work. Attention to the composition of good sentences and paragraphs should be accompanied by a discriminating choice of words.

5:38   To help you select the right word, and avoid the wrong one, a reputable dictionary is an indispensable tool. There will be times when you will want to consult a large dictionary, such as the *Oxford English Dictionary* or *Webster's Third New International Dictionary,* but, for ready reference, every student should possess the smaller college dictionary, *Webster's Eighth New Collegiate Dictionary*. Like all reference works, a dictionary is completely useful only when the introductory notes, with their explanations of symbols and abbreviations, are understood. Besides the spelling, syllabication, pronunciation, and definition of a word—those uses most often required—the dictionary gives synonyms and antonyms and such labels as "archaic," "colloq.," "dial.," "obs." (obsolete), "slang," "nonstand." (nonstandard) and "substand." (substandard) to indicate the particular level of writing and speaking to which the word belongs. In both Webster's dictionaries French and Latin words and expressions that are often used in English writing appear in the straight alphabet list. Some few of the more commonly recognized words and expressions in other languages are included as well.

5:39   In most research papers colloquialisms, dialect, slang, and jargon are out of place. In general, too, technical words that are not a part of the vocabulary of the subject matter should be avoided. And trite expressions should be everywhere excluded. Be alert to the proper meanings of the many pairs of words that are often mistakenly used for each other. A few of them follow:

accept--except	credible--credulous
adverse--averse	emigrant--immigrant
advice--advise	fewer--less
affect--effect	formally--formerly
allude--elude	imply--infer
allusion--illusion	judicial--judicious
already--all ready	luxuriant--luxurious
altogether--	moral--morale
all together	practicable--
born--borne	practical
censor--censure	principal--principle
childish--childlike	their--there--they're
complement--	tortuous--torturous
compliment	uninterested--
continual--continuous	disinterested

5:40   Avoid, too, the pretentious, the flowery, the poetic expressions that will seem forced and artificial—the first of the following, for example: "ancestral mansion" for "home," "beauteous" for "beautiful," "domicile" for "house," "esteemed forebears" for "grandparents," "better half" for "wife," "halcyon" for "peaceful," "gentleman of the cloth" for "clergyman" or "priest," "native of the Emerald Isle" for "Irishman," "Honest Abe" for "Lincoln," "the Father of His Country" for "Washington," "knight of the road" for "tramp," "minion of the law" for "policeman," "liquidate" for "kill," "prevaricate" for "lie."

5:41   Strive for exactly the right word to convey your meaning at a given place. Use the dictionary in selecting synonyms and antonyms and pay attention to the *precise* meanings of the words you choose. The synonyms listed for a word cannot always be used interchangeably with it; so notice particularly what the dictionary says of the different implications of the synonyms. Aim at a style that is simple and direct—and one that is your own.

Transitional Expressions

5:42   To keep ideas moving in orderly fashion from one sentence to another, appropriate transitional expressions are used. Besides the familiar *and, also, too, but, or, nor,* the following frequently appear:

first	also	meanwhile
second	at the same	nevertheless
third	time	however
next	accordingly	notwithstanding
then	consequently	on the other
last	similarly	hand
finally	in like	on the whole
again	manner	to sum up
further	likewise	to conclude
moreover	hence	so
besides	thus	therefore
in addition		

5:43   Guard against overuse, or too constant use, of the transitional expression; one does not need a transitional word in every sentence.

5:44   In addition to paragraph and sentence structure and diction, there are particular matters of style that must be attended to in writing the paper. These are treated in the following chapter.

REVISING THE FIRST DRAFT

5:45   If you can spare the time after completing the first draft, put it aside for twenty-four hours. Returning to it afresh, you will be able the more readily to spot errors, omissions, need for curtailment, for rearrangement.

5:46   It is well to revise the draft in two separate operations.

5:47   *First,* take note of whether the central idea has been adequately developed in accordance with the outline; whether the sentences are effective, the paragraphs properly developed, the transitions satisfactory, the diction concise. In the light of this examination make the necessary alterations for clarification, expansion, curtailment, and rearrangement, not forgetting to revise the outline if the order of the parts has been changed. For copy with extensive revisions, cutting and pasting produces a corrected draft that is far easier to follow than one with changes made between the lines, along the margins, and on the backs of the pages.

5:48   *Second,* scrutinize the copy for correctness of grammar, spelling, capitalization, punctuation, and expression of quotations; completeness and proper style of footnotes; and attention to those mechanics of style set forth in chapter 6.

5:49   Finally, reread the corrected draft with great care. And do not rule out the possibility that *your* paper—because of its length or complexity, or both—may require more than one draft.

WRITING THE FINAL COPY

5:50   When you have done the best job of revision of which you are capable and have put the rough copy in order, you are ready for the final typing. Some institutions have special requirements with respect to paper, margins, pagination, and so forth, which of course you must follow. But if you are not bound by special regulations, you should observe the following.

PAPER

5:51   Use theme paper 8½ × 11 inches—the ruled variety if you write in ink, the unruled if you typewrite. Write on only one side and use black or blue-black ink, or a black ribbon. Be sure that the ribbon is new or nearly new and that the type is clean. If you want a carbon copy, choose a hard-finish black carbon paper rather than a soft-finish one, which tends to smudge.

MARGINS

5:52   Leave a margin of 1½ inches on the left and 1 inch on the other three sides of the paper, except on the first page, which should have a margin of 2 inches at the top to allow space for the title. Indent paragraphs eight spaces (i.e., begin typing at the eighth space).

SPACING

5:53   Double-space the text if you typewrite. Single-space footnotes, long prose quotations, and poetry (see pars. 5:60, 6:3, 6:6).

5:54   Always leave two spaces after a period, question mark, and exclamation mark. Leave one space after a colon except when it separates chapter from paragraph number (as in this book), hour from minute, and chapter from verse in scriptural references, when no space is left. Leave one space after other marks of punctuation, except the dash, which should consist of two hyphens, without space between or at either side.

```
There is no question--there can be none--of
who is right in this case.
```

5:55   Never put a subheading at the foot of a page unless there is space beneath it for at least one line of text.

TITLE

5:56   Put the title 2 inches from the top of the first page, center it on the page, and capitalize all letters in it. If the title is so long that it would extend into the margins if typed in one line, divide and double-space in two lines. Triple-space before beginning text.

PAGINATION

5:57   Place the page number at the top of the sheet, centering it about ¼ inch from the top, except on the first page, where the number should be centered at the foot of the sheet, about ¼ inch from the lower edge.

ARRANGEMENT OF FOOTNOTES

5:58   Footnote numbers should follow each other in numerical order on the page. They may begin with "1" on each page or they may be numbered consecutively throughout the paper. Beginning with "1" on each page is recommended, because this scheme permits a mistake in the footnoting to be easily corrected. Under the second scheme a mistake necessitates renumbering all notes from the error to the end of the paper.

5:59   Indicate a footnote with a raised numeral placed *at the end* of the matter it supports, letting it follow any mark of punctuation. Use no period or slash after the footnote numeral. Every footnote numeral in the text must be represented by a footnote of the corresponding number at the foot of the page.

5:60   Indent the first line of each footnote eight spaces and begin the note with the raised numeral. Carry succeeding lines of the note to the margin. Single-space within the notes but double-space between individual notes.

5:61   The typing of pages that require insertion of footnotes calls for special care. Before starting to type a page, look at the copy and make note of the footnotes that the page is likely to include. (At this point you will see one of the advantages of having the footnotes in final form in the first draft.) To estimate the amount of space required for the notes, for the proper space between the notes, and for correct margin at the bottom, figure as follows:

5:62   Allow two spaces (i.e., two *single-spaced* lines) between the last line of the text and the first footnote. Add to this the number of lines required for the note; then add to that number five single spaces to allow for the 1-inch margin at the bottom (on most typewriters there are approximately five lines to the inch). Thus, if there were one two-line footnote to be accommodated, you would need to allow nine spaces, or about 2 inches at the foot of the page. In other words, your text could occupy (together with the top margin) about 9 inches on the page. To avoid typing text below the point at which you should stop in order to take care of the footnotes, put a light pencil mark at the margin. Actually, marking the point at which typing of the text should stop is helpful when there is only the lower margin to consider. If there is more than one footnote to be allowed for, be sure that your estimate allows not only for the number of lines in each additional note but for the extra space between individual notes as well.

5:63   Separate text and footnotes either with an unbroken line (made with the key used for underlining) extending the width of the typing area or with an eight-space line beginning at the left margin. Single-space after typing the last line of text before beginning to type the separating line; then double-space before beginning the footnote.

BIBLIOGRAPHY

5:64   Assemble the bibliography cards in alphabetical order according to the last names of the authors. A work for which no author is given is alphabetized according to the first word of the title (disregarding "A," "An," or "The"). Enter in the bibliography every work—books, articles, primary sources if any such were used—that supplied valuable information for your paper.

5:65   Begin the bibliography on a new page, dropping down from the top about 1½ inches and centering the heading

BIBLIOGRAPHY

5:66   The bibliographic form for various kinds of works is illustrated in the examples in paragraphs 7:78–129. Begin each entry at the left-hand marginal line and, if necessary to carry over to another line, indent (eight spaces suggested) for each line of runover. Single-space within each entry and double-space between the entries. Center the page number ½ inch from the bottom of the sheet. If there is more than one page of bibliography, number the succeeding pages in the center, ¼ inch from the top of the sheet.

OUTLINE

5:67   If an outline is required to accompany the paper, type it on a separate page, using the form set forth in the section "Outlining" (pars. 4:37–54). Center the heading

OUTLINE

about 1½ inches from the top of the page.

TITLE PAGE

5:68   Your instructor may require that the title page be in a special form. If there is no special requirement, type the title of the paper slightly above the center of the page, using capital letters throughout and double-spacing if two lines are necessary. The first line should not exceed 5 inches. Center the word "By" four spaces below the title, and your name two spaces below it. The course number and the date, each on a separate line, should be centered on the lower part of the page so as to allow a margin of 1½ inches.

PROOFREADING

5:69   Proofreading your paper should consist of comparing the final copy with the first draft; not as some students may think, of merely rereading the final typescript.

CORRECTIONS

5:70   Errors in typing found in the proofreading may ordinarily be corrected in ink if they are slight and if there are no more than two or three on a page. If there are more, the page should be retyped.

6 Some Matters of Style

FOOTNOTES

6:1 Elsewhere we have pointed out the importance of acknowledging all the sources in developing your paper (see pars. 4:59–60). As the writing progresses, your note cards will be constantly in use, and, as the substance of each card takes its place in the composition, the proper footnote should be inserted. In order that the train of thought may not be unduly disrupted, footnotes in the rough draft should be inserted into the page immediately after the section to which the individual note belongs, separated from the text by a short rule above and below the note. For the same reason, the writing of the footnote citations in acceptable form may be postponed until the draft is finished. Then, however, they should be reviewed at once with the bibliography cards, and the footnotes set up in the proper style before the typing of the final copy is undertaken. (The various forms of footnotes are discussed in chap. 7.) This timing will ensure early discovery of any missing items of information and allow omissions to be repaired before the final typing begins.

QUOTATIONS

6:2 The correct presentation of quotations, which must be understood while notes are being made from source materials, is discussed in the section "Notetaking" (pars. 4:55–72). Here it is important to mention some customary ways of displaying and punctuating quotations in typewritten matter.

6:3 Following the general practice of publications, short, direct prose quotations should be incorporated into the text of the paper and enclosed in double quotation marks. Longer quotations—two or more sentences which would occupy four or more typewritten lines—should be set off from the text in single spacing and indented in their entirety four spaces from the left marginal line of text, omitting quotation marks at beginning and end. (See example in par. 6:5.) If paragraph indention is necessary, indent another four spaces for the beginning of the paragraph.

6:4 Since these long quotations (block quotations, as they are called) omit quotation marks at beginning and end, any quotation appearing within the excerpt should be enclosed in quotation marks as in the original.

6:5 If in a quotation of two or more paragraphs, there is an omission of a paragraph or more, that omission should be indicated by a period and three ellipsis points at the end of the paragraph preceding the omission.

```
When Chief Justice Warren retired from the
Supreme Court, it was most appropriate
for him to assume the office of Chairman of
the United Nations Association of the
United States. . . .
    Earl Warren believed that the effort
to bring the rule of law to govern the
relations between sovereign states--the
central effort of the United Nations--is of
the highest priority.
```

6:6 Quotations of poetry should be set off from the text in single spacing and centered upon the page—if possible, line for line as in the original. None of the lines should be allowed to extend beyond the margins of the text; allow the end of a very long line to run over to the next line. Omit quotation marks at the beginning and end.

6:7 If a line or more is omitted from the quotation, the omission should be indicated by a full line of ellipsis points approximating in length the line of poetry immediately above it:

```
Hark! Hark! the sweet vibrating lyre
Sets my attentive soul on fire:
 . . . . . . . . . . . . . . .
```

```
        And the more slow and solemn bass
        Adds charm to charm and grace to grace.
```

FOREIGN WORDS AND EXPRESSIONS

6:8   Underline foreign words in English text, but make exceptions of the following foreign words which by continued use in English have became anglicized. Notice that some foreign words have dropped the accent marks proper to their native forms. Among them are *debris, denouement, entree, regime, role.* Accent marks, where necessary, should be inserted in ink, by hand. The following words and expressions should not be underlined:

a posteriori	entree
a priori	entrepreneur
ad hoc	ex officio
ad infinitum	exposé
antebellum	facade
apropos	genre
attaché	habeas corpus
barranca	kapellmeister
beau idéal	laissez faire
bête noire	mea culpa
blitzkrieg	mélange
bona fide	ménage
bourgeoisie	milieu
carte blanche	mores
chargé d'affaires	naiveté
cliché	par excellence
communiqué	pasha
contretemps	per annum
coup d'état	per capita
coup de grace	percent
debris	per se
denouement	pro rata
de rigueur	rapport
dilettante	rapprochement
élan	recherché
émigré	regime

```
remuda                 versus
résumé                 via
role                   vice versa
status quo             vis-à-vis
subpoena               visa
tête-à-tête            weltanschauung
trattoria              weltschmerz
```

6:9 In general, foreign words and expressions that are not included in the foregoing list should be underlined. *The Oxford English Dictionary, Webster's Third New International Dictionary,* and *Webster's [Eighth] New Collegiate Dictionary* include in their straight alphabetic listing foreign words and expressions that occur frequently in English publications. Further, the *Oxford Dictionary* marks as "alien" those words and expressions that have not been accepted into the English language; they should, therefore, be underlined unless they appear in the foregoing list.

6:10 Do not underline foreign titles preceding proper names (Mme, M., Mlle, Sr., etc.), or foreign names of persons, places, institutions, or the like.

```
Alliance française     Freiherr von Schwenau
Bibliothèque nationale the rue Royale
Père Lagrange          Academia española
```

Note that following Mme and Mlle there is no abbreviation period.

6:11 Do not underline the words in a quotation entirely in a foreign language. In the following excerpt the words *songe réalisé* are properly underlined since they occur within a sentence in which the other words are English.

```
"We drove out one evening to Chambord and
experienced there a songe réalisé."
```

6:12 But the following excerpt contains within it a quotation that is entirely in French, and this is not underlined:

```
"Our local folder of attractions carried an
appealing advertisement which stated that
'chaque soir d'été les scènes oubliées, les
```

```
mots évanouis s'animent, resonnent, grâce
à la magie du son et de la lumière.' "
```

ABBREVIATIONS

6:13   Few abbreviations are permissible *in text,* except in scientific and technical writing. In footnotes, bibliographies, and tabular matter and in some kinds of illustrations (*e.g.*, maps, graphs, charts), however, abbreviations not only are permitted but are normally preferred. In all quoted matter, the exact expression of the original must be followed.

WITH PERSONAL NAMES

6:14   Use the following abbreviations for social titles before names: Mr., Messrs., Mrs., Ms., Mlle, M., MM., Mme, Sr., and corresponding abbreviations in other foreign languages.

6:15   Use the abbreviation Dr. before a name, but spell out the word *doctor* when it appears without a name:

```
Dr. Chase is the physician in charge.
Her doctor was out of town.
```

6:16   Use abbreviations for scholastic degrees and professional affiliations after names: M.A., Ph.D., Litt.D., M.D., F.R.S., F.R.G.S., and so on. A comma is placed between name and abbreviation:

```
Marcus Ledbetter, Ph.D.
David Bonham, F.R.G.S.
```

6:17   Use the abbreviations Sr. and Jr., for Senior and Junior, and II and III for designating Second and Third (see par. 6:61), following a full name. Never use the spelled-out words or the abbreviations with the surname alone. (In informal writing, such as letters, it is permissible to use the terms with given names.) Note that a comma precedes Sr. and Jr., but not II and III:

```
Mrs. Paul Taylor, Sr.
Christopher Morley, Jr.
but: Adlai Stevenson III
```

6:18   Spell out a civil, military, professional, or religious title when it precedes the surname alone:

```
Senator Jackson    Professor Cate
Governor McCall    General Abrams
        Father O'Brien
```

But use the appropriate abbreviation before the full name:

```
Sen. Henry M. Jackson    Prof. James L. Cate
Gov. Thomas McCall    Gen. Creighton W. Abram
        Fr. Lawrence O'Brien
```

6:19   Spell out *Reverend* and *Honorable* if preceded by *the*; otherwise abbreviate to Rev. and Hon. *Never* use the title, either spelled out or abbreviated, with the surname alone, but only when it is followed by the person's full name, or by Dr. or Mr. as may be appropriate:

```
Wrong: Rev. White (or the Rev. White)
Right: Rev. Edward S. White (or the Reverend
       Edward S. White, or the Reverend
       Dr. White, or Rev. Mr. White)
```

6:20   *Saint* standing before the name of a saint may be abbreviated, St. (plural, SS.):

```
St. Thomas Aquinas
SS. Augustine and Benedict
```

6:21   Names preceded by *Saint* are spelled out or abbreviated, as personal preference on the part of the bearers of such names may determine:

```
Etienne Geoffroy Saint-Hilaire
Louis Stephen St. Laurent
```

BOOKS OF THE BIBLE

6:22   Spell out the names of the books of the Bible and of the Apocrypha, except when they occur with exact references. Acceptable abbreviations may be found in the front matter of the Bible, in the *Shorter Oxford English Dictionary,* and in the University of Chicago Press *Manual of Style.* Place a colon between chapter and verse number(s), leaving no space either before or after the colon:

```
The first of the Gospels to be written
was Mark.
```

```
The Beatitudes are found in Matt. 5:3-12
and in Luke 6:20-23.
```

GEOGRAPHIC NAMES

6:23   Spell out the names of countries (except that USSR is now commonly used for Union of Socialist Soviet Republics), states, counties, provinces, territories, bodies of water, mountains, and the like.

6:24   Spell out the prefixes of geographic names: Fort, Lake, Mount, Point, Port, Saint:

```
Fort Worth          Mount Prospect
Lake Michigan       Port Huron
```

6:25   Spell out *north, south, east, west,* as well as *northeast, southwest,* and so on, capitalizing when they are part of a name, and abbreviating when they follow a street name:

```
The seminary is in West Newton,
Massachusetts.
```

```
The shop is at 425 Seventeenth Street NW.
```

```
High-rise apartments are going up on the
northwest side of the city.
```

6:26   Spell out all such words as *avenue, street, drive, road, court, square, terrace, building,* capitalizing only when they are used as part of a name:

```
Many members of the faculty live in
College Terrace.
```

TIME

6:27   Spell out the names of the months and of days when they occur in text, whether alone or in dates. And in footnotes, bibliographies, tables (and other closely set matter), the following designations are permissible if used consistently: Jan.,

Feb., Mar., Apr., May, June, July, Aug., Sept., Oct., Nov., Dec.; Sun., Mon., Tues., Wed., Thurs., Fri., Sat.

6:28   Use the abbreviations A.M., P.M., and M. after numerals indicating time of day. Note that the abbreviation for noon is M., that for midnight, P.M.

6:29   For era designations use the abbreviations B.C., A.D., B.C.E., or C.E. ("before Christ," "Anno Domini," "before the common era," "common era"). A.D. should precede the year number, and the other designations should follow it:

```
Solomon's Temple was destroyed by the
Babylonians in 587 B.C. Rebuilt in 515
B.C., it was destroyed by the Romans in
A.D. 70.
```

MEASUREMENTS

6:30   Spell out expressions of dimension, distance, measure, weight, degree, and so on (but see par. 6:66).

PARTS OF A BOOK

6:31   Spell out the words *book, chapter, part, volume, section, scene, verse, column, page, figure,* and so on, except that when such a term is followed by a number in footnote or parenthetical material, abbreviation is preferred: bk(s)., chap(s)., pt(s)., vol(s)., sec(s)., sc., v. (vv.), col(s)., p. (pp.), fig(s). The words *act, line,* and *table* should never be abbreviated.

ORGANIZATIONS

6:32   It is now general practice to refer to many government agencies, unions, service and fraternal organizations, network broadcasting companies, and so on, by the initials of their names, omitting periods (these designations are called acronyms). For unfamiliar abbreviations, the name should be spelled out at its first occurrence and the abbreviation placed in parentheses immediately after. Following are some of the better-known abbreviations:

AMA	AFL–CIO	IOOF	CORE
NATO	NBC	YMCA	CIA
UNESCO	UN	YMHA	HEW

6:33 Some abbreviations should be used in giving the names of companies, even though the individual firm name does not abbreviate the word: &, Bro., Bros., Co., Corp. *The* before a name, and *Inc.* or *Ltd.* following it, are usually omitted; when *the* is needed in the context, it is not treated as part of the title and therefore is not capitalized:

```
The book was published by the University
of Chicago Press.
```

NUMBERS

GENERAL RULE

6:34 In nonscientific text matter in which numbers appear in isolation, the general rule is to spell out all numbers up through one hundred—e.g., sixty-five, eighty-nine—and all round numbers that can be expressed in two words—e.g., one hundred, three hundred, forty-five hundred, five thousand:

```
Tractor sales in Russia in 1969 totaled
twelve hundred.
```

6:35 Exact numbers over one hundred are written in figures:

```
The school has 526 pupils.
```

6:36 Now note the following in which exact numbers over one hundred and those under one hundred appear:

```
More than half of the 440 families who
applied for apartments came from distances
of fifty to seventy-five miles.
```

6:37 It must be understood that there is considerable latitude in applying this *general rule* and that there are a good many exceptions, as the special cases discussed in the following paragraphs show.

SERIES

6:38 The general rule is changed when numbers above *and* below one hundred appear in a group or series, all of which apply to the same kind of thing. Here all are expressed in figures.

```
In the area studied, there were 186 such
buildings, the smaller housing anywhere
from 50 to 65 persons each, and the larger
from 650 to 900 each, with a single room
sometimes occupied by 8 to 10.
```

INITIAL NUMBERS

6:39   A sentence should never begin with a figure, even when there are figures in the rest of the sentence. Either spell out the first number or, better, recast the sentence.

<u>Wrong</u>:
```
250 passengers escaped injury;
68 sustained minor injuries;
and 110 were so seriously hurt
that they required hospitaliza-
tion.
```

<u>Right</u>:
```
Two hundred and fifty passengers
escaped injury; 68 sustained
minor injuries; and 110 were so
seriously hurt that they re-
quired hospitalization.
```

<u>Or, better</u>:
```
There were 250 passengers who
escaped injury; 68 who sustained
minor injuries; and 110 so se-
riously hurt that they required
hospitalization.
```

ROUND NUMBERS

6:40   Although round numbers occurring in isolation are spelled out (par. 6:34), several round numbers coming close together are usually expressed in figures:

```
There were 1,500 books in the first ship-
ment, 8,000 in the second, and 100,000
in the third; altogether there were now
1,000,000 books in the warehouse.
```

6:41   Very large round numbers are frequently expressed in figures and units of millions or billions:

```
In Latin America the number of unemployed
```

climbed from 2.5 million in 1950 to 8.5
million in 1965.

PERCENTAGES AND DECIMALS

6:42   Figures should be used to express percentages and decimals.
The word *percent* should be written out, except in scientific
writing, where the symbol % may be used:

With interest at 8 percent, the monthly
payment would amount to $12.88, which he
noted was exactly 2.425 times the amount he
was accustomed to save monthly.

FRACTIONS

6:43   A fraction standing alone should be spelled out, but a numerical unit composed of a whole number and a fraction should
be expressed in figures:

Trade and commodity services accounted for
nine-tenths of all international receipts
and payments.

<u>But</u>: The rent of the house was almost 2½
times that of the apartment.

MONEY

6:44   *United States currency.* The general rule (par. 6:34) applies
in isolated references to amounts of money in United States
currency.* If the amount is spelled out, so are the words
dollars and *cents*; if figures are used, the dollar symbol ($)
precedes them:

His allowance was five dollars a week.

<u>But</u>: The report showed $135 collected in
fines.

6:45   Fractional amounts of money over one dollar appear in figures
like other decimal fractions ($1.75). When both fractional
amounts and whole-dollar amounts are used in the same sen-

---

* The student whose paper must deal with sums of money in cur-
rencies other than United States is advised to consult the table "Foreign
Money" in the United States Government Printing Office *Manual*.

tence (and only in such circumstances), the whole-dollar amounts are shown with decimal point and ciphers:

```
The same article is sold by some stores for
$1.75, by others for $1.95, and by still
others for $2.00.
```

6:46   The expression of very large amounts of money, which may be cumbersome whether spelled out in full or written in figures, may well follow the rule for expressing large round numbers (par. 6:41), using units of millions or billions with figures preceded by the dollar sign:

```
Japan's exports to Taiwan, which averaged
$60 million between 1954 and 1958, rose
sharply to $210 million in 1965, and to
$250 million in 1966.
```

6:47   *British currency*. Since decimalization went into effect in February 1971, British currency has been expressed in pounds and pence, very like dollars and cents:

```
two pounds     twenty-five pence
£3.50     25 p.
```

Before decimalization, British currency was expressed in pounds, shillings, and pence:

```
threepence     seventeen shillings
four pounds two shillings and sixpence
£12 17s. 6d.   or:     £12.17.6
£48 million          £1,238 million
```

A sum of money might also be expressed in guineas (twenty-one shillings equaled a guinea):

```
30 guineas (gns.)     342 guineas
```

The term *billion* should not be used for British sums, since *billion* as employed by the British means *trillion* in United States terminology.

PARTS OF WRITTEN WORKS

6:48   With few exceptions, all the numbered parts of printed works are referred to in arabic numerals. If, however, a reference is made to the preliminary pages of a work that designates those pages with small roman numerals (i, iii, viii, ix, x), the reference should also employ that style.

6:49 Citations to public documents or other manuscript material should use exactly the kind of numerals found in the source.

DATES

6:50 *Day, month, and year.* Full dates may be expressed in one of two styles:

```
10 June 1974    or: June 10, 1974
```

The first, in which no punctuation is used, is preferred. Use one form consistently throughout the paper.

6:51 When the month is omitted, or when the day is separated from the month by one or more words, the preferred style is to spell out the date:

```
The date set was the twenty-second.
The sequence of events of the twenty-first
of March is unclear.
```

6:52 When month and year alone are mentioned, the preferred style is to omit punctuation between them: March 1974.

6:53 In informal writing it is permissible to abbreviate reference to the year:

```
The class of '74 is already planning next
year's reunion.
```

6:54 *Centuries.* References to particular centuries should be spelled out, uncapitalized:

```
the eighteenth century
the mid-twentieth century
```

6:55 *Decades.* References to decades take two forms:

```
the 1890s    or, less formal: the nineties
```

TIME OF DAY

6:56 Except with A.M. or P.M., when figures must always be used, time of day should usually be spelled out in text. Never add *in the morning* after A.M. or *in the evening* after P.M., and never use *o'clock* with either A.M. or P.M., or with figures.

6:57   Where the context makes clear whether morning or evening is meant, you might write simply:

```
The first class was at eight.
The evening program ran from eight to
eleven.
```

But where there is the possibility of misinterpretation, you should write:

```
The first class was at eight o'clock in the
morning.
```

6:58   When the exact time should be emphasized, figures should be used:

```
The train is due to arrive at 7:10 A.M.
Station XORT broadcasts the news at 7:00
and 8:00 A.M. and at 5:00, 6:00, and
7:00 P.M.
```

6:59   Midnight is written as 12:00 P.M., noon as 12:00 M.

NUMBERS WITH NAMES

6:60   *Rulers.* In a succession of emperors, kings, queens, or popes with the same name, identification is by numerals, traditionally capital roman:

```
Napoleon III    Elizabeth I
Louis XIV       John XXIII
```

6:61   *Family names.* Male members of families with identical names are sometimes differentiated in the same way as monarchs:

```
Adlai Stevenson III
```

See also paragraph 6:17.

6:62   *Governmental designations.* Particular dynasties, governments, governing bodies, political divisions, and military subdivisions are commonly designated by an ordinal number before the noun and are capitalized. Numerals up through one hundred should be spelled out; those over one hundred, written in figures:

Nineteenth Dynasty   Ninety-third Congress
Fifth Republic   Twenty-fourth Con-
                                gressional District
but: 173d Airborne Division

6:63   *Lodges, unions.* Local branches of fraternal lodges and of unions bear numbers, which should be expressed in arabic numerals following the name:

Typographical Union No. 16
American Legion, Department of California,
    Leon Robart Post No. 1248

6:64   *Churches.* Numerals standing before the names of churches or religious organizations are usually spelled-out ordinals:

First Church of Christ, Scientist
Seventh Day Adventists

6:65   *Street addresses, highways, telephone numbers, page numbers.* It is preferable to spell out the names of numbered streets under one hundred, for the sake of appearance and ease of reading, but street (as well as building) addresses, highway numbers, telephone numbers, and page numbers should be expressed in figures:

The address is 20 Eighty-first Street; the
    telephone number, 461-2630.
33 N. State St.
1040 First National Bank Building
California 17   Interstate 80
U.S. Route 30 or U.S. 30
The Bibliography is on pages 239-60.

SCIENTIFIC USAGE

6:66   In mathematical, statistical, technical, or scientific text, where physical quantities for distances, lengths, areas, volumes, pressures, and so on, are frequently referred to, all amounts should be expressed in figures, whether they are under or over one hundred:

```
30 milliliters          2,200 miles
3 cubic feet            125 volts
12 meters               10 picas
60 pounds               10°C, 10.5°C
180 hectares            10° (of arc)
```

THE COMMA WITH NUMBERS

6:67   For the most part, in numbers of one thousand or more, the thousands are marked off with commas:

```
1,500      12,275,500      1,475,525,000
```

No comma is used, however, in page numbers, street address and telephone numbers, four-digit year numbers, chapter numbers, fraternal organizations and the like, and decimal fractions of less than one:

```
The Bibliography is on pages 1012-20.
The address is 10314 Hale Avenue; the
telephone number, 238-4728.
In the Coastal district the peel thick-
ness ÷ the pulp diameter of the Eureka
lemon was 0.1911 for fruit from the top of
the tree and 0.2016 for fruit from the
bottom.
The Leon Robart Post was established in
1946.
```

Note, however, that in year dates of more than four figures, the comma is employed: 10,000 B.C.

CONTINUED NUMBERS

6:68   The term *continued numbers* (or *inclusive numbers*) refers to the first and last number of a sequence of numerical designations, such as pages or years. Continued numbers are separated by a hyphen in a typewritten work and expressed according to the following scheme, which is based on the way one normally speaks these numbers:*

* The table is taken from the University of Chicago Press *Manual of Style,* 12th ed. (1969), p. 205.

FIRST NUMBER	SECOND NUMBER	EXAMPLES
Less than 100	Use all digits	3-10; 71-72
100 or multiple	Use all digits	100-104; 600-615
More than 100 but less than 110 (in multiples of 100)	Use changed part only (i.e., omit 0)	107-8; 1002-3
More than 109 (in multiples of 100)	Use last two digits (or all if more than last two digits change)	321-25; 415-532; 1536-38; 1890-1954

The principal use of the foregoing scheme is for page numbers and other numbered parts of written works, and for inclusive year dates:

pp. 2-14, 45-46, 125-26, 200-210, 308-9

the years 1933-36 of the Great Depression

the Napoleonic victories of 1800-1801

PLURALS

6:69   Plurals of numbers expressed in figures are formed by the addition of *s* alone (i.e., not apostrophe and *s*):

Mercedes-Benz 220s are popular with the affluent young marrieds.

Pilots of 747s receive special training.

There was a heavy demand to trade 6½s for 8¾s.

6:70   Plurals of spelled-out numbers are formed like the plurals of nouns:

Twelves and fourteens, but few thirty-fours or thirty-sixes, were on sale.

Most of the women were in their forties or fifties.

ENUMERATIONS

6:71   *Run-on in text.* Numbers (or letters) used to enumerate items in text stand out better when they are set in parentheses, either single or double, than when they are followed by periods:

```
He gave three reasons for his resignation:
(1) his age, 63, (2) failing eyesight,
(3) desire to live under less pressure.
```

6:72   *Beginning a new line or paragraph.* When numbered items in an enumeration without subdivisions begin each on a new line, they are most often indicated by arabic numerals followed by a period. The items may be treated like the paragraphs of the text, that is, given paragraph indention and the runover lines begun at the margin:

```
          1. The nature of the relationship
between library quality and library use
```

Or the items may be set flush with the margin, and the runover lines aligned with the first line of substantive matter:

```
1. The concept of organization as a function
   of library service
2. The concept of information in librarian-
   ship
3. The concept of formal relations
4. Topological and intellectual relations
   of information classes: new solutions
```

In both styles, periods following numerals must be aligned. Periods at the ends of lines should be omitted, whether or not the items are composed of complete sentences.

6:73   *In outline form.* For an outline or other enumeration in which there are subdivisions, the following scheme of notation and indention is recommended. It is not necessary to use a capital roman numeral for the first level when there are fewer divisions than shown in the example. The first level may well begin with A or with 1 (arabic 1):

```
I. Wars of the Nineteenth Century
   A. United States
      1. Civil War, 1861-65
         a) Causes
            (1) Slavery
               (a) Compromise
                   i) Missouri Compromise
                   ii) Compromise of 1850
```

> II. Under the head of . . .
>   A. Under the head of . . .
>   1. Under the head of . . .
>   ETC.

SPELLING

6:74 Spelling should accord with the best American usage and must be consistent—except, of course, in quotations, where the original must be followed exactly. The authority recommended for spelling and for syllabication (which generally determines the division of words at ends of lines) is *Webster's Third New International Dictionary* or its abridgment, *Webster's New Collegiate Dictionary* (the eighth). (Use the first spelling where there is a choice.) For the spelling of personal names, refer to *Webster's Biographical Dictionary,* and of geographical names, to *Webster's Geographical Dictionary.*

PLURALS

6:75 *Proper names.* Plurals of the names of persons and of other capitalized names are formed by the addition of *s* or *es* without the change of a final *y* to *i* as required for common nouns.

> There are three Bettys in the class.

6:76 Add *s* to all names except those ending in *s, x,* or *z,* or in *ch* or *sh*:

> the Johnsons   the Pattullos   the Blys
> the Coreys   the Boyces   the Allees

6:77 Add *es* to names ending in *s, x,* or *z,* or in *sh* or *ch*:

> the Hugheses   the Coxes   the Cashes
> the Jenkinses   the Alvarezes   the Marches

6:78 *Capital letters.* Form the plurals of most single and multiple capital letters used as nouns by adding *s* alone:

> The three Rs are taught at the two YMCAs.

6:79 *Small letters.* Form the plurals of all small letters, of capital letters with periods, and of capital letters that would be confusing if *s* alone were added, by adding an apostrophe and *s*:

```
All the examples were labeled by letters:
the a's were tested first, the b's second,
and so on.

The B.A.'s and B.S.'s conferred were almost
ten times the number of M.A.'s, M.S.'s,
and Ph.D.'s.

The A's, I's, and S's in the directory were
checked by the same group.
```

POSSESSIVES

6:80 Form the possessive case of a proper name in the singular by adding an apostrophe and *s*:

```
Hughes's contribution      Marx's ideology
Bly's poems                Berlioz's music
Johnson's essays           Cash's program
```

But see the exceptions noted in paragraphs 6:81 and 6:82.

6:81 The possessive case of the names of Jesus and Moses, and of Greek (or hellenized) names of more than one syllable ending with *es,* is formed by adding an apostrophe alone:

```
Jesus' ministry            Aristophanes' plays
Moses' leadership          Xerxes' campaigns
```

6:82 For some common nouns as well, a regard for euphony sets aside the rule for forming the possessive by adding an apostrophe and *s,* and instead adds only an apostrophe:

```
for appearance' sake    for conscience' sake
            for righteousness' sake
```

6:83 Form the possessive case of a plural proper name (the Coreys, the Pattullos, etc.) by adding an apostrophe to the accepted form of the plural of the name. (See pars. 6:76 and 6:77.)

```
the Coreys' garden      the Alvarezes' ranch
the Pattullos' house    the Marches' boat
```

PLURALS AND POSSESSIVES OF PREPOSITIONAL-PHRASE COMPOUNDS

6:84 The plurals of prepositional-phrase compounds are formed according to the rule governing the first noun of the compound:

```
brothers-in-law    commanders-in-chief
              men-of-war
```

But the possessive case of the same compound words is:

```
my brother-in-law's business
the commander-in-chief's dispatches
the man-of-war's prow
```

COMPOUND WORDS

6:85   The hyphen is used in many compound words; others are left open; others are spelled as one word. For most noun forms and for many adjective forms, Webster's unabridged dictionary gives the correct forms, but all are not included. Principles of hyphenation for some forms not included in the dictionary are given in the following paragraphs.

6:86   Compounds made up of a word of relationship plus a noun should be spelled as separate words:

```
brother officer        foster child
father figure          parent organization
mother church          sister ship
```

6:87   Compounds made up of two nouns that are different but of equal importance should be hyphenated:

```
author-producer    composer-director
          sculptor-painter
```

6:88   Compounds ending with *-elect* should be hyphenated except when the name of the office is in two or more words:

```
president-elect    but: county clerk elect
```

6:89   Combinations of words including a prepositional phrase that describe a character should be hyphenated:

```
stay-at-home            stick-in-the-mud
Alice-sit-by-the-fire   Johnny-on-the-spot
```

6:90   When spelled out, fractional numbers should be hyphenated unless either numerator or denominator already contains a hyphen:

```
one-half              but: sixty-five hundredths
two-thirds                 six and two-thirds
```

6:91   Spell as separate words adjective forms composed of an adverb ending in *-ly* plus an adjective or a participle:

```
highly developed species
newly minted coins
easily seen result
```

6:92   Compounds with *better-*, *best-*, *ill-*, *lesser-*, *little-*, *well-*, and the like, should be hyphenated when they precede the noun unless there is a modifier:

```
better-planned program
ill-advised move
little-foreseen outcome
well-intentioned suggestion
but: a very well intentioned man
```

But as predicate adjectives they are generally spelled as two words:

```
The program was better planned.

The outcome had been little foreseen.

The move was ill advised.
```

6:93   An adjective form composed of a present participle preceded by its object should be hyphenated when it precedes a noun:

```
tool-making tribes      problem-solving test
oil-producing wells     thought-provoking
                            lecture
```

But noun forms similarly constructed are usually treated as two words:

```
Problem solving is part of the daily lesson.

Environmentalists strongly oppose strip
coal mining.
```

6:94   Compounds with *all-* should be hyphenated whether they precede or follow the noun:

```
all-powerful ruler
all-encompassing aim
```

```
all-out effort
all-inclusive title
The ruler is all-powerful.
The title is all-inclusive.
```

6:95   Hyphenate phrases used as adjectives before a noun:

```
better-than-average turnout
behind-the-scenes maneuvers
up-to-date figures
on-the-job training
six-to-ten-year-old group
around-the-clock surveillance
```

But note that as predicate adjectives, such combinations should not be hyphenated:

```
The figures were brought up to date.
Training was given on the job.
```

6:96   Most compounds made up of adjective plus past participles should be hyphenated before a noun and spelled as two words after a noun:

```
rosy-cheeked boy          fine-grained powder
straight-sided dish       open-handed person
but: For a city child he was beautifully
       rosy cheeked.
```

6:97   Adjective forms ending with the suffix *-like* should be spelled as one word except when they are formed from proper names, word-combinations, or words ending with *ll* (double ell):

```
mosslike           but: fall-like
catlike                 kitchen-cabinet-like
businesslike            Stalin-like
```

6:98   An adjectival compound composed of a cardinal number and a unit of measurement should be hyphenated when it precedes a noun:

```
twelve-mile limit
eight-space indention
two-inch margin
but: 15 percent increase
```

6:99   An adjectival compound composed of a cardinal number and the word *-odd* should be hyphenated before or after the noun:

```
forty-odd       twenty-five-hundred-odd
175-odd         fifteen-hundred-odd
```

6:100   Adjectival compounds with *-fold* are written as one word, unless figures are used:

```
tenfold                    manifold
hundredfold        but: 75-fold
```

6:101   The trend in the spelling of compound words has for some years been away from the use of hyphens. This is noticeable especially in words with such common prefixes as *pre-*, *post-*; *pro-*, *anti-*; *over-*, *under-*; *intra-*, *extra-*; *infra-*, *ultra-*; *sub-*, *super-*; *re-*; *un-*; *non-*; *semi-*; *pseudo-*; *supra-*:

```
pretrial        intramural      supercharge
postwar         extramural      reactor
antifreeze      infrared        unappreciated
overqualified   ultraviolet     nonentity
undersupplied   subculture      semicomatose
            pseudoclassical suprarenal
```

6:102   Adjectives with the foregoing prefixes are spelled as one word, unless the second element is capitalized or is a figure:

```
pro-Arab     un-American     pre-1914
```

or it is necessary to distinguish homonyms:

```
re-cover     re-creation
```

or the second element consists of more than one word:

```
non-food-producing people
pre-nuclear-age civilization
```

6:103   Other than as suggested above, there is no hard-and-fast rule about when the hyphen should be used and when it should not; but it is safe to say that the hyphen is often used (*a*) when the terminal letter of the prefix is the same as the first letter of the word to which it is joined:

```
co-owner      anti-industrial
non-native    post-trial
but:   cooperate    reestablish
```

or (*b*) when the combination is not a common one and might suggest mispronunciation:

```
pro-ally    anti-college
```

CAPITALIZATION

PROPER NAMES

6:104 In all languages written in the Latin alphabet proper nouns—the names of persons and places—are capitalized:

```
John and Jane Doe    Niagara Falls
```

6:105 In English, proper adjectives—adjectives derived from proper nouns—are also capitalized:

```
European    Shakespearean
```

But proper nouns and adjectives that have lost their original meanings and become part of everyday language are not capitalized:

```
french doors    india ink
```

OTHER NAMES

6:106 In modern American usage, the practice of capitalization of names other than proper names varies widely. Official names of organizations are capitalized; names of political divisions and titles of persons are usually capitalized. The writer of a paper should decide, *before the final typescript is prepared,* which terms are to be capitalized and which are not. The neglect of care in this matter only results in additional work later. Detailed suggestions for capitalization of many terms occurring in run of text may be found in chapter 7 of the University of Chicago Press *Manual of Style,* 12th edition (Chicago: University of Chicago Press, 1969).

TITLES OF WRITTEN WORKS

6:107 The titles of written works, published or unpublished, as referred to in text, footnotes, and bibliographies are capitalized to accord with the rule stated in paragraph 4:17.

DIVISION OF WORDS

6:108   Correct division of words and other separations at the ends of
lines promote ease of reading. Except that a break at the end
of the last line on a page is not permissible, there is no rule
about the number of breaks that are allowable on a page. It
is obvious, however, that a great number of hyphens at the
right-hand margin—especially if they occur in succession—
detract from the appearance of the page and slow the reader,
to some extent at least.

GENERAL RULES

6:109   In general, divide words at the ends of lines according to their
syllabication as shown in the dictionary (*Webster's Third
International* or *Webster's New Collegiate* as suggested in
par. 6:74). In some dictionaries the syllables are separated
with a dot; in others, with a hyphen. Stress of pronunciation
is indicated by an accent mark before the syllable in some
dictionaries; after it, in others. Also, in some dictionaries the
dot or hyphen separating the accented syllable from the syllable that follows or precedes it is omitted and the accent
mark serves the dual purpose of indicating syllabication as
well as stress of pronunciation: *syl·lab·i·ca'tion*. Webster's
dictionaries use a different scheme: instead of placing an accent mark *after* the accented syllable, they place the mark
before the syllable in the phonetic transcription following each
main word entry.

6:110   In general divide according to the pronunciation (rather than
derivation). This means that when dividing after an accented
syllable, the consonant stays with the vowel when the vowel
is short:

```
signif-icant      param-eter      philos-ophy
democ-racy        hypoth-esis     prej-udice
```

but goes with the following syllable when it is long:

```
stu-dent      lo-cal       divi-sive
asy-lum       pota-to      crea-tor
```

6:111   When *-ing* or *-ed* is added to a word whose final syllable contains the liquid *l* (e.g., *cir·cle*, *han·dle*), the final syllable of the parent word becomes a part of the added syllable:

```
cir-cling  brist-ling  chuck-ling  han-dling
cir-cled   brist-led   chuck-led   han-dled
```

6:112   Notice that in words whose ending consonant is *doubled* before *-ing* or *-ed*, the added consonant is joined to the final syllable:

```
win-ning  set-ting  permit-ting  permit-ted
```

But for words *originally* ending in a double consonant, the second consonant is not joined to *-ing* or *-ed*:

```
will-ing  add-ing  add-ed
```

But see par. 6:116

EXCEPTIONS AND SPECIAL RULES

6:113   Some divisions, although syllabically correct, should never be made.

6:114   Never make a one-letter division:

<u>Wrong</u>: `u-nite  a-mong  e-nough  man-y`

6:115   Never divide the final syllables *-able* and *-ible*:

<u>Wrong</u>: `inevita-ble  permissi-ble`
`allowa-ble`
<u>Right</u>: `inevi-table  permis-sible  allow-able`

Note that these words may be divided after the first syllable as well.

6:116   It is recommended that *-ed* not be carried over, whether it is pronounced as a separate syllable or not. Never carry over *-ed*, *-bed*, *-ged*, *-led*, *-ned*, *-ped*, *-red*, *-sed*, *-zed* in words where these combinations are not pronounced as separate syllables:

<u>Wrong</u>: `help-ed  vex-ed  mark-ed  climb-ed`
`pass-ed  club-bed  bag-ged`
`control-led  cap-ped  man-ned`
`scar-red  gas-sed  whiz-zed`

6:117   Never divide the following suffixes:

```
-cious  -geous  -cial  -cion  -sion
-ceous  -gious  -sial  -gion  -tion
        -tious  -tial
```

6:118   Avoid two-letter divisions, especially when the division would give a misleading appearance:

```
wo-man  of-ten  pray-er  mon-ey  loss-es
```

6:119   Avoid division of hyphenated words except at the hyphen:

<u>Wrong</u>: `self-evi-dent  gov-er-nor-elect`
`well-in-tentioned`

<u>Right</u>: `self-evident  governor-elect  well-`
`intentioned`

6:120   Avoid division of a proper name unless it is one in which the correct division is evident:

<u>Right</u>: `Wash-ing-ton  Went-worth  Bond-field`
`John-son`

A biographical dictionary should be consulted before risking division of most proper names.

6:121   Never divide initials used in place of given names. It is best to write given names or initials on the same line as the surname, but it is allowable to place all the initials on one line and the surname on the next:

<u>Wrong</u>:   `T./S. Eliot    J./ B. S. Haldane`
<u>or</u> `J. B. / S. Haldane`

<u>Allowable</u>: `T. S. / Eliot  J. B. S. / Haldane`

6:122   Never divide capital letters used as abbreviations for names of countries or states (U.S., N.Y.); or for names of organizations (YMCA, NATO); or for names of publications or radio or television stations (*PMLA*, KKHI, KQED; but two sets of initials separated by a hyphen, e.g., KRON-FM, may be divided after the hyphen). Similarly, never divide the abbreviations for academic degrees (B.A., M.S., LL.D., Ph.D.).

6:123   Never divide a day of the month from the month, and never divide any such combinations as the following:

104

```
£6 4s. 6d.   A.D. 1895   6:40 P.M.   1:45-47
       245 mi.   10%
```

6:124 Never end a line with a divisional mark, such as (*a*) or (1), or with a dollar sign or an opening quotation mark or an opening parenthesis or an opening bracket; and never begin a line with an ending quotation mark or an ending parenthesis or an ending bracket or with any mark of punctuation save only a dash (—).

6:125 For rules on the division of words in foreign languages, the University of Chicago Press *Manual of Style,* 12th edition, should be consulted.

PUNCTUATION

6:126 Punctuation in some of its specialized uses is treated in the sections on abbreviations, numbers, quotations, footnotes, and bibliographies. Here, the general use of the various marks of punctuation—chiefly in running text—is dealt with briefly, the primary aim being to provide answers to questions that frequently puzzle writers. The rules are based on those set forth in the University of Chicago Press *Manual of Style.*

PERIOD

6:127 A period, or full stop, should be placed at the end of a complete declarative sentence, a moderately imperative sentence, and a sentence containing an indirect question:

```
They took the long road that ran at the
foot of the hill.
```
```
Take the long road that runs at the foot of
the hill.
```
```
The driver asked which road he should take.
```

6:128 In compound sentences two or more subject-predicate elements may be separated with semicolons, but commas are sometimes seen instead. This substitution is ordinarily to be avoided:

```
Wrong: We should recognize this as the
        moment for intelligent decisions,
```

```
            the right ones could benefit Amer-
            icans for years to come.
```

Right : We should recognize this as the
            moment for intelligent decisions; the
            right ones could benefit Americans
            for years to come.

In a short compound sentence, however, commas may be used
to separate two or more subject-predicate elements:

```
John is going to Europe, Debby is going to
Maine, I am going to summer school.
```

6:129   A period is used after most abbreviations. If an abbreviation
period comes at the end of a sentence, this period serves also
as the terminal period. But if the sentence ends with a question
mark or an exclamation point, the appropriate mark is added
after the abbreviation period:

```
The meeting adjourned at 9:00 P.M.
```

```
Was the committee called for 10:00 A.M.?
```

```
How incredible to have given the date as
700 B.C.!
```

6:130   It has been noted (par. 6:72) that the period is omitted at the
ends of items in a vertical list or enumeration, whether or not
the items are composed of sentences.

6:131   Periods are omitted at the ends of all of the following:
(*a*) display headings for chapters, tables, illustrations, and so
on; (*b*) any subheading that is typed on a line by itself;
(*c*) headings in tables; (*d*) address and date lines in communications, and signatures.

6:132   Periods in series (ellipsis dots) are used to mark omissions in
quoted matter (pars. 6:5, 6:7).

QUESTION MARK

6:133   A question mark is used at the end of a whole sentence containing a query or at the end of a query making up a part of
a sentence:

```
What has been the result of these studies?
```

Would high prices for gasoline cut down significantly the use of the automobile? was the question the opposition wanted answered in the affirmative before they would support the measure.

The question put by the Board was, Would the taxpayers vote another bond issue that would raise their taxes? [Note the capitalization of the first word of the sentence that asks the question, even though it is only a part of the whole sentence.]

6:134   A question mark may be used to indicate an uncertainty:

Pedro de Cieza de León (1518?-1560) wrote one of the most richly detailed accounts of the Spanish conquest of South America.

EXCLAMATION POINT

6:135   An exclamation point is used to mark an outcry or an emphatic or ironical comment (but don't overuse this device). Like the question mark, it may occur within a declarative sentence:

"Great heavens! He has hanged himself!"

"It is really <u>too</u> kind of you to warn me of the slights I am about to encounter!"

"I saw my sixteen-year-old son leap to his feet--if only I could have stopped him!--and loudly challenge the speaker."

6:136   Do not use an exclamation point to call attention to an error in a quotation, but place the word *sic* enclosed in square brackets after the error (see par. 4:69).

COMMA

6:137   Although the comma indicates the smallest interruption in continuity of thought or sentence structure, when it is correctly used it does more for ease of reading and ready understanding than any other mark of punctuation.

6:138   In sentences containing two independent clauses joined by a coordinate conjunction (*and, but, or, nor, for*), a comma is usually placed before the conjunction. This is not an unalterable rule, however; where the sentence is short and clarity not an issue, no comma is needed.

> This summer many Americans will look for vacation spots near their homes, but many students will stay at home and take vacation jobs.

> <u>But</u>: Mary came by bus but John bicycled over.

6:139   A series of three or more words, phrases, or clauses (like this) takes a comma between each of the elements and before a conjunction separating the last two:

> New York, Chicago, and Los Angeles were the cities mentioned.

> Dishes were broken, spoons lost, and carpets and upholstery damaged.

6:140   No commas should be used, however, when the elements in a series are all joined by conjunctions:

> Good taste and planning and a considerable expenditure of money had produced delightful rooms.

6:141   A series of three or more words, phrases, or clauses ending with the expression *and so forth* or *and so on* or *and the like* or *etc.,* should have commas both preceding and following the expression:

> Wages, hours, working conditions, benefits, and so on, can be improved by worker participation in the deliberations of management.

6:142   When commas occur within one or more of the elements of a series, semicolons instead of commas should be used to separate the elements:

> Three cities that have had notable success with the program are Hartford, Connecticut;

> Kalamazoo, Michigan; and Pasadena, California.

> Our marshlands are being filled in for housing developments, industrial sites, roads, parks, and airports; suffocated with dredge soil, garbage, and trash; or gouged out for gravel and sand.

6:143 A comma may be used to mark the omission of a word or words made clear by the context:

> In the autumn I shall take a course in American literature; in the winter, European literature; in the spring, creative writing.

6:144 Use commas to set off a nonrestrictive clause or phrase following a main clause. An element is nonrestrictive if it is not essential to the meaning of the main clause:

> These books, which are placed on reserve in the library, are required reading for the course.

The clause is nonrestrictive, since the meaning of the main clause, "These books are required reading for the course," is unchanged if the parenthetical clause is omitted. But in the following sentence, the clause identifies the books placed on reserve as those "that are required reading for the course," and the clause is therefore restrictive. No commas should be used:

> The books that are required reading for the course are placed on reserve in the library.

6:145 A word, phrase, or clause in apposition to a noun may also be restrictive or nonrestrictive. When it is nonrestrictive, it must be set off with commas:

> His brother, a Yale graduate, is pursuing a graduate program in economics at Stanford.

> A veteran of the Korean war, the man volunteered for service in Vietnam, where he was taken prisoner in 1969.

If, however, the appositive limits the meaning of the noun and is therefore restrictive, no commas should be used:

> The American philosopher William James was the brother of the novelist Henry James.

> Verdi's opera <u>Falstaff</u> is based on Shakespeare's play <u>The Merry Wives of Windsor.</u>

6:146   Although commas are generally used to set off a phrase indicating place of residence immediately following a personal name, in practice their use may be determined by the length and complexity of the sentence. For ease of reading, the usage shown in the second of the examples is to be preferred:

> The revived power of the states has produced a new breed of politicians: Governor Thomas McCall, of Oregon; Governor Robert Ray, of Iowa; Governor James Carter, of Georgia; Governor Francis Sargent, of Massachusetts.

> Or:
> The revived power of the states has produced a new breed of politicians: Governor Thomas McCall of Oregon, Governor Robert Ray of Iowa, Governor James Carter of Georgia, Governor Francis Sargent of Massachusetts.

6:147   Note, further, that the person's name and place name are not separated by commas in those cases where the place name has practically become a part of the person's name:

> St. Francis of Assisi   Eleanor of Aquitaine
>   Philip of Navarre

6:148   Use commas to set off words identifying a position or title following a person's name:

> Mr. Mitsugo Hirayama, a family counselor for the Tokoyo Family Court, gives advice that saves many a marriage.

> Robert Darnton, Professor of History at Princeton University, is the author of <u>Mesmerism and the End of the Enlightenment in France.</u>

6:149 Use commas, and remember to use both of them, to set off a parenthetical element in the middle of a sentence:

Wrong: The bill, you will be pleased to hear
   passed at the last session.

Wrong: The bill you will be pleased to hear,
   passed at the last session.

Right: The bill, you will be pleased to
   hear, passed at the last session.

Wrong: The problem of communication is less
   serious it is held, with the new
   generation than with the old.

Wrong: The problem of communication is less
   serious, it is held with the new
   generation than with the old.

Right: The problem of communication is less
   serious, it is held, with the new
   generation than with the old.

6:150 Set off with commas interjections, transitional adverbs, and the like, when they cause a distinct break in the flow of thought:

His statement, therefore, cannot be
verified.

Indeed, this was precisely what he had
feared.

6:151 But note that when such elements do not cause a break in continuity and do not require a pause in reading, the commas should be omitted:

It is therefore clear that no deposits were
made.

This is indeed the crux of the matter.

6:152 Use a comma following *namely, that is, for example, i.e., e.g.* There must be a punctuation mark before each of these expressions, but the kind of mark varies with the nature and complexity of the sentence:

Two other countries, namely, Greece and
Turkey, already are half-members of EEC.

> The President said that the next Cabinet
> meeting would deal with France's most press-
> ing problem: that is, inflation and the
> economy.

> India, for example, imports three critical
> products--fertilizer, food grains, and fuel.

> Restrictions on the sulfur content of fuel
> oil are now in effect in some large cities
> (e.g., Paris, Rome, Milan, Stockholm).

6:153   When a dependent clause or a long participial or prepositional phrase begins a sentence, it is usually followed by a comma:

> After suffering years of mounting inflation,
> people--and especially the elderly--are
> fearful for their future.

> If there should be long traffic delays,
> they would miss the plane.

6:154   No comma should follow a participial phrase that is part of the main verb or an adverbial phrase that immediately precedes the verb it modifies:

> Working with the Sierra Club is a group
> interested in recycling paper.

> Through the mountain runs a two-lane
> highway.

And a comma is usually unnecessary after a short prepositional phrase:

> On Saturdays they usually take the children
> to the park.

6:155   When each of several adjectives preceding a noun modifies the noun individually, they should be separated with commas:

> It was a large, well-placed, well-
> landscaped, handsome house.

> We strolled out into the warm, luminous,
> scent-filled night.

But note that if the last adjective *identifies* the noun rather than merely modifying it, no comma precedes it:

112

It was a large, well-placed, well-
landscaped, handsome brick house.

Then in the procession came the tall,
dignified third-year students.

He was a surly, impudent, old blue-suited
pensioner.

6:156   Set off with commas contrasted elements and two or more
complementary or antithetical phrases or clauses referring to
a single word following:

Disciplined conditioning, not merely skill
with the racquet, is what produces tennis
stars.

She both delighted in, and was disturbed
by, her new leisure and freedom.

The work presents a tactfully worded, yet
mainly candid, view of two economic rivals.

6:157   A comma should be used to prevent misreading of such sentences as the following:

From the British, educated Indians learned
the principles of parliamentary democracy.

After attacking, the hawk continued the
nesting activities he had taken over after
the loss of his mate.

SEMICOLON

6:158   A semicolon marks a greater break in the continuity of a
sentence than that indicated by a comma. Use a semicolon
between the parts of a compound sentence (two or more independent clauses) when they are not connected by a conjunction:

More than one hundred planned communities
are in various stages of completion; many
more are on the drawing boards.

6:159   If the clauses of a compound sentence are very long and there
are commas within them, they should be separated with semicolons even though they are connected by a conjunction:

Although productivity per man in U.S. industry is almost twice that in West European
industry, Western Europe has an increasingly
well-educated young labor force; and the
crucial point is that knowledge, which is
not transferable between peoples, has become by far the most important world
economic resource.

6:160 When used transitionally between clauses of compound sentences, the words *hence, however, indeed, so, then, thus,* and
sometimes *yet* are considered adverbs, not conjunctions, and
should therefore be preceded by semicolons rather than
commas:

This Pentagon adviser wants limits on arms
which will enhance world stability; however, he believes that we should begin at
once on new weapons programs.

Aerosols interfere with the earth's ability
to absorb solar radiation; thus they influence the temperature.

6:161 For the use of a semicolon instead of a comma, see paragraphs
6:142, 6:143, 6:158, 6:159, and 6:160.

COLON

6:162 The colon indicates a discontinuity of grammatical construction greater than that indicated by the semicolon. Whereas
the semicolon is used to separate parts that are usually of
equal significance, the colon is used to introduce a clause or
phrase that expands, clarifies, or exemplifies the meaning of
what precedes it:

Oil and gas are nonrenewable resources: when
they are burned in cars, planes, and home
furnaces, or used to make synthetic shirts,
plastic toys, or sandwich wrap, they are
gone.

The same underlying cause has been weaken-
ing governments throughout the free world:
the failure to check inflation.

6:163   A colon should be placed at the end of a grammatical element introducing a formal statement, whether the statement is quoted or not. It is usually placed after *following* or *as follows* or *in sum* when the enumerated (not necessarily numbered) items come immediately after:

```
His "laws" are as follows:
1. Books are for use
2. For every reader his book
3. For every book its reader
```

6:164   As noted elsewhere in this *Guide,* a colon is used between chapter and verse in scriptural references (par. 6:22), between hours and minutes in notations of time (par. 6:58), between place and publisher in footnote and bibliographical references (pars. 7:8, 7:36), and between volume and page references in citations (pars. 7:9, 7:16).

DASH

6:165   The dash, which in printing is a continuous line, in typescript consists of two hyphens without space between or on either side of them. (See the examples in par. 6:166.)

6:166   A dash or a pair of dashes may indicate a sudden break in thought that disrupts the sentence structure:

```
The Fuji looks like a crude-oil tanker--and
is large enough to be one--but it is, in
fact, the world's largest refrigerated
carrier of liquefied petroleum gas.

Banana splits, spaghetti with meat sauce,
and fried eggs and bacon--Japanese tastes in
food are changing--are served in many
restaurants in Tokyo.
```

6:167   Use a dash to introduce an element that emphasizes or explains the main clause through repetition of a key word or words:

```
The Mayor discovered that planning and de-
sign considerations could become political
issues--issues the electorate could sink its
teeth into.
```

6:168   In a sentence that includes several elements referring to a word that is the subject of a final, summarizing clause, a dash should precede the final clause:

Sarong-clad girls, superb stone temples and palaces, breathtaking panoramas of mist-wreathed peaks, palm-fringed beaches--all add up to what has been called the loveliest place on earth.

6:169   A word or phrase set on a line by itself, the meaning of which is completed by two or more parallel elements that follow on lines by themselves, may end with a dash:

Answering some pertinent questions, environmentalists say--
1. that shale-oil technology is not perfected;
2. that wide-scale extraction of shale oil may do immense damage to the environment;
3. that nuclear power is also not without threat to the environment.

The introductory phrase with the enumerated elements that complete its meaning forms a sentence and thus is punctuated as one. When such parallel elements are run into text, no dash is used at the end of the introductory words:

Answering some pertinent questions, environmentalists say (1) that shale-oil technology is not perfected; (2) that wide-scale extraction of shale oil may do immense damage to the environment; (3) that nuclear power is also not without threat to the environment.

6:170   For the use of numbers to enumerate items in the text, see paragraph 6:71.

6:171   Breaks in faltering speech or interruptions should be indicated by dashes:

"Well, it's as I said, difficult to explain --but the service, being considered so im-

portant by us Russians--if you were absent
--I don't know how to put it--people might
think--might think--"

PARENTHESES

6:172   The principal uses of parentheses in the text of a paper are
(*a*) to set off parenthetical elements, (*b*) to enclose the source
of a quotation or other matter when a footnote is not used for
the purpose, and (*c*) to set off numbers or letters in an enumeration (like that in this sentence). The first use is a matter of
choice, since both commas and dashes are also used to set off
parenthetical material. In general, commas are used for material most closely related to the main clause, dashes and parentheses for material more remotely connected. The following
examples illustrate some instances where parentheses might
be used:

The conference has been divided (with some
malice aforethought) into four main areas.

"Most of the scapegoats for Portugal's old
misfortunes have gone now--some of them
to jail--and the real shape of power has
yet to be determined" (Kenneth Maxwell, "The
Hidden Revolution in Portugal," New York
Review, 17 April 1975).

6:173   For the use of other punctuation with parentheses, see paragraphs 6:185-86.

BRACKETS

6:174   Brackets, often called *square brackets,* are used (*a*) to enclose
an interpolation in a quotation and (*b*) to enclose parenthetical matter within parentheses:

"These masters [Picasso, Braque, Matisse]
appeared to be throwing away or rebelling
against academic training, and thus they
discredited art teaching itself."

A biography of the author of Six Characters
in Search of an Author is now available in
translation (see Gaspare Giudice, Pir-

andello: A Biography, translated by Alastair
Hamilton [Oxford: Oxford University Press,
1975]).

6:175 If within the bracket further parenthesis is required, use
parentheses again:

The various arguments advanced (these include certain anonymous writers [Public
Economy (New York, 1848)]) may be formulated
thus: . . .

OTHER PUNCTUATION MARKS

6:176 The use of quotation marks is described in paragraphs 6:2–7.
The hyphen, sometimes considered a mark of punctuation, is
discussed in paragraphs 6:85–103 (compound words and
word division) and in paragraph 6:68 (continued numbers).

MULTIPLE PUNCTUATION

6:177 The term *multiple punctuation* means the conjunction of two
marks of punctuation—for example, a period and a closing
parenthesis. Where such conjunction occurs, certain rules
must be observed concerning (*a*) whether to omit one mark
or the other—as a period when an abbreviation ends a sentence (see par. 6:129) or (*b*) which mark to put first when
both marks are kept.

6:178 A comma is generally omitted following a stronger mark of
punctuation:

Wrong: If he had watched "What's My Line?",
       he would have known the answer.

Right: If he had watched "What's My Line?"
       he would have known the answer.

6:179 The comma is retained when it falls after an abbreviation with
a period:

Never use the abbreviations St., Ave., or
Rte. in formal correspondence.

6:180 Two marks of punctuation fall in the same place chiefly where
quotation marks, parentheses, or brackets are involved.

6:181 In American usage, with quotation marks, a final comma or period always goes inside (i.e., before the final quotation mark), whether it is part of the quotation or not. This is done even when the quotation marks enclose only one letter or figure (e.g., "a," "2b," "4e,").

In closing, the Senator said, "We need this bill to awaken conscience."

"I've been trying to figure that out," said George.

Because the school focuses on "the basics," the students "get none of the curricular extras" of the traditional comprehensive high school.

Every public official and every professional person is called upon "to join in the effort to bring justice and hope to all people."

6:182 Where a period (or a comma) and ending quotation marks both single and double come together, the period is placed inside both quotation marks.

The article to which he referred is in the Journal of Political Economy:

"Comment on 'How to Make a Burden of the Public Debt.' "

6:183 Semicolons and colons go outside the quotation marks, as part of the sentence containing the quotation. (If the quoted matter ends with a semicolon or a colon in the original, the mark would normally be changed to a period or a comma to accord with the structure of the main sentence.)

The author contends that The Hobbit is "a book addressed to children, symbolically expressing their fears and wishes about growing up"; it is a simply conceived story which Tolkien reconceived.

Coal has been called "the legacy of the ages"; it is nothing less than "the captured essence of nature."

6:184   Question marks and exclamation points go inside the quotation marks if they are part of the quoted matter, outside if they pertain to the entire sentence of which the quotation is a part:

In 1932 my father asked Bernard Baruch, "Things are pretty bad in the stock market, aren't they?"

But:
Do we accept Jefferson's concept of "a natural aristocracy among men"?

Charged by a neighbor with criminal mistreatment of her child and threatened with police action, the woman retorted, "Just you call the police, and you'll regret it to your dying day!"

How frightening it was to hear her reply-- calmly--"We'll let the law decide that"!

6:185   When a complete sentence enclosed in parentheses or brackets stands alone, the terminal period for that sentence is placed within the parentheses or brackets:

The President has ordered offshore oil leases sold at the rate of ten million acres a year, beginning in 1975. ("It's not all going to be leased, even if it's offered," says one knowledgeable oil geologist.)

When, however, the parenthetical sentence appears inside another sentence, the period is omitted:

Some of the strongest criticism comes from specialists (this criticism is glossed over by government leaders) worried about future energy supplies.

6:186   No punctuation should be placed between a parenthetical element (whether it is placed in parentheses or in brackets) and the element it modifies or to which it is closely connected. Therefore, internal sentence punctuation normally

120

follows the parenthetical element and no punctuation precedes it:

President Giscard's real problem is not
whether to shelve frills (like the S.S.
France and the Concorde), but how to stifle
inflation.

"We [the French people] feel we are in a
hinge of history."

Theta H. Wolf, Alfred Binet (Chicago: University of Chicago Press, 1973), p. 49.

"If he [the believer] stops here [feeling
sure of his election], who shall blame him?"

6:187 Numbers or letters in an enumeration belong with the items
following them, and therefore sentence punctuation precedes
them and no punctuation mark comes between them and the
item to which they apply:

He gave three reasons for resigning:
(1) age, (2) gradually failing health, and
(3) a desire to enjoy the fruits of leisure.

6:188 Square brackets used to set off words or expressions supplied
to fill in incomplete parts of a quotation or dates supplied in
footnote references are ignored in punctuating—i.e., punc-
tuate as if there were no brackets:

"These masters [Picasso, Braque, Matisse],
some of whose works are currently on exhibit
at a Paris gallery, appear to be throwing
away or rebelling against academic training." New York: Macmillan Co., [1910].

7   Footnote and Bibliographic Forms

7:1   Footnotes are of two kinds, *reference* and *content*. Reference footnotes are used to cite the authority for statements in text and to make cross-references (i.e., references to other parts of your paper). Content footnotes are used to make incidental comments upon, to amplify or to qualify textual discussion— in short, to provide a place for material which the writer thinks it worthwhile to include but which he feels would disrupt the flow of thought if introduced into the text. Also, they are sometimes used to make acknowledgments of aid received in the preparation of the paper, such as use of papers in private files or special interviews.

7:2   The place in the text at which a footnote is introduced, whether it is of the reference or of the content variety, is marked with an arabic numeral, as already discussed under "Arrangement of Footnotes" (pars. 5:58–63).

REFERENCE FOOTNOTES

FIRST, FULL REFERENCES

7:3   The first time a work is mentioned, the footnote should give complete information about it: author's name, title of the work, facts of publication, specific reference (volume number, if any, and page number). Thereafter, the full form ordinarily is not repeated. Proper styles of footnote entries for subsequent references to works once cited in full are discussed in paragraphs 7:136–53.

7:4   With some exceptions, such as legal, classical, and biblical references and references to some classes of public documents and those used in scientific papers (all discussed hereinafter), reference footnotes citing a published work the first time are arranged and punctuated as indicated below. Although not every entry will include all the items of information mentioned, the order should be maintained regardless of the items omitted. The source of the information should be the title page of the book, with reference in some cases to the library catalog card.

Book

7:5   (1) Name of author, with first name or initials first; the last name followed by a comma:

```
James Joyce,
```

7:6   (2) Title of the book, underlined, followed by a comma. *But note* that if the facts of publication come immediately after the title, the comma after the title is transferred to follow the parentheses. (See par. 7:78.)

Within the following book title is the title of another book. In such case, the title within a title is enclosed in quotation marks.

```
James Joyce, A First-Draft Version of
        "Finnegans Wake,"
```

7:7   (3) Name of editor or translator (if any):

```
James Joyce, A First-Draft Version of
        "Finnegans Wake," ed. and annotated
        by David Hayman

Ivar Lissner, The Living Past, trans. J.
        Maxwell Brownjohn
```

7:8   (4) Facts of publication, consisting of (*a*) number of the edition (if other than the first), (*b*) total number of volumes (if two or more), and (*c*) series title (if any). Separate these items with commas. Enclose in parentheses (*d*) place of publication, followed by a colon, (*e*) name of publishing agency, followed by a comma, and (*f*) date of publication, and place a comma after the final parenthesis.

7:9   (5) Volume number (if necessary) in arabic numerals, followed by a colon.

123

7:10   (6) Page number or numbers, followed by a period. Following is a complete reference which illustrates those elements pertinent to the work:

> James Joyce, <u>A First-Draft Version of</u>
>   <u>"Finnegans Wake</u>," ed. and annotated
>   by David Hayman (Austin: University
>   of Texas Press, 1963), pp. 180-81.

Magazine Article

7:11   The following numbers correspond to those given above for the items included in a reference to a book.

7:12   (1) Same as (1) above:

> Robert Edwin Blank,

7:13   (2) Title of the article, placed between quotation marks, with a comma before the final quotation mark; then the name of the magazine, underlined and followed by a comma:

> Robert Edwin Blank, "Days of Grace,"
>   <u>Atlantic</u>,

7:14   (3) Rare, but given the same way as for a book.

7:15   (4) Seldom given, except for the date of publication, which may be the full date necessary for a weekly magazine:

> Stephen Spender, "Is a New Literature Pos-
>   sible?" <u>Saturday Review</u>, 22 Septem-
>   ber 1962, pp. 16-19.

Or month and year, which identifies monthly, semimonthly, and quarterly magazines:

> Robert Edwin Blank, "Days of Grace,"
>   <u>Atlantic</u>, February 1962, pp. 60-65.

Note that in both cases the date is not enclosed in parentheses, and that no comma comes between month and year. But in both cases a comma follows the date.

7:16   (5) Volume number is omitted except for scholarly publications. When used, it comes immediately after the journal title, with no comma between, and is followed by the month and year, enclosed in parentheses. A colon precedes the page numbers:

> Granville D. Davis, "Douglas and the Chicago
>   Mob," <u>American Historical Review</u> 54
>   (April 1949): 553-54.

7:17   (6) Inclusive page numbers should be given in most instances; but since they are meaningless for an article that begins at the front of a magazine and finishes at the back, in such a case only the first page should be given.

7:18   Note that in the citation to the *Atlantic* (par. 7:15), the page numbers are preceded by the abbreviation "pp." and that the citation to the *American Historical Review* (par. 7:16) omits the abbreviation before the numbers. This is the preferred style for a reference that includes both volume number and page numbers (see par. 7:52).

Detail of Forms

7:19   Under their separate heads the items of information included in a footnote will now be discussed in detail.

7:20   (1) *Name of author*. Give the author's full name—Robert Edwin Blank—unless the title page or the byline at the head of the article gives only initials. Titles, as "Doctor," "Professor," or "President," the author's position, degrees held, should be omitted unless their inclusion is of special significance for the subject under discussion.

7:21   If the title page mentions no author, or if it indicates that the work is anonymous, and the authorship of the work has been definitely established, the author's name may be enclosed in brackets and placed before the title (see par. 7:83).

7:22   If the title page bears a pseudonym known to be that of a certain author, the real name should be given as the author, since most library catalog cards list pseudonymous authors under their own names. The pseudonym, enclosed in brackets, may follow the real name (see par. 7:84).

7:23   If a pseudonym is indicated as such on the title page and the author's real name is not known, the abbreviation "pseud." is placed *in parentheses* after the name. But if pseudonymity is not indicated on the title page and it is nevertheless an established fact, the abbreviation "pseud." may appear *in brackets* after the name.

7:24   If the work is that of two or three authors, all the names are set down in normal order (see pars. 7:79–80). If there are more than three authors, it is usual to mention only the name of the first and to add either "and others" or the equivalent Latin abbreviation "et al." (see par. 7:81).

7:25   Some works are compilations and are listed under the name of a compiler or of an editor in place of an author (see par. 7:86).

7:26   The "author" may be the name of a corporate body—a country, state, city, legislative body, institution, society, business firm (see par. 7:85).

7:27   (2) *Title of the work.* Enter the title of a book as it appears on the title page. Enter the title of an article in a periodical as it appears at the head of the article. In both cases, follow the peculiarities of spelling and the punctuation within the title, but capitalize in conformance with the general rule (see pars. 7:59–61).

7:28   Underline the title of a *whole published work;* that is, underline the title of a book and of a periodical. "Quote" (i.e., place between quotation marks) the title of an *article in a periodical,* a chapter in a book, an essay or a short story in a collection (see pars. 7:55–58).

Guy B. Hammond, "Tillich on the Personal God," <u>Journal of Religion</u> 44 (October 1964): 291.

James Norman Hall, <u>The Far Lands</u>, chap. 17, "Escape," pp. 164–70 (Boston: Little, Brown & Co., 1950).

Willa Cather, "Two Friends," in <u>Fifty Years, Being a Retrospective Collection</u> . . . (New York: Alfred A. Knopf, 1965), pp. 527–39.

7:29   It is said above that, in giving the title of a book or of a periodical, peculiarities of spelling and punctuation within the title should be followed. But an exception to this must be pointed out. Since display headings, both on title pages and at the heads of articles, frequently set a title in two or more lines, and since punctuation is commonly omitted at the ends of display headings, it is often necessary to add one or more marks of punctuation to a title as it is given in your paper. This addition is most often required to separate a main title from its subtitle, since a subtitle on a title page nearly always begins on a line by itself, and the main title above it carries no ending punctuation. Notice what happens when the following title is copied from the title page, where the main title appeared on a line without ending punctuation:

Wrong : <u>The Early Growth of Logic in the</u>
          <u>Child Classification and Seriation</u>

Adding a colon after *Child* clarifies the meaning.

Right : <u>The Early Growth of Logic in the</u>
         <u>Child: Classification and Seriation</u>

7:30   (3) *Name of editor, compiler, or translator.* Enter the name and the designation "ed.," "comp.," or "trans." before it. When placed before the name, these abbreviations stand, respectively, for "edited by," "compiled by," and "translated by" (see par. 7:87).

7:31   (4) *Facts of publication.* As listed in paragraph 7:8 the facts of publication are:

7:32   (*a*) *Number of edition.* Write, e.g., "2d ed." or "1st ed., rev." (for "1st edition, revised"), or "2d ed., rev. and enl." (for "2d edition, revised and enlarged").

7:33   (*b*) *Total number of volumes.* This information may be omitted except in a note that refers to a work as a whole. When it is included, write, e.g., "2 vols.," not "vols. 2" or "II vols."

7:34   (*c*) *Series title.* Capitalize to accord with the scheme chosen for listing books, articles, periodicals, etc. (see par. 7:59). Do not underline. In some series, as illustrated in the following example, the publications are given volume numbers. But notice that the volume number is only an indication of the place of the work in the series; it must not be interpreted to mean that the *work itself* is in several volumes.

> W. Kendrick Pritchett, <u>Ancient Athenian
> Calendars on Stone</u>, University of
> California Publications in Classical
> Archaeology, vol. 4, no. 4 (Berkeley
> and Los Angeles: University of
> California Press, 1963), p. 24.

7:35   If more than one of the "facts" mentioned in *a, b,* and *c* is included, separate them with commas.

7:36   (*d*) *Place of publication.* When the name of more than one city appears under the publisher's imprint, the first is assumed to be the location of the editorial offices, and that is the one to list. Follow with a colon. If the city is one whose location is not commonly known, give both city and state, separating the two with a comma and placing a colon after the state. Abbreviate the name of the state.

7:37   Occasionally a title page is found that omits the place of publication. The library catalog card may give the information and, if it does, you may include it, placing the name between square brackets. But if the information cannot be found, write "n.p." ("no place") before the publisher's name.

7:38   (*e*) *Name of publishing agency.* This is copied from the title page. It is recommended that if the name begins with "The" or ends with "Inc." or "Ltd.," these elements be omitted; also, that the ampersand (&) be used in place of "and" in a name, that "Company" be abbreviated as "Co.," and "Brother" or "Brothers" as "Bro." or "Bros." All this must be done consistently, however.

7:39   If neither the title page nor the library catalog card gives the publisher's name, write "n.p." ("no publisher") after the name of the place of publication. If the information is recorded on the catalog card, it is written between square brackets and put after the place name.

7:40   If neither place of publication nor publisher's name can be given, write "n.p." before the date. In this case the abbreviation stands for both "no place" and "no publisher."

7:41   (*f*) *Date of publication.* If the date of publication is not given on the face of the title page or on the copyright page, it may be found on the catalog card and set down between square brackets in your reference. If the date is not found, write "n.d." ("no date") as the last item of the facts of publication.

7:42   For a work of more than one volume published in different years, give the inclusive dates of publication as shown on the library catalog card, as, e.g., "1935–40."

7:43   For a work of more than one volume, publication of which is still in progress, indicate the ongoing publication by giving the first publication date and placing a dash after it, as, e.g., "1955–."

7:44   From the foregoing, it will be seen that the facts of publication may present different faces from time to time. If only two are found, they should be separated by a comma, as, e.g.: "(Boston, 1852)."

7:45   It may be noted that in some fields it is common practice to omit the name of the publisher. But without the express permission of your instructor, do not omit from your footnote and bibliographic entries the names of publishers.

7:46   (5) *Volume number*. Write the volume number in *arabic* numerals, *regardless of whether the work itself numbers its volumes in roman or in arabic numerals*. In legal, scientific, and technical writing, the more convenient arabic numeral long ago replaced the roman for expressing volume numbers. Gradually in other fields as well this practice has been adopted. Now, this *Guide*'s only specification for the use of roman numerals is in exact quotations, in citations to public documents or other manuscript material in which roman numerals are employed, in outlines, and in references to the preliminary pages of a book when the book itself so expresses them.

7:47   If a book is in more than one volume, the reference must include volume number as well as page. If the volumes were published in different years, the footnote must show this in one of the following ways: (*a*) Give the inclusive dates of publication and place the volume number *after* the facts of publication:

```
George Grote, History of Greece, 5 vols.
        (New York: Harper & Bros., 1853-
        72), 5: 249.
```

Or (*b*), give only the publication date of the specific volume referred to and place the volume number *before* the facts of publication:

```
George Grote, History of Greece, 5 (New
          York: Harper & Bros., 1860): 249.
```

7:48   If all the volumes were published in the same year, the volume number may be placed with equal correctness either before or after the facts of publication. However, placing the volume after the facts of publication makes it clear to the reader that the entire work, not merely the volume noted, was published in the year mentioned.

7:49   In references to magazines, the volume number is sometimes omitted and the issue identified by date alone. The different forms of reference are discussed in full under "Magazine Articles," paragraphs 7:15–18.

7:50   (6) *Page number*. Refer to a single page as, e.g., "p. 60." The rules for expressing continued numbers are given in paragraph 6:68.

7:51   The citation of exact page references is preferable to the use of, say, "pp. 60 f." (page 60 and following page) and "pp. 140 ff." (page 140 and following pages).

7:52   *Omission of abbreviations for "vol." and "p."* In a reference which includes both a volume number and a page number, it is permissible to omit the abbreviations "vol." and "p." or "pp."

```
W. T. Jones, A History of Western Philosophy
          (New York: Harcourt, Brace & Co.,
          1952), 2: 156.
```

7:53   But if in addition to volume and page some other division is mentioned, that division must be appropriately designated.

```
Arnold Toynbee, A Study of History, 12 vols.
          (London: Oxford University Press,
          1935-61), 1, pt.1: 45.
```

7:54   Also, in a reference such as the following in which volume and page number are widely separated, the abbreviations should be retained:

> T. C. Chamberlin and R. D. Salisbury, <u>Geology</u>, vol. 1: <u>Geologic Processes and Their Results</u>, 2d ed., rev. (New York: Henry Holt & Co., 1906), p. 155.

Titles

7:55   *Underlined or "quoted."* In general, titles of written works, published or unpublished, are either underlined or "quoted" (i.e., placed between double quotation marks), depending upon their form. The general rule is to underline the titles of *whole published works* (which in printed matter are usually italicized) and to quote the titles of their *component parts* (see par. 7:57) and of *unpublished materials.* This scheme should be followed wherever the titles appear in the paper.

7:56   *Underline* the titles of all the following kinds of published materials: books, pamphlets, bulletins, periodicals (magazines, technical and scholarly journals), newspapers, yearbooks, plays, motion pictures, symphonies, and operas, as well as poems, essays, lectures, sermons, proceedings, and reports appearing as *separate publications.* If the separate volumes of a work with an overall title have titles of their own, underline the titles of both, as in the example in paragraph 7:54.

7:57   *Quote* the titles of chapters or other divisions of books; subdivisions of whole publications, such as articles in periodicals; essays, poems, lectures, sermons, etc., published as parts of collections; radio and television programs; short musical compositions; and unpublished works, such as typed or "processed" reports, lectures, minutes, theses. But note that when a processed work (lithoprinted, multilithed, multigraphed, etc.) appearing as a separate publication bears a publisher's imprint, the title should be underlined.

7:58   *Neither underlined nor "quoted."* The names of the books of the Bible and of all sacred scriptures (Koran, Upanishads, Vedanta, etc.) and the titles of series (e.g., University of California Publications in English) are neither underlined nor quoted.

7:59   *Capitalization.* In titles of English works, capitalize first and last words and all nouns, pronouns, verbs, adverbs, and adjectives, and subordinate conjunctions (*after*, *because*, *if*, *since*, *until*, and *when*, *where*, and *while*). Use this scheme wherever the titles appear in the paper.

7:60   In the titles of French, Italian, and Spanish works, capitalize the first word and all proper nouns.

Dictionnaire illustré de la mythologie et
         des antiquités grecques et romaines

Bibliografia di Roma nel' Cinquecento

Historia de la Orden de San Gerónimo

7:61   In the titles of German works, capitalize the first word and all nouns, both common and proper, but not proper adjectives.

Reallexikon zur deutschen Kunstgeschichte

7:62   An exception to the schemes of capitalization here given may be made in a paper concerned, for example, with a specific edition of a work or with a manuscript when the exact way in which the title appeared originally is significant.

Parts of a Work

7:63   *Numbering.* Use arabic numerals to refer to all parts into which a written work may be divided (volume, part, chapter, act, scene, etc.).

7:64   *Abbreviating.* An abbreviation designating a part ("vol.," "pt.," "bk.," etc.) may never be used unless it is preceded or followed by a number ("vol. 8," "2 vols.," "chap. 3," "p. 10," etc.).

Abbreviations

7:65   It has been pointed out that few abbreviations are permissible in the *text* of the paper (see pars. 6:13–33). In footnotes, bibliographies, tabular matter, and in some illustrative matter, there is greater latitude, and the abbreviations listed in paragraph 7:68 are often used.

7:66   In the list, only "MS" is capitalized, but the first letter of any abbreviation should be capitalized when it is the first item in a footnote and whenever the usual rule for capitalization applies.

7:67   The Latin abbreviations here shown are not underlined (*sic* is the exception), and it is permissible not to underline them also in footnotes, bibliography, tabular matter, and parenthetic matter.

LIST OF ABBREVIATIONS

7:68   app., appendix
art., article (plural, arts.)
b., born
bk., book (plural, bks.)
c., copyright
ca., circa, about, approximately
cf., confer, compare [Note that confer is
  the Latin word for "compare"; cf. must not
  be used as the abbreviation for the English "confer"; nor should cf. be used to
  mean "see."]
ch., chapter, in legal references only
chap., chapter (plural, chaps.)
col., column (plural, cols.)
comp., compiler (plural, comps.); compiled
  by
d., died
dept., department (plural, depts.)
div., division (plural, divs.)
e.g., exempli gratia, for example
ed., editor (plural, eds.); edition; edited
  by
et al., et alii, and others
et seq., et sequens, and the following
etc., et cetera, and so forth
fig., figure (plural, figs.)
ibid., ibidem, in the same place
id., idem, the same [used to refer to persons, except in law citations; not to
  be confused with ibid.]
infra, below

1. (ell), line (plural, ll.) [Not recommended because l. might be mistaken for
"one" and ll. for "eleven." Spell out
"line" and "lines."]
loc. cit., <u>loco citato</u>, in the place cited
MS, manuscript (plural, MSS)
n., note, footnote (plural, nn.)
n.d., no date
n.p., no place; no publisher
no., number (plural, nos.)
n.s., new series
op. cit., <u>opere citato</u>, in the work cited
o.s., old series
p., page (plural, pp.)
par., paragraph (plural, pars.)
passim, here and there
pt., part (plural, pts.)
q.v., <u>quod vide</u>, which see
sc., scene
sec., section (plural, secs.)
<u>sic</u>, so, thus
supp., supplement (plural, supps.)
supra, above
s.v., <u>sub verbo</u>, <u>sub voce</u>, under the word
trans., translator; translated by
v., verse (plural, vv.)
v., <u>vide</u>, see
viz., <u>videlicet</u>, namely
vol., volume (plural, vols.)
vs., <u>versus</u>, against (v. in law references)

CROSS-REFERENCES

7:69   Cross-references are used to refer to other parts of the paper.
They may consist of a simple reference, as, e.g., "Supra, p. 6"
or "Infra, p. 12" (or the English equivalents, "Above, p. 6"
and "Below, p. 12"), or they may be combined with reference
to another work, as in the following:

Ruth Benedict, <u>Patterns of Culture</u> (Boston:
Houghton Mifflin Co., 1934), p. 48.
See also supra, p. 11.

Also, a cross-reference may occur as part of a content footnote (see n. 2 under "Content Footnotes," par. 7:154).

7:70   Be consistent in using only one form, the Latin or the English words.

EXAMPLES: BASIC FORMS

7:71   In this section and the following, we shall illustrate the principles of footnote and bibliographic forms as discussed earlier by showing their application to various kinds of source materials.

7:72   Students sometimes ask why there is a difference between footnote and bibliographic forms. The reasons for the differences seem to be logical ones.

7:73   First, concerning the difference in the way of giving the author's name: In the footnote, the normal order is used because there is no reason to alter it; but in the bibliographic entry, the surname is given first because the bibliography is usually arranged in alphabetic order according to surnames of the authors.

7:74   Second, concerning the difference in punctuation: A primary purpose of the footnote is to give the reader the specific location—page, or volume and page, number—of the source from which a statement in the text was drawn; and since it is logical to link page number with the name of the author and the title of the work, the loose separation with commas is employed, and the minor importance of the facts of publication is shown by their insertion in parentheses. The primary purpose of the bibliographic entry is to give the reader the means of identifying the *work,* as distinct from a specific part of it. The importance of all three main items of information —author, title, facts of publication—is shown by separating them with periods and by dropping the parentheses around the facts of publication.

7:75   It will be noticed that in references to articles, where volume and page number are necessary means of identifying the work, the forms for footnote and bibliographic entries differ scarcely at all.

7:76   The following examples illustrate basic forms for references in books, magazine and journal articles, and reports in all papers except those in scientific fields. Special forms, including those suitable for use in scientific papers, are discussed below in paragraphs 7:108–35.

7:77   The abbreviations "N." and "B." preceding the entries stand for footnote entry and the corresponding bibliographic entry. The difference in indentions illustrates the way footnote and bibliographic entries are indented in the finished paper.

BOOKS

7:78   *One author*

N.   [1]Hyatt H. Waggoner, <u>Emerson as Poet</u> (Princeton, N.J.: Princeton University Press, 1975), p. 43.

B.   Waggoner, Hyatt H. <u>Emerson as Poet</u>. Princeton, N.J.: Princeton University Press, 1975.

7:79   *Two authors*

N.   [2]Bernard Berelson and Gary A. Steiner, <u>Human Behavior: An Inventory of Scientific Findings</u> (New York: Harcourt, Brace & World, 1964), pp. 282–84.

B.   Berelson, Bernard, and Steiner, Gary A. <u>Human Behavior: An Inventory of Scientific Findings</u>. New York: Harcourt, Brace & World, 1964.

7:80   *Three authors*

N.   [3]Gordon W. Allport, Philip E. Vernon, and Gardner Lindzey, <u>Study of Values: A Scale for Measuring the Dominant Interests in Personality</u> (New York: Houghton Mifflin Co., 1951), p. 35.

B.   Allport, Gordon W.; Vernon, Philip E.;
          and Lindzey, Gardner. <u>Study of
          Values: A Scale for Measuring the
          Dominant Interests in Personality</u>.
          New York: Houghton Mifflin Co.,
          1951.

[Notice that in the footnote the names are separated with commas, but that in the bibliographic entry, where the individual names are reversed, semicolons are used.]

7:81   *More than three authors.* Note that for more than three authors, it is permissible in the footnote to give only the first name and add "et al." (or "and others"), but that in the bibliography, the preferred style is to give all the names. Note also that if you choose to shorten the footnote as here suggested, the name of only the first author should be mentioned (not some one of the others or the first two). Choose one style and follow it consistently.

N.   [4]Angus Campbell et al., <u>The
      American Voter</u> (New York: John Wiley &
      Sons, 1964), p. 148.

B.   Campbell, Angus; Converse, Philip E.;
          Miller, Warren E.; and Stokes,
          Donald E. <u>The American Voter</u>. New
          York: John Wiley & Sons, 1964.

7:82   *No author given.* The use of "Anonymous" or "Anon." should be avoided. The date enclosed in square brackets is an indication that it was not found in the book itself.

N.   [5]<u>The Lottery</u> (London: J. Watts
      [1732]), pp. 20-21.

B.   <u>The Lottery</u>. London: J. Watts [1732].

7:83   *No author given; name supplied*

N.   [6][Henry K. Blank], <u>Art for Its
      Own Sake</u> (Chicago: Nonpareil Press,
      1910), p. 32.

B.   [Blank, Henry K.] <u>Art for Its Own Sake</u>.
          Chicago: Nonpareil Press, 1910.

7:84   *Pseudonymous author; real name unknown* (see par. 7:22)

N.   [7]Elizabeth Cartright Penrose [Mrs. Markham], <u>A History of France</u> (London: John Murray, 1872), p. 95.

B.   Penrose, Elizabeth Cartright [Mrs. Markham]. <u>A History of France</u>. London: John Murray, 1872.

7:85   *Institution, association, or the like, as "author"*

N.   [8]Special Libraries Association, <u>Directory of Business and Financial Services</u> (New York: Special Libraries Association, 1963), p. 25.

B.   Special Libraries Association. <u>Directory of Business and Financial Services</u>. New York: Special Libraries Association, 1963.

7:86   *Editor as "author"; same form used for compiler.* When the name of an editor or compiler, and no name of an author, appears on a title page, the editor's or compiler's name appears in footnote and bibliographic entries in place of an author. Notice the difference between the following form and that under paragraph 7:87.

N.   [9]Lawrence H. Seltzer, ed., <u>New Horizons of Economic Progress</u> (Detroit: Wayne State University Press, 1964), pp. 11-12.

B.   Seltzer, Lawrence H., ed. <u>New Horizons of Economic Progress</u>. Detroit: Wayne State University Press, 1964.

7:87   *Author's work translated by another; same form if edited by another*

N.   [10]Ivan Lissner, <u>The Living Past</u>, trans. J. Maxwell Brownjohn (New York: G. P. Putnam's Sons, 1957), p. 68.

B.   Lissner, Ivan. The Living Past.
         Translated by J. Maxwell Brown-
         john. New York: G. P. Putnam's
         Sons, 1957.

N.   11Edward Chiera, They Wrote on
     Clay: The Babylonian Tablets Speak
     Today, ed. George G. Cameron (Chicago:
     University of Chicago Press, 1938),
     p. 48.

B.   Chiera, Edward. They Wrote on Clay: The
         Babylonian Tablets Speak Today.
         Edited by George G. Cameron. Chi-
         cago: University of Chicago Press,
         1938.

7:88   *Author's work contained in his collected works*

N.   12Samuel Taylor Coleridge, The
     Complete Works of Samuel Taylor
     Coleridge, ed. W. G. T. Shedd, vol. 1:
     Aids to Reflection (New York: Harper
     & Bros., 1884), p. 18.

B.   Coleridge, Samuel Taylor. The Complete
         Works of Samuel Taylor Coleridge.
         Edited by W. G. T. Shedd. Vol. 1:
         Aids to Reflection. New York:
         Harper & Bros., 1884.

7:89   *Separately titled volume in a multivolume work with a general*
           title and editor

N.   13Gordon N. Ray, gen. ed., An
     Introduction to Literature, 4 vols.
     (Boston: Houghton Mifflin Co., 1959),
     vol. 2: The Nature of Drama, by
     Hubert Hefner.

B.   Ray, Gordon N., gen. ed. An Introduction
         to Literature. 4 vols. Boston:
         Houghton Mifflin Co., 1959. Vol.
         2: The Nature of Drama, by Hubert
         Hefner.

7:90   *Separately titled volume in a multivolume work with a general title and one author*

N.   [14]Will Durant, The Story of Civilization, 10 vols. (New York: Simon & Schuster, 1935–67), vol. 1: Our Oriental Heritage, p. 88.

B.   Durant, Will. The Story of Civilization. 10 vols. New York: Simon & Schuster, 1935–67. Vol. 1: Our Oriental Heritage.

7:91   *Book in a series*

N.   [15]Verner W. Clapp, The Future of the Research Library, Phineas W. Windsor Series in Librarianship, no. 8 (Urbana: University of Illinois Press, 1964), p. 12.

B.   Clapp, Verner W. The Future of the Research Library. Phineas W. Windsor Series in Librarianship, no. 8. Urbana: University of Illinois Press, 1964.

7:92   *Paperback series.* Reference to a paperback should always give the name of the paperback series (e.g., Bantam Books, Capricorn Books, Harper Torchbooks, Phoenix Books). If the paperback was published at an earlier date in hardcover, it is desirable to give the full reference as, for example:

N.   [16]George F. Kennan, American Diplomacy, 1900–1950. (Chicago: University of Chicago Press, 1951; Phoenix Books, 1970), p. 48.

B.   Kennan, George F. American Diplomacy, 1900–1950. Chicago: University of Chicago Press, 1951; Phoenix Books, 1970.

7:93   *Edition other than the first*

> N.   [17]Katharine S. Diehl, <u>Religions,
> Mythologies, Folklores: An Annotated
> Bibliography</u>, 2d ed. (New York:
> Scarecrow Press, 1962), pp. 84–86.

> B.   Diehl, Katharine S. <u>Religions,
>   Mythologies, Folklores: An Anno-
>   tated Bibliography</u>. 2d ed. New
>   York: Scarecrow Press, 1962.

If an edition is edited by someone other than the author,
the edition number is followed by "ed. John Doe" in the
footnote and "Edited by John Doe" in the bibliography.

7:94   *Book privately printed*

> N.   [18]John G. Barrow, <u>A Bibliography
> of Bibliographies of Religion</u> (Austin,
> Tex.: By the Author, 716 Brown Bldg.,
> 1955), p. 10.

> B.   Barrow, John G. <u>A Bibliography of
>   Bibliographies of Religion</u>.
>   Austin, Tex.: By the Author, 716
>   Brown Bldg., 1955.

7:95   *Title within a title.* A title of another work appearing within
an underlined title is enclosed in double quotation marks:

> N.   [19]Arnold B. Come, <u>An Introduction
> to Barth's "Dogmatics" for Preachers</u>
> (Philadelphia: Westminster Press, 1963),
> pp. 90–92.

> B.   Come, Arnold B. <u>An Introduction to
>   Barth's "Dogmatics" for Preachers</u>.
>   Philadelphia: Westminster Press,
>   1963.

7:96   When the title of a book occurs within a title that is in quotation marks, such as the title of an article in a journal, the
book title is underlined:

N.   [20]Cedric H. Whitman, "Two Passages
in the <u>Ion</u> of Euripides," <u>Classical
Philology</u> 59 (October 1964): 257.

B.   Whitman, Cedric H. "Two Passages in
        the <u>Ion</u> of Euripides." <u>Classical
        Philology</u>, 59 (October 1964):
        257-59.

7:97   When the title of an article appears within the title of another
article, single quotation marks are used: "Comment on 'How
to Make a Burden of the Public Debt.' "

7:98   *Component part by one author in a work edited by another*

N.   [21]Paul Tillich, "Being and Love,"
in <u>Moral Principles of Action</u>, ed. Ruth
N. Anshen (New York: Harper & Bros.,
1952), p. 663.

B.   Tillich, Paul. "Being and Love." In
        <u>Moral Principles of Action</u>, edited
        by Ruth N. Anshen. New York:
        Harper & Bros., 1952.

REPORTS—PUBLISHED

7:99   *Personal author named*

N.   [1]John H. Postley, <u>Report on a
Study of Behavioral Factors in Informa-
tion Systems</u> (Los Angeles: Hughes
Dynamics, [1960]), p. 15.

B.   Postley, John H. <u>Report on a Study of
        Behavioral Factors in Information
        Systems</u>. Los Angeles: Hughes
        Dynamics, [1960].

7:100   *Chairman of committee named*

N.   [2]<u>Report of the Committee on
Financial Institutions to the President
of the United States</u>, Walter W. Heller,

chairman (Washington, D.C.: U.S. Government Printing Office, 1963), p. 12.

B.   Report of the Committee on Financial Institutions to the President of the United States. Walter W. Heller, chairman. Washington, D.C.: U.S. Government Printing Office, 1963.

MAGAZINE ARTICLES

7:101   Notice the difference in form between references to popular magazines and to scholarly journals (see pars. 7:15–16).

7:102   *Article or story in a popular magazine*

N.   [1]Wilfred Sheed, "The Good Old Days in California," Atlantic, September 1968, pp. 48-53.

B.   Sheed, Wilfred. "The Good Old Days in California." Atlantic, September 1968.

7:103   *Book review in a popular magazine*

N.   [2]Granville Hicks, "Voyage of Life," review of Ship of Fools, by Katherine Anne Porter, Saturday Review, 31 March 1962, pp. 15-16.

B.   Hicks, Granville. "Voyage of Life," review of Ship of Fools, by Katherine Anne Porter. Saturday Review, 31 March 1962.

[A book review does not always carry its own title, and sometimes the name of the reviewer is not mentioned. An entry might begin, therefore, Review of. . . .]

7:104   *Article in a scholarly journal*

N.   [3]William C. Hayes, "Most Ancient Egypt," Journal of Near Eastern Studies 23 (October 1964): 217-74.

B.   Hayes, William C. "Most Ancient Egypt."
     Journal of Near Eastern Studies
     23 (October 1964): 217-74.

7:105   *No author given*

N.   [4]"The Victor--for the Moment,"
     Time, 10 August 1962 p. 15.

B.   "The Victor--for the Moment." Time, 10
          August 1962, p. 15.

ENCYCLOPEDIA ARTICLES; SAME FORM
USED FOR DICTIONARY

7:106   *Signed article*

N.   [5]Encyclopaedia Britannica, 11th
     ed. (1910-11), s.v. "Blake, William,"
     by J. W. Comyns-Carr.

B.   Encyclopaedia Britannica. 11th ed.
          (1910-11), s.v. "Blake, William."
          By J. W. Comyns-Carr.

7:107   *Unsigned article*

N.   [6]Encyclopedia Americana, 1963
     ed., s.v. "Sitting Bull."

B.   Encyclopedia Americana. 1963 ed., s.v.
          "Sitting Bull."

N.   [7]Grove's Dictionary of Music and
     Musicians, 5th ed. (1954), s.v.
     "Harp Lute."

B.   Grove's Dictionary of Music and
          Musicians. 5th ed. (1954), s.v.
          "Harp Lute."

EXAMPLES: SPECIAL FORMS

7:108   References to some kinds of source materials require special
     forms, as explained and illustrated below.

NEWSPAPERS

7:109   In general, the name of the newspaper and the date are sufficient, but many large metropolitan papers—especially Sunday editions—are made up in sections that are separately paginated. For these, section number (or letter) and page number must be given. The title of an article and the author may be given. If the name of the paper does not include the name of the city, the city should be named and placed in parentheses after the title of the paper. The definite article as part of the title is omitted. Footnote and bibliographic entries are identical.

> [1]<u>Palo Alto Times</u>, 11 January 1969.

> [2]"Amazing Amazon Region," <u>New York Times</u>, 12 January 1969, sec. 4, p. E11.

RADIO AND TELEVISION PROGRAMS

7:110   References vary, depending upon whether the circumstances at the time of the broadcast would make the title and narrator of special significance. The indispensable information is name of network and date, with perhaps name of the series. The name of the local station is not necessary. Footnote and bibliographic entries are identical, if bibliographic entry is made.

> [1]CBS, "Twentieth Century," 28 October 1962, "I Remember: Dag Hammarskjöld," Walter Cronkite, narrator.

PUBLIC DOCUMENTS

7:111   Public documents are of many kinds, and no one style of reference is suitable for all. Whatever the form, it should be one that would make it easy to locate the reference. When in doubt of how much to include in a reference to a public document, remember that it is better to have too much than too little. The "author" is usually the name of a country, state, city, town, or government district, together with the name of the legislative body, court, executive department, bureau, board, commission, or committee responsible for the work. Sometimes a work bears in addition the title of an official, as, e.g., "State Entomologist"; and sometimes it bears the name of a personal author.

7:112 The examples are far from covering all classes of documents, but it is thought that they include those most frequently cited.

Statutory Material

7:113 The United States Constitution is referred to by article and section (by clause as well, if relevant). Reference to an amendment must give the number of the amendment following "Constitution."

```
N.        1U.S., Constitution, art. I, sec.
4.

B.   U.S. Constitution. Art. I, sec. 4.

N.        2U.S., Constitution, amend. xiv,
sec. 1.

B.   U.S. Constitution. Amend. xiv, sec. 1.

N.        3U.S., Statutes at Large, vol. 55.

B.   U.S. Statutes at Large, vol. 55.

N.        4Illinois, Revised Statutes
(1949), c. 20.

B.   Illinois. Revised Statutes (1949),c. 20.
```

[The date is essential in citing revised statutes. The abbreviation "c." for "chapter" is permissible in referring to public documents.]

Debates

7:114 Congressional debates are printed in the *Congressional Record*. Unless the subject of the speech, or merely of the remarks, is mentioned in the text, it is proper to include it in the citation. The name of the speaker may also be included.

N.   [1]U.S., Congress, Senate, <u>Congres-sional Record</u>, 84th Cong., 2d sess., 1960, 87, pt. 6: 2750.

B.   U.S. Congress. Senate. <u>Congressional Record</u>, 84th Cong., 2d sess., 1960, 87, pt. 6: 2750.

N.   [2]U.S., Congress, Senate, Senator Blank speaking for the <u>Amendment of the Standing Rules of the Senate</u>, S. Res. 103, 89th Cong., 1st sess., 14 November 1965, <u>Congressional Record</u> 102: 6522.

B.   U.S. Congress. Senate. Senator Blank speaking for the <u>Amendment of the Standing Rules of the Senate</u>, S. Res. 103, 89th Cong., 1st sess., 14 November 1965, <u>Congressional Record</u> 102: 6522.

[Here the name of the speaker is included in the reference, which is to the bound volume of the *Congressional Record* rather than to the *Daily Digest*. The pagination differs in the two.]

Reports and Hearings

7:115 N.   [1]U.S., Congress, House, Committee on Interstate and Foreign Commerce, <u>National Foundation Act of 1949: Report to Accompany H.R. 4846</u>, 81st Cong., 1st sess., 1949, H. Rept. 796, p. 15.

B.   U.S. Congress. House. Committee on Interstate and Foreign Commerce. <u>National Foundations Act of 1949: Report to Accompany H.R. 4846</u>, 81st Cong., 1st sess., 1949, H. Rept. 796.

N.   [2]U.S., Department of State, <u>A Plan for the Establishment in Hawaii of a Center for Cultural and Technical</u>

Interchange between East and West, 86th
Cong., 2d sess., 1960, p. 28.

B.   U.S. Department of State. A Plan for the
Establishment in Hawaii of a
Center for Cultural and Technical
Interchange between East and
West, 86th Cong., 2d sess., 1960.

N.   [3]U.S., Congress, Joint Economic
Committee, The Low-Income Population and
Economic Growth, paper prepared for the
Joint Committee, by Robert J. Lampman,
Joint Committee Print, Study Paper 12
(Washington, D.C.: U.S. Government
Printing Office, 1959), pp. 15-16.

B.   U.S. Congress. Joint Economic Committee.
The Low-Income Population and Eco-
nomic Growth, paper prepared for
the Joint Committee, by Robert J.
Lampman. Joint Committee Print,
Study Paper 12. Washington, D.C.:
U.S. Government Printing Office,
1959.

N.   [4]U.S., Congress, House, Committee
on Ways and Means, Narcotics, Marihuana,
and Barbiturates: Hearing on H.R. 3490,
82d Cong., 1st sess., 15 November 1951,
p. 28.

B.   U.S. Congress. House. Committee on Ways
and Means. Narcotics, Marihuana,
and Barbiturates: Hearing on H.R.
3490, 82d Cong., 1st sess.,
15 November 1951.

Executive Departmental Documents

7:116   Departmental documents consist of reports of executive departments and bureaus, bulletins, circulars, and miscellaneous
materials. Many departmental publications are classified in
series, and some have personal authors (n. 2). It is not ad-

visable, however, to cite government publications by names of authors, since few libraries catalog them except under the names of the sponsoring agencies.

N.   [1]U.S., Department of State, <u>Decla-ration of the U.N. Conference on Food and Agriculture</u>, War Documents Series, no. 2162 (1944), pp. 8-10.

B.   U.S. Department of State. <u>Declaration of the U.N. Conference on Food and Agriculture</u>. War Documents Series, no. 2162 (1944).

N.   [2]U.S., Department of Agriculture, <u>Sheep Migration in the Inter-Mountain Region</u>, Department of Agriculture Circular no. 624, by H. R. Hockmuth, Earl R. Franklin, and Marion Clawson (Washington, D.C.: U.S. Government Printing Office, 1942), pp. 11-12.

B.   U.S. Department of Agriculture. <u>Sheep Migration in the Inter-Mountain Region</u>. Department of Agriculture Circular no. 624, by H. R. Hockmuth, Earl R. Franklin, and Marion Clawson. Washington, D.C.: U.S. Government Printing Office, 1942.

N.   [3]U.S., Department of Commerce, Bureau of the Census, <u>Eighteenth Census of the United States, 1960: Population</u>, 2: 98.

B.   U.S. Department of Commerce. Bureau of the Census. <u>Eighteenth Census of the United States: Population</u>, vol. 2.

Presidential Papers

7:117   Presidential proclamations, executive orders of general in-interest, and any other documents that the president submits or orders to be published are carried in the *Federal Register,* issued on every day following a government working day. These are compiled at regular intervals and published in book form, with sections devoted to each of the presidents whose papers are included.

N.   [1]U.S., President, Proclamation, "Supplemental Quota on Imports of Long-Staple Cotton," <u>Federal Register</u>, vol. 15, no. 196, 10 October 1950, pp. 6801-2.

B.   U.S. President. Proclamation. "Supplemental Quota on Imports of Long-Staple Cotton." <u>Federal Register</u>, vol. 15, no. 196, 10 October 1950.

N.   ·   [2]U.S., President, <u>Public Papers of the Presidents of the United States</u> (Washington, D.C.: Office of the <u>Federal Register</u>, National Archives and Records Service, 1953-), Dwight D. Eisenhower, 1956, pp. 223-24.

B.   U.S. President. <u>Public Papers of the Presidents of the United States</u>. Washington, D.C.: Office of the <u>Federal Register</u>, National Archives and Records Service, 1953-. Dwight D. Eisenhower, 1956.

COURT CASES

7:118   In a paper on a predominantly legal subject, the style of reference set forth in *A Uniform System of Citation,* 11th edition, published by the Harvard Law Review Association, is recommended. But since papers on nonlegal subjects sometimes refer to court cases, examples of their form are given. A feature of legal references is their use of abbreviations and their lack of underlining. Volume number precedes the abbreviation for the name of the law report, and page number follows. The date, enclosed in parentheses, comes at the end. Some early reports are named for reporters (n. 2). "(U.S.)" after the name indicates a reporter of the United States Supreme Court. Footnote and bibliographic references are identical, except that the latter omit page notation.

> [1]How v. State, 9 Mo. 690 (1946).

> [2]Slaughterhouse Cases, 16 Wallace (U.S.) 97–111.

> [3]Ex parte Mahone, 30 Ala. 49 (1847).

NOVELS

7:119 Novels, many of which appear in various editions with different pagination, are best referred to by chapter (or by part or book, and chapter) rather than by page.

N.   [1]Conrad Richter, The Fields (New York: Alfred A. Knopf, 1946), chap. 7.

B.   Richter, Conrad. The Fields. New York: Alfred A. Knopf, 1946.

7:120 In a paper on a particular novel, the edition is specified and page references given in footnotes where necessary.

N.   [2]Jane Austen, Pride and Prejudice, ed. R. W. Chapman, The Oxford Illustrated Jane Austen, 3d ed., Vol. 2 (London: Oxford University Press, 1932), pp. 93–95.

B.   Austen, Jane. Pride and Prejudice. Edited by R. W. Chapman. The Oxford Illustrated Jane Austen, 3d ed. Vol. 2. London: Oxford University Press, 1932.

CLASSICAL WORKS

7:121 Arabic numerals are used to indicate all divisions and subdivisions of classical works. The different levels of division are separated by periods; several references to the same division are separated by commas; and continuing numbers are separated by hyphens. A superior number or letter (as for a footnote number) placed after a number designating a division of the work indicates another subdivision (n. 3). Notice the absence of punctuation between name of author and title, and between title and the first number.

N.   [1]Cicero <u>De officiis</u> 1. 133, 140.

B.   Cicero <u>De officiis</u>.

N.   [2]Ovid <u>Amores</u> 1. 7. 27–29.
B.   Ovid <u>Amores</u>.

N.   [3]Aristotle <u>Poetics</u> 20. 1456^{b}20. 8, 12, 15.

B.   Aristotle <u>Poetics</u>.

PLAYS AND LONG POEMS

7:122   The citing of English classics may be in the style of Greek and Latin classical works, except that a comma follows the title of the work and the name of the part precedes each number designating a part.

N.   [1]Shakespeare <u>Romeo and Juliet</u>, act 3, sc. 2, lines 6–34.

B.   Shakespeare <u>Romeo and Juliet</u>.

N.   [2]Milton <u>Paradise Lost</u>, bk. 2, lines 39–45.

B.   Milton <u>Paradise Lost</u>.

7:123   Although references to classical works do not require the facts of publication, they must be given for modern plays.

N.   [3]Louis O. Coxe and Robert Chapman, <u>Billy Budd</u> (Princeton, N.J.: Princeton University Press, 1951), act 1, sc. 2.

B.   Coxe, Louis O., and Chapman, Robert. <u>Billy Budd</u>. Princeton, N.J.: Princeton University Press, 1951.

SHORTER POEMS

7:124   Titles of shorter poems are placed between quotation marks; verses and lines are so designated. Although the poem cited

may have been read in a volume devoted to that one poem,
it is best to give the title of a collection in which it can be
found.

N.   [1]Francis Thompson, "The Hound of
          Heaven," The Oxford Book of Modern
          Verse (New York: Oxford University
          Press, 1937), v. 3, lines 7-10.

B.   Thompson, Francis. "The Hound of
              Heaven." The Oxford Book of Modern
              Verse. New York: Oxford University
              Press, 1937.

THE BIBLE

7:125   The names of sacred scriptures, both Christian and non-
Christian, are not underlined, nor are the names of the books
underlined. Chapter and verse are both indicated by arabic
numerals, separated by a colon. The King James Version of
the Bible is assumed unless a different version is mentioned,
as in note 2 below.

N.   [1]Psalm 103:13, 14.

B.   The Bible.

N.   [2]1 Corinthians 13:9-12 (Revised
          Standard Version).

B.   The Bible. Revised Standard Version.

MANUSCRIPT COLLECTIONS

7:126   The location, title, and number, or similar designation are
given. If a specific document or letter is referred to, it should
be mentioned at either the beginning or the end of the note,
as in note 2 below.

N.   [1]British Library, Arundel MSS,
          285, fol. 165b.

B.   British Library. Arundel MSS.

[Note that manuscript collections formerly referred to as in
the British Museum (BM) are now (since 1973) a part of the
British Library.]

N.   [2]A. H. Strong to W. R. Harper,
       23 December 1890, University of Chicago,
       Archives, Harper Letter File.

B.   University of Chicago. Archives. Harper
            Letter File.

MISCELLANEOUS UNPUBLISHED MATERIALS

7:127   Unpublished materials are of many kinds, and references to
       them necessarily vary in form. However different the form,
       it should always indicate the location of the material. If there
       is a title, the reference "quotes" it; if you give it a general, de-
       scriptive title, that title appears without quotation marks. The
       information given about a personal letter may be much or
       little, depending upon its importance as source material. Thus
       one may be referred to by the name of the writer, and others
       give the name, official position, place, and date as well.

N.   [1]John Doe, personal letter,
       5 August 1959.

B.   Doe, John. Personal letter, 5 August
            1959.

N.   [2]Letter to Marin County Board of
       Supervisors, from Alan Cranston, Cali-
       fornia State Controller. Sacramento,
       22 October 1962.

B.   Cranston, Alan. California State Con-
            troller. Letter to Marin County
            Board of Supervisors. Sacramento,
            22 October 1962.

N.   [3]Helen Margaret Reynolds, "Uni-
       versity Library Buildings in the United
       States, 1890-1939" (Master's thesis,
       Library School, University of Illinois,
       1946), p. 48.

B.   Reynolds, Helen Margaret. "University
            Library Buildings in the United
            States, 1890-1939." Master's

thesis, Library School, University
of Illinois, 1946.

N.   [4]Minutes of the Meeting of the
Board of the Library, Everyman's College, New City, Virginia, 10 April 1961.

B.   Everyman's College. New City, Virginia.
Board of the Library, Minutes of
the Meeting of 10 April 1961.

INTERVIEWS

7:128   Although not written sources, personal interviews are much
relied upon in some kinds of research and require mention in
footnotes. By general consent, they are given a place in bibliographies as well. References to them follow the same general
pattern as that used for letters.

N.   [1]Interview with John Nought,
Primus Realty Company, San Jose, California, 12 May 1962.

B.   Nought, John. Primus Realty Company,
San Jose, California. Interview,
12 May 1962.

CITATIONS TAKEN FROM A SECONDARY SOURCE

7:129   References to the works of other writers appear frequently in
reading matter. If you wish to cite from the work of one author as found in that of another, your reference must indicate
the work in which you found the material as well as the original
source. Following is an example:

N.   [1]William Stubbs, Lectures on
Medieval History, p. 210, as quoted in
[or "cited by," if the material is not
a direct quotation] G. G. Coulton,
Medieval Panorama (New York: Meridian
Books, 1957), p. 366, n. 2.

[This entry would not be represented in the bibliography except as it might be covered by the entry of Coulton's book.]

REFERENCES IN THE SCIENCES

7:130   Papers in scientific fields use different forms of citation from any of those discussed earlier in this chapter. Moreover, the forms vary not only among the several fields but sometimes within the fields themselves.

7:131   One scheme omits footnotes for references to sources, collecting all the references in a list at the end of the paper under some such heading as "List of References" or "Literature Cited." Short references to items in the list—regardless of its heading—appear in the text in two forms:

7:132   The surname of the author and the year date of the publication, given in parentheses, or year date alone if the author's name occurs in the sentence:

```
These results were later confirmed
(Naismith 1971).
```

```
Naismith (1971) was able to confirm these
results.
```

Under this first form, the list of references at the end of the paper is arranged alphabetically by authors' surnames. Works by the same author are listed chronologically (by date of publication). Two or more works by the same author published in the same year are identified as, for example, 1973*a*, 1973*b*. For works edited by the same author, the abbreviation "ed." follows the name. And for works of which he is coauthor, the names of the other coauthors follow his name. The list is then numbered, beginning with "1" at the top.

7:133   The second style of reference places a number after the author's name in the text, enclosing the number either in parentheses or in square brackets [ ].

```
Boulger [1] classifies Coleridge as a
voluntarist-traditionalist.
```

```
Some interesting work has been done with
Schleiermacher (2, 3, 4).
```

7:134   Be consistent in using one style of reference or the other throughout your paper.

7:135   Although the following styles of entries do not illustrate a common form in the sciences, they do illustrate some features that are more or less common.* Notice the omission of the title of the article in reference 12, the underlining of some titles, the difference in capitalization of titles of articles and of journals, the use of abbreviations. The first three are articles; the last two are books.

> Mohr, H. 1962. Primary effect of light on growth. <u>Ann. Rev. Plant Physiol</u>. 13:465-88.

[Note that capitalization of the title of the article is that used in a sentence.]

> 7. Damas, J. Some further experiments on the relation of light to growth. Amer. Jour. Bot. 12:398-412. 1925.

> 12. S. R. Palit, <u>J. Org. Chem</u>., 12, 752 (1947).

> Kramer, P. J., and Kozlowski, T. T. 1960. <u>Physiology of trees</u>, p. 11. New York: McGraw-Hill.

["Sentence" capitalization for book title.]

> 9. C. H. Goulden, Methods of Statistical Analysis, 2d ed. (New York: John Wiley & Sons, 1952), p. 42.

REFERENCE FOOTNOTES: SECOND OR LATER REFERENCES

7:136   When a work has once been cited in complete form, later references to it are made in shortened forms. For these the Latin abbreviation "ibid." and shortened titles are used.

---

* For a more comprehensive discussion of the format of papers in the sciences, we refer you to Kate L. Turabian, *A Manual for Writers of Term Papers, Theses, and Dissertations,* 4th ed. (Chicago: University of Chicago Press, 1973), pp. 180–87.

WHEN TO USE "IBID."

7:137   When references to the same work follow each other without any intervening reference, even though the references are separated by several pages, the abbreviation "ibid." (for the Latin *ibidem*, "in the same place") is used to repeat as much of the preceding reference as is appropriate for the new entry.

> [1]Max Plowman, <u>An Introduction to the Study of Blake</u> (London: Gollancz, 1952), p. 32.

[A first, and therefore complete, reference to the work.]

> [2]Ibid.

[With no intervening reference, a second mention of the same page of Plowman's work requires only "ibid." Notice that "ibid." is not underlined.]

> [3]Ibid., p. 68.

[With no intervening reference since the last to Plowman's work, "ibid." is still correct, but here the reference is to a different page.]

7:138   Since "ibid." means "in the same place," it must not be used to repeat an author's name when references to two works by the same author follow each other without intervening reference. Although repetition of the author's name in the second reference is the style preferred by many scholars, "idem" may be used. This Latin word, meaning "the same," is properly used only of a person. It may be abbreviated to "id." if the abbreviation is consistently used. Do not confuse "ibid." and "idem": notice that in footnote 2 "ibid." stands for *all* the items of the preceding reference except page number. "Idem," referring only to a person, could not serve here:

> [1]Arthur Waley, <u>The Analects of Confucius</u> (London: George Allen & Unwin, 1938), p. 33.
>
> [2]Ibid., p. 38.

7:139   On the other hand, in the following examples, "ibid." in the second footnote would be incorrect, since it is used to repeat only the author's name from the preceding footnote, all the other items being changed. "Idem," meaning the same person, is correct here.

> [1]Arthur Waley, <u>The Analects of Confucius</u> (London: George Allen & Unwin, 1938), p. 33.

<u>Wrong</u>: [2]Ibid., <u>Chinese Poems</u> (London: George Allen & Unwin, 1946), p. 51.

> [1]Arthur Waley, <u>The Analects of Confucius</u> (London: George Allen & Unwin, 1938), p. 33.

<u>Right</u>: [2]Idem, <u>Chinese Poems</u> (London: George Allen & Unwin, 1946), p. 51.

[Repetition of the author's name would be equally correct; but, again, consistency is necessary. There is no period after "idem"; it is a complete word, not an abbreviation.]

7:140 If a number of pages separate references to a given work, the writer may prefer, for the sake of clarity, to repeat the title rather than to use "ibid." even though no reference to another work has intervened, and the abbreviation is technically correct.

WHEN NOT TO USE "IBID."

7:141 Reference to a work which already has been cited in full form, *but not in the reference immediately preceding,* is made in one of two ways, which we shall call Method A and Method B.

Method A

7:142 Method A uses the author's last name (but not the first name or initials unless another author of the same surname has been cited), a shortened form of the title of the work, and the specific reference.

7:143 For a book, a shortened form of reference omits the facts of publication, series title, edition (unless more than one edition of the same work has been cited), and the number of volumes. It includes author's last name, short title of the work, and page number (volume *and* page numbers if necessary). Examples of a full footnote reference to a book and its corresponding shortened form are shown in notes 1 and 6, below.

7:144   For an article in a magazine or journal, or for any component part of a work, such as the chapter in a book, essay or poem in an anthology, a shortened form of reference omits the name of the periodical, or book, or anthology; the volume number; and the date. It includes author's last name; title of the article, chapter, essay, or poem—in shortened form, if desired—and page number. Examples of a full footnote reference to an article in a scholarly journal and its corresponding shortened form are shown in notes 4 and 7 below.

7:145   The following succession of footnotes illustrates the use of Method A:

[1]Max Plowman, <u>An Introduction to the Study of Blake</u> (London: Gollancz, 1952), pp. 58-59.

[2]Plowman, in William Blake's <u>The Marriage of Heaven and Hell</u>, reproduced in facsimile from an original drawing, with a note by Max Plowman (London: J. M. Dent & Sons, 1927), pp. ix-xii.

[Reference to another work by Plowman. The page numbers in small numerals are those in the front of the book carrying Plowman's note.]

[3]Review of <u>An Introduction to the Study of Blake</u>, by Max Plowman, <u>Times Literary Supplement</u>, 8 June 1952, p. 12.

[A reference to a popular magazine, which is identified by date alone.]

[4]Elspeth Longacre, "Blake's Conception of the Devil," <u>Studies in English</u> 90 (June 1937): 384. (Hereinafter referred to as "Blake's Devil.")

[Reference to a scholarly journal.]

> [5] Ibid.

[The same as the footnote immediately above.]

> [6] Plowman, <u>Blake</u>, p. 125.

[Since two works by Plowman have already been introduced, the title, here given in shortened form, is necessary.]

> [7] Longacre, "Blake's Devil," p. 381.

[Another reference to Miss Longacre's journal article, using a short title. Other works having intervened since the complete reference in n. 4, "ibid." cannot be used.]

Shortened Titles

7:146   A shortened title uses the key words of the main title, omitting an initial "A," "An," or "The." A title beginning with "A Dictionary of," "A Study of," "Readings in," or similar initial words, should omit those words in a shortened title. In general, no part of a subtitle should be included in a shortened title. For such works, then, as *The Pound Sterling: A History of English Money* and *Henry P. Davison: A Biography,* the short titles come ready made.

7:147   Generally speaking, titles of from two to five words should not be shortened, but length of the words is a consideration and such a title as the following lends itself well to shortening:

> <u>Financial Aspects of Economic</u>
>   <u>Development</u>

shortened to

> <u>Economic Development</u>

Titles like the following, however, should not be shortened except by omitting the initial article:

> <u>Human Destiny</u>
> <u>The Far Eastern Dilemma</u>
> <u>The Dollar Crisis</u>

7:148   Here are some examples of full titles with their short titles:

Full Main Title	*Short Title*
A Guide to Rehabil- itation of the Handicapped	Handicapped
The Rise of the Evangelical Con- ception of the Ministry in America	Ministry in America
Classification and Identification of Handwriting	Handwriting
The American Dream of Destiny and Democracy	American Dream or: Destiny and Democracy
Creation Legends of the Ancient Near East	Creation Legends
"Blake's Conception of the Devil"	"Blake's Devil"

7:149   Neither the order of the words of the original title nor the form of the words should be changed. *Creation Legends of the Ancient Near East,* for example, should not be given the short title of *Near Eastern Legends.*

7:150   When a shortened title that is to be used in later references is not readily identifiable, it is usual to give that title, within parentheses, at the end of the original citation: "(Hereinafter referred to as ———.)"

"Op. cit." and "loc. cit."

7:151   Scholarly usage has made readers familiar with the Latin abbreviations "op. cit." (*opere citato*, "in the work cited") and "loc. cit." (*loco citato,* "in the place cited") in footnotes refer- ring to previously cited works given in full form. But this usage is not without disadvantage and it can be a real stumbling block. Consider the conscientious reader who has been intro- duced in earlier footnotes to a good many authors and their works and then meets "Gates, op. cit., p. 80" in footnote 65. Not remembering Gates's work, he turns to the bibliography, only to find two or more works listed for Gates. Nothing for it, then, but to examine all the preceding footnotes. If he is lucky, he may not go far before locating the original citation. But he may not be lucky: he may have to go back to the beginning; he may even discover that the writer has mentioned two works by Gates, or none at all! One of the pitfalls of rearranging text —and rearranging is probably more common than uncommon—is keeping the footnotes in order, especially being sure that abbreviated forms do not appear before full forms have been given. Should the writer slip up, if he has used the "short-title" form of abbreviated reference rather than "op. cit." or "loc. cit.," the work will be identifiable to the reader—at least to the extent that he can find in the bibliography any additional information desired.

Method B

7:152   Method B uses the author's last name (without first name or initials unless another author of the same surname has been cited) and the page number (or volume and page number, if necessary). And this is all, unless more than one work by the same author has been cited, in which case the appropriate title—in shortened form, if desired—must be included in the reference. Works in which an association, or institution, or company stands as author must always include the title in the shortened form of reference.

7:153   An example of a succession of footnotes illustrating the use of Method B follows. It consists of the same works that have been used to illustrate footnote practice under Method A, thus pointing up the differences in the two methods.

> [1]Max Plowman, <u>An Introduction to the Study of Blake</u> (London: Gollancz, 1952), pp. 58-59.

> [2]Idem, in William Blake's <u>The Marriage of Heaven and Hell</u>, reproduced in facsimile from an original drawing, with a note by Max Plowman (London: J. M. Dent & Sons, 1927), pp. ix-xii.

[Reference to another work by Plowman. Here "idem" is used to repeat the author's name. With no intervening reference, this is permissible (see par. 7:139). Notice the page numbers in small roman numerals, indicating their reference to pages in the front of the book that are so expressed.]

³Review of <u>An Introduction to the</u> <u>Study of Blake</u>, by Max Plowman, <u>Times</u> <u>Literary Supplement</u>, 8 June 1952, p. 12.

[A reference to a popular weekly magazine identified by date.]

⁴Elspeth Longacre, "Blake's Con- ception of the Devil," <u>Studies in En-</u> <u>glish</u> 90 (June 1937): 384-88.

[A reference to a scholarly journal identified by both volume and date.]

⁵Ibid.

[The same as the footnote immediately above.]

⁶Plowman, <u>Blake</u>, p. 125.

[Since two works by Plowman have already been introduced, the title, here given in shortened form, is necessary.]

⁷Longacre, p. 381.

[Another reference to Miss Longacre's article. Since no other works by her have been previously mentioned, the name and page number are sufficient under the style of Method B.]

CONTENT FOOTNOTES

7:154   Content footnotes consist of explanations or amplifications of the textual discussion, sometimes supported by references to the works of others, sometimes by references to other parts of the paper (cross-references [see par. 7:69]), sometimes without any supporting references. Where there are references, they may be placed in any one of several ways, depending upon the position which seems most appropriate in a given instance. If the reference is to a work that has not been cited before, the notation must include the facts of publication, as in the first note below.

> [1]It has been estimated that in the early days of the Republic 120,000 out of 4,000,000 inhabitants had the right to vote. Woodrow Wilson, <u>History of the American People</u>, cited by David C. Coyle, <u>The United States Political System and How It Works</u> (New York: New American Library, 1954), p. 14.

Following are two other examples of content footnotes:

> [1]Sexson and Harbeson state that George A. Merrill, the principal of the Wilmerding School, "might well be called the father of the 6-4-4 plan of . . . school organization" (p. 27).

[Here reference is made to a work previously cited in full form, and therefore the page number is sufficient.]

> [2]Burton, too, believed it is the "central business of a college to develop, not ideas in the abstract, nor the human tools of the trades, but personalities capable of a large contribution to life" (p. 59). See also Harper's statement, p. 6, supra.

SPLIT REFERENCES

7:155 If at the first mention of a work, the author's full name is given in the text close to the footnote number, the name may be omitted in the footnote. After the first reference, mention in the text of the surname alone permits its omission in the note.

7:156 Similarly, if both name and title of a work occur in the text, both may be omitted in the footnote, which then would consist either of the facts of publication (unless they had been given in an earlier note) and the volume and page number, or of the volume and page number or of the page number alone.

Appendix A
Sample Research Paper

LIBERTY AND EQUALITY: CAN THEY BE RECONCILED?
Robert D. Falk

Political Science 101A

LIBERTY AND EQUALITY: CAN THEY BE RECONCILED?

For centuries liberal theorists and statesmen have tried to reconcile the ideals of liberty and equality in the democratic version of the good society. The American experiment is one such attempt, and American theorists have been among the most articulate expounders of the dual concepts of liberty and equality--not as contradictions, but as complementary facets of the same ideological gem. We have put into practice many of the democratic doctrines we preach. In a world where oppression and privilege are the political norms, we have enjoyed relative liberty and relative equality. As we become more equal, are we becoming less free?

"All men are created equal," states the Declaration of Independence. Yet observation tells us men do not remain equal. Thomas Jefferson, who drafted the Declaration, also wrote:

> There is a natural aristocracy among men. The grounds of this are virtue and talent. . . .

1

2

> The natural aristocracy I consider as the most precious gift of nature, for the instruction, the trusts, and government of society.[1]

A similar view was expressed by John Adams. Why, asked the French statesman Anne Robert Jacques Turgot, should there be "orders" in republics "founded on the equality of all citizens"? Adams replied:

> But what are we to understand here by equality? Are the citizens to be all of the same age, sex, size, strength, stature, activity, courage, hardiness, industry, patience, ingenuity, wealth, knowledge, fame, wit, temperance, constancy, and wisdom? Was there, or will there ever be, a nation whose individuals were all equal in natural and acquired qualities, in virtues, talents, and riches? The answer of all mankind must be in the negative.[2]

Adams's definition of equality is given in the same document:

> In this society of Massachusettensians then there is,it is true, a moral and political equality of rights and duties among all the individuals and as yet no appearance of artificial inequalities of conditions, such as hereditary dignities, titles, magistracies, or legal distinctions; and no established

---

[1] Saul K. Padover, ed., Thomas Jefferson on Democracy (New York: New American Library, Mentor Books, 1953), p. 150.

[2] George A. Peek, Jr., ed., The Political Writings of John Adams (New York: Liberal Arts Press, 1954), p. 133.

marks as stars, garters, crosses, or
ribbons. . . .[3]

Equality, then, means to Adams equality
of rights and duties, and the absence of artificial distinctions. What kind of equality is
provided for in the United States Constitution?

1. Both Federal and State governments are
   prohibited from granting titles of
   nobility. (Art. I, sec. 9, par. 8;
   Art. I, sec. 10, par. 1.)

2. "The Citizens of each State shall be
   entitled to all Privileges and Im-
   munities of Citizens in the several
   States."•(Art. IV, sec. 2, par. 1.)

3. Slavery is forbidden. (Amendment XIII.)

4. "No State shall . . . deny to any
   persons within its jurisdiction the
   equal protection of the laws." (Amendment XIV, sec. 1.)

5. "The right of citizens of the United
   States to vote shall not be denied or
   abridged by the United States or by
   any State on account of race, color,
   or previous condition of servitude."
   (Amendment XV.)

6. "The right of citizens of the United
   States to vote shall not be abridged
   by the United States or by any State on
   account of sex." (Amendment XIX.)

Political equality has been extended still
further by various provisions of the state
constitutions, and by liberal judicial inter-

---

[3] Ibid.

pretations of constitutions and laws. Social
equality, intellectual equality, and economic
equality have also been increased through legis-
lation: progressive income and inheritance taxes,
free and subsidized education, public libraries,
minimum wage laws, and "Fair Employment Practices"
acts.

However, constitutional guarantees and
public policy do not provide a complete picture
of the relative status of individuals within a
society. There is more to equality than equality
of opportunity, distributive justice, equal
protection of the laws, mass suffrage, and the
absence of hereditary titles. Equality is also a
state of mind. The "feeling" or "sense" of
equality determines the nature of public policy;
at the same time it pervades those areas of national life which are beyond the reach of laws,
administrative acts, and judicial decisions. An
early visitor to this nation began his classic
study of the American scene by attempting to
describe the nature and source of the equalitarian
climate which he found so prevalent:

> Among the novel objects that attracted my
> attention during my stay in the United States,
> nothing struck me more forcibly than the
> general equality of condition among the peo-
> ple. I readily discovered the prodigious
> influence that this primary fact exercises

on the whole course of society; it gives a
peculiar direction to public opinion and
a peculiar tenor to the laws; it imparts new
maxims to the governing authorities and
peculiar habits to the governed.

I soon perceived that the influence of
this fact extends far beyond the political
character and laws of the country, and that
it has no less effect on civil society than
on government; it creates opinions, gives
birth to new sentiments, founds novel customs,
and modifies whatever it does not produce.
The more I advanced in the study of American
society, the more I perceived that this
equality of condition is the fundamental fact
from which all others seem to be derived
and the central point at which my observations constantly terminated.[4]

What is meant by liberty? I would define
it broadly. Liberty is less than license, and
more than the absence of governmental restraints.
It has to do with "the pursuit of happiness,"
though it does not guarantee happiness. And to
the extent that restraints--social, economic,
political--become arbitrary, liberty is dimin-
ished. Liberty is the opportunity to develop
one's natural endowments to the fullest possible
extent.

Can liberty and equality be reconciled?
Peter Viereck, of the American neo-conservative
movement, attempts to summarize a negative view:

---

[4]Alexis de Tocqueville, <u>Democracy in Amer-
ica</u> (New York: Vintage Books, 1959), 1: 3.

6

According to conservative historians,
parliamentary and civil liberties were created
not by modern liberal democracy but by medieval feudalism, not by equality but by
privilege. These free institutions--Magna
Cartas, constitutions, Witens, Dumas, and par-
liaments--were originally founded and bled
for by medieval noblemen, fighting selfishly
and magnificently for their historic rights
against both kinds of tyranny, the tyranny
of kings and the tyranny of the conformist
masses. Modern democracy merely inherited from
feudalism that sacredness of individual
liberty and then, so to speak, mass-produced
it. Democracy changed liberty from an individual privilege to a general right, thereby
gaining in quantity of freedom but losing
in quality of freedom. . . .[5]

Viereck continues his interpretation of
the conservative historians' case against equality
by citing the great English libertarians--Pitt,
Burke, Sheridan--who were sent to Parliament by
aristocratically controlled "rotten boroughs."
It might be argued just as convincingly that
American liberties, where they are not part of
our English heritage, were established by the
representatives of a domestic aristocracy.[6] The

[5]Peter Viereck, Conservatism: From John
Adams to Churchill (Princeton, N.J.: D. Van
Nostrand Company, Anvil Original, 1956), p. 28.

[6]It has been estimated that in the early
days of the Republic 120,000 out of 4,000,000
inhabitants had the right to vote. Woodrow Wilson, History of the American People, cited by
David Cushman Coyle, The United States Political
System and How It Works (New York: New American
Library, Signet Key Book, 1954), p. 14.

basic defect in this kind of argument is that it
assumes the particular to be universal. Increases
in liberty and the rise of an aristocracy may
be seen together at certain times and in certain
places; but not always and everywhere. Nor are
strong rulers inevitably tyrants, the masses
forever ignorant and overbearing. Which is the
more oppressive: the Sedition Act of 1918, or that
of 1798? Congressional witch-hunts (sanctioned
by the mob), or slavery (an aristocratic institution)? And have the traditional liberties of
Englishmen and Americans actually suffered at the
hands of their present heirs?

Whatever the relative merits of privilege
and equality, the world appears to be moving
generally in the direction of the latter
condition.

> The various occurrences of national exis-
> tence have everywhere turned to the advantage
> of democracy. . . . The gradual development
> of the principle of equality is, therefore, a
> providential fact. It has all the chief
> characteristics of such a fact: it is
> universal, it is lasting, it constantly eludes
> all human interference, and all events as
> well as all men contribute to its progress.[7]

And ethnic minorities continue to aspire
to positions which are denied them; workers
demand still higher wages; and colonial subjects

---

[7]Tocqueville, _Democracy_, 1: 6.

clamor for independence, and celebrate independence by threatening their neighbors. Those
who feel that equality leads to mediocrity and
disorder call attention to the present state of
the arts and mass communications media, and to the
endless fashions, fads, and fancies of nations
which seem so often in doubt as to what they
want and where they are going. They ask whether
disorder and mediocrity, the decline of custom
and culture, can be other than a prelude to the
eventual withering away of freedom itself. In
short, will Western democracy continue to survive,
and evolve, or does it contain the seed of its
own destruction: ever greater equality. Or: can
liberty and equality be reconciled?

Perhaps the final verdict of history will
be that equality is not incompatible with liberty,
but essential to liberty. Do we accept Jefferson's concept of "a natural aristocracy among
men"? It is important that we decide. For such
an aristocracy cannot rise to its rightful position in a society based upon inequality, and
it cannot flourish where men limit the reservoir
of talent and leadership from which they might
draw by subjecting large segments of the population to perpetual ignorance and poverty.

LIST OF REFERENCES

Coyle, David Cushman. *The United States Political System and How It Works*. New York: New American Library, Signet Key Book, 1954.

Padover, Saul K., ed. *Thomas Jefferson on Democracy*. New York: New American Library, Mentor Books, 1953.

Peek, George A., Jr., ed. *The Political Writings of John Adams*. New York: Liberal Arts Press, 1954.

Tocqueville, Alexis de. *Democracy in America*. 2 vols. New York: Vintage Books, 1959.

U.S. *Constitution*.

Viereck, Peter. *Conservatism: From John Adams to Churchill*. Princeton, N.J.: D. Van Nostrand Company, Anvil Original, 1956.

9

Appendix B

Select List of Reference Works

The following list is divided into general reference works and works in the major subject fields. Under General Reference Works you will find items that are useful, in greater or lesser degree, in every subject field. But also under each of the major subject fields (Humanities, History, Social Sciences, and Biological and Physical Sciences) is a section headed "General" or "General Studies" which lists reference works pertaining to the various subjects within that division. It is important, therefore, to take note of the General Reference Works and the works listed under "General" or "General Studies" in the division in which your subject falls before giving attention to the recommendations under the name of the subject field. Also helpful are the comments on some of the general reference works that appear in chapter 3, "Collecting Material."

CONTENTS

GENERAL REFERENCE WORKS

BIBLIOGRAPHICAL GUIDES

Besterman, Theodore. *A World Bibliography of Bibliographies.* 4th
ed., revised and greatly enlarged. 5 vols. Lausanne: Societas Bibliographica, 1965–66.

With over 117,000 bibliographies, the most generally useful
work in its field.

*Bibliographic Index, The: A Cumulative Bibliography of Bibliog-
raphies.* New York: H. W. Wilson, 1938–. (Semimonthly, with
annual and larger cumulations.)

The standard current bibliography of bibliographies.

Walford, A. J. *Guide to Reference Material.* 2d ed. 3 vols. London:
Library Assn., 1966–70.

Vol. 1: *Science and Technology* (1966). Vol. 2: *Philosophy and
Psychology, Religion, Social Sciences, Geography, Biography and
History* (1968). Vol. 3: *Generalities, Languages, the Arts, and
Literature* (1970). A third edition is in progress: Vol. 1 (1973);
Vol. 2 (1975).

Winchell, Constance M. *Guide to Reference Books.* 8th ed. Chicago:
American Library Assn., 1967.

Kept up to date by supplements at two-year intervals.

ENCYCLOPEDIAS

Chambers's Encyclopaedia. New Revised Edition. 15 vols. London:
International Learning Systems Corp., 1973.

Collier's Encyclopedia. 24 vols. New York: Crowell-Collier Educational Corp., 1968.

All the bibliographies are collected in Vol. 24, which also
contains (pp. 219–1073) the index.

Columbia Encyclopedia, The New. 4th ed. 1 vol. New York: Columbia
Univ. Press, 1975.

Encyclopaedia Britannica, The New. 15th ed. 30 vols. Chicago:
Encyclopaedia Britannica, Inc., 1974.

The encyclopedia is divided into three sections: (1) *Propaedia,*
1 volume, containing an "outline of knowledge" and guide to the
encyclopedia; (2) *Micropaedia,* 10 volumes, containing shorter

articles "for ready reference" and indexes; and (3) *Macropaedia,* 19 volumes, with longer articles ("knowledge in depth").

Encyclopedia Americana, The. International Edition. 30 vols. New York: Americana Corp., 1972.

SUBJECT INDEXES

The following items constitute, in various forms, universal subject indexes, i.e., they point to materials on almost any subject under investigation.

To Books

A.L.A. Catalog 1926: An Annotated Basic List of 10,000 Books. Edited by Isabella M. Cooper. Chicago: American Library Assn., 1926.

Book titles arranged according to the Dewey decimal system, with comments. Continued by supplements.

A.L.A. Index: An Index to General Literature. . . . Edited by William I. Fletcher. 2d ed. enl. Boston and Chicago: American Library Assn., 1901. Reprint: Freeport, N.Y.: Books for Libraries Press, 1971.

Supplement, 1914. Continued by the *Essay and General Literature Index* (below).

American Book Publishing Record. New York: R. R. Bowker, 1960–.

The books listed in the *Publishers' Weekly* rearranged according to the Dewey decimal system. Cumulated monthly, and annually.

Book Review Digest. New York: H. W. Wilson, 1905–.

Published monthly, except February and July, with semiannual cumulation in August and annual cumulation in February. Cumulated subject and title indexes published at five-year intervals.

Book Review Index. Detroit: Gale Research Co., 1965–68, 1972–.

Indexes by author, giving title of work and location of reviews. Now published bimonthly.

British Museum, Department of Printed Books. *Subject Index of the Modern Works Added to the Library . . . in the Years 1881–1900.* Edited by G. K. Fortescue. 3 vols. London: British Museum, 1902–3.

Continued by similar subject indexes published every five years.

British National Bibliography. London: Council of the B.N.B., British Museum, 1950–. (Weekly.)

Each issue indexed by subject and author. Books are arranged by the Dewey decimal system. The last issue for each month has a cumulated author, title, and subject index. Quarterly cumulations and cumulated subject indexes every five years.

Cumulative Book Index: A World List of Books in the English Language 1928/32–. New York: H. W. Wilson, 1933.

Originally a supplement to the *United States Catalog,* 4th ed. (1928). Now published monthly, except July and August, cumulating semiannually and at larger intervals. Indexed by author, title, and subject.

Dickinson, Asa D. *The World's Best Books.* . . . New York: H. W. Wilson, 1953.

Essay and General Literature Index, 1900–1933: An Index to about 40,000 Essays and Articles in 2,144 Volumes of Collections of Essays and Miscellaneous Works. Edited by Minnie E. Sears and Marian Shaw. New York: H. W. Wilson, 1934.

Continued by supplements and periodic cumulations.

Paperbacks in Print: A Reference Catalogue of . . . Paperbacks in Print and on Sale in Great Britain. London: Whitaker, 1960–. (Semiannually.)

The 1973 edition lists over 38,000 books, indexed by author, title, and subject.

Paperbound Books in Print. New York: R. R. Bowker, 1955–. (Monthly.)

The 1973 edition lists over 114,000 books, indexed by title, author, and subject.

Publishers' Trade List Annual. New York: R. R. Bowker, 1873–.

Publishers' catalogs and announcements, arranged alphabetically by names of publishers. See also *Books in Print: An Author-Title-Series Index to the Publishers' Trade List Annual.* New York: R. R. Bowker, 1948–. Published annually in two volumes until 1974 and 1975, when it was published in four volumes, two for authors and two for titles. Useful for locating information on new books. A companion work, *Subject Guide to Books in Print,* was published in one volume annually until 1973; in two volumes since then. (New York: R. R. Bowker, 1957–).

Reader's Adviser, The: A Guide to the Best in Literature. 11th ed., rev. and enl. by Winifred P. Courtney. 2 vols. New York: R. R. Bowker, 1968–69.

A valuable annotated guide to important books in all fields of learning and imaginative literature.

U. S. Library of Congress. *Catalog. Books: Subjects, 1950–1954. A Cumulated List of Books Represented by Library of Congress Printed Cards.* 20 vols. Ann Arbor, Mich.: Edwards Bros., 1955.

A continuation for the years 1955–59; Paterson, N.J.: Pageant Books, 1960 (22 vols.). Continued by quarterly and annual supplements, with cumulations at five-year intervals.

Watt, Robert. *Bibliotheca Britannica; or, A General Index to British and Foreign Literature. In Two Parts: Authors and Subjects.* 4 vols. Edinburgh: Constable, 1824.

A valuable source for earlier literature.

To Periodicals

Annual Magazine Subject Index, 1907–49: A Subject Index to a Selected List of American and English Periodicals and Society Publications. Compiled by F. W. Faxon. 43 vols. Boston: F. W. Faxon, 1908–52.

Indexes by subject only.

Canadian Periodical Index, 1928–1947. Toronto: Public Libraries Branch, Ontario Department of Education, 1928–47.

Continued by *Canadian Index to Periodicals and Documentary Films, 1948–59* (Ottawa: Canadian Library Assn., 1962); and *Canadian Periodical Index* (Ottawa: Canadian Library Assn., 1964–). Monthly, with annual and five-year cumulations. Indexes by author and subject.

Catholic Periodical Index. Washington, D.C.: Catholic Library Assn., 1930.

Beginning with July 1968 combined with the *Guide to Catholic Literature,* edited by Walter Ronig (Detroit: Ronig, 1940–) under the title *Catholic Periodical and Literature Index* (Vol. 14, 1967–68), Haverford, Pa.: Catholic Library Assn., 1968–.

Goode, Stephen H. *Index to Little Magazines, 1943–1947.* Denver: Alan Swallow, 1965.

Continued by *Index to Little Magazines, 1948–* (Denver: Alan Swallow, 1949–). Annually through 1961; biennially from 1962/63.

———. *Index to Little Magazines, 1940–42.* New York: Johnson Reprint Corp., 1967.

————. *Index to American Little Magazines, 1920–1939*. Troy, N.Y.: Whitston Publishing Co., 1969.

————. *Index to American Little Magazines, 1900–1919. To Which Is Added a Selected List of British and Continental Titles for the Years 1900–1950, Together with Addenda and Corrigenda to Previous Indexes*. 3 vols. Troy, N.Y.: Whitston Publishing Co., 1974.

International Index to Periodicals. See *Social Sciences and Humanities Index* (below).

Poole's Index to Periodical Literature, 1802–1881. Rev. ed. 2 vols. Boston: Houghton Mifflin, 1891.

    Indexes over 450 American and English periodicals, but by subject only. Five supplementary volumes continue the index to January 1907. Supplemented by Helen G. Cushing and Adah V. Morris, *Nineteenth-Century Readers' Guide to Periodical Literature, 1890–1899, with Supplementary Indexing, 1900–1922* (2 vols.), New York: H. W. Wilson, 1944. See also Marion V. Bell and Jean C. Bacon, *Poole's Index, Date and Volume Key* (Chicago: Assn. of College and Reference Libraries, 1957) and C. Edward Wall et al., *Cumulative Author Index for Poole's Index to Periodical Literature, 1802–1906* (Ann Arbor, Mich.: Pierian Press, 1971).

Readers' Guide to Periodical Literature. New York: H. W. Wilson, 1900–.

    Issued semimonthly from September to June, monthly in July and August, with annual and five-year cumulations. The standard index for U. S. periodicals of nonprofessional and nontechnical nature. Coverage has varied from the beginning. A very useful subject index, since indexing is by author, subject, and title.

Social Sciences and Humanities Index. New York: H. W. Wilson, 1907–.

    Originally published as a supplement to *Readers' Guide to Periodical Literature*. Vol. 1 covers the years 1907 to 1915. Issued quarterly with annual and two-year cumulations. From 1955 to January 1965 it was entitled *International Index to Periodicals* and included references to a number of foreign journals. The present title has been used since March 1965. Essentially an index to the more scholarly journals.

Subject Index to Periodicals [1915–61]. London: Library Assn., 1919–62. Annual. (Quarterly, 1954–61, cumulated annually.)

Now divided into three specialized periodical indexes: *British Technology Index,* 1962–; *British Humanities Index,* 1963–; *British Education Index,* 1964–.

BIOGRAPHICAL AIDS

General (items marked with asterisk include living persons)

Biography Index. A Cumulative Index to Biographical Material in Books and Magazines. New York: H. W. Wilson, 1947–.*

A quarterly index to a wide range of biographical material, with annual and three-year cumulations.

Boase, Frederic. *Modern English Biography, containing many thousand Concise Memoirs of Persons who have died since 1850, with an index of the most interesting Matter.* 6 vols. Truro: Netherton, 1892–1923; New York: Barnes & Noble, 1965.

Useful for nineteenth-century persons not included in the *Dictionary of National Biography.*

Chambers's Biographical Dictionary. Edited by J. O. Thorne. Rev. ed. Edinburgh: W. & R. Chambers; New York: St. Martin's Press, 1969.*

Includes (pp. 1398–1432) a valuable subject index, including such subjects as Art & Architecture, Cinema, Exploration & Geography, and History.

Dictionary of American Biography. Published under the Auspices of the American Council of Learned Societies. 21 vols. (Vol. 21 = Index.) New York: Scribner, 1928–37. Supplement One (to 31 December 1935), 1944. Supplement Two (1936–40), 1958.

A scholarly work, with long, signed articles and bibliographies. See also the one-volume *Concise Dictionary of American Biography* (New York: Scribner, 1964).

Dictionary of Canadian Biography. Toronto: Univ. of Toronto Press, 1966–.

Dictionary of National Biography. Edited by Leslie Stephen and Sidney Lee. 63 vols. London: Smith, Elder, 1885–1900. Published since 1917 by Oxford University Press in 22 volumes (Vol. 22 = Supplement).

Includes notable persons of Great Britain and the colonies from the earliest historical period. Supplements at ten-year intervals, the latest (covering 1951–60) published in 1971.

Encyclopedia of American Biography. Edited by John A. Garraty and Jerome L. Sternstein. New York: Harper & Row, 1974.*

Each entry consists of a factual summary, followed by an interpretative essay.

Hyamson, Albert M. *A Dictionary of Universal Biography of All Ages and of All Peoples.* 2d ed., entirely rewritten. London: Routledge, 1951.

Not a collection of biographies, but a key to other collections where biographies may be found.

Ireland, Norma O. *Index to Women of the World from Ancient to Modern Times: Biographies and Portraits.* Westwood, Mass.: F. W. Faxon, 1970.*

James, Edward T., et al. *Notable American Women, 1607–1950: A Biographical Dictionary.* 3 vols. Cambridge, Mass.: Harvard Univ. Press, Belknap Press, 1971.*

National Cyclopaedia of American Biography. New York: James T. White, 1892–.* In progress.

Old-fashioned and less scholarly than the *Dictionary of American Biography,* but includes more minor figures. Volumes A to K are devoted to living persons. *Revised Index: Permanent and Current Series,* compiled by H. A. Harvey and Raymond D. McGill. New York: James T. White, 1971 (= Index to Vols. 1–32).

New York Times Obituary Index, 1858–1968. New York: New York Times, 1970.

Lists over 350,000 names; very useful, especially for less famous figures.

Thomas, Joseph. *Universal Pronouncing Dictionary of Biography and Mythology.* 5th ed. Philadelphia: Lippincott, 1930.

First published in 1870; usually referred to as *Lippincott's Biographical Dictionary.*

Webster's Biographical Dictionary. Springfield, Mass.: G. & C. Merriam, 1962.

Who Was Who (1897–1960). 5 vols. London: A. and C. Black, 1929–61.

Who Was Who in America: Historical Volume, 1607–1896. Chicago: Marquis, 1963.

Who Was Who in America. 4 vols. Chicago: Marquis, 1942–68.

Vol. 4 contains a cumulative index to Vols. 1–4 and to the *Historical Volume.*

Living Persons

Current Biography. New York: H. W. Wilson, 1940–. (Monthly, except August.)

An annual cumulation (*Current Biography Yearbook*). Very useful for figures in current news. The 1973 volume begins with Claudio Abbado (orchestra conductor), Dick Allen (baseball player), and Idi Aman (president of Uganda).

International Who's Who. London: Europa Pubns., 1935–.

Who's Who: An Annual Biographical Dictionary. London: A. and C. Black, 1849–.

Mainly British, but includes some prominent world figures from other countries.

Who's Who in America: A Biographical Dictionary of Notable Living Men and Women. Chicago: Marquis, 1899–.

Now published in two volumes, biennially. The same publishers issue a number of sectional volumes (*Who's Who in the Midwest,* etc.).

Who's Who in the World. Chicago: Marquis, 1970–.

This reference work and the *International Who's Who* do not entirely duplicate each other.

BIBLIOGRAPHIES OF PERIODICALS

Ayer, N. W., publisher. *N. W. Ayer & Son's Directory of Newspapers and Periodicals,* Philadelphia: N. W. Ayer & Son, 1880–. (Annual.)

Covers the United States and its possessions; Canada; Bermuda; Panama; and the Philippines.

Mott, Frank Luther. *A History of American Magazines.* 5 vols. Cambridge, Mass.: Harvard Univ. Press, 1930–68.

Muller, Robert H.; Spahn, Theodore J.; and Spahn, Janet M. *From Extreme Left to Extreme Right.* 2d ed., rev. and enl. Vol. 1. Ann Arbor, Mich.: Campus Publishers, 1970.

Subtitle: "A bibliography of current periodicals of protest, controversy, advocacy, or dissent, with dispassionate content-summaries to guide librarians and other educators through the polemic fringe."

Ulrich's International Periodicals Directory. New York: R. R. Bowker, 1932–. (Biennial.)

Beginning with the 15th edition (1974) published in one volume.

Union List of Serials in Libraries of the United States and Canada. 3d ed. Edited by Edna Brown Titus. 5 vols. New York: H. W. Wilson, 1965. Continued by the following item.

New Serial Titles. A Union List of Serials Commencing Publication after December 31, 1949. 1950–1970 Cumulation. 4 vols. Washington, D.C.: Library of Congress; New York: R. R. Bowker, 1973.

    Published in eight monthly issues, four quarterly issues, and annual cumulations. Cumulated over five- and ten-year periods.

White, Cynthia L. *Women's Magazines, 1693–1962.* London: Michael Joseph, 1970.

DICTIONARIES

Unabridged

A Dictionary of American English on Historical Principles. Edited by Sir William A. Craigie and James R. Hulbert. 4 vols. Chicago: Univ. of Chicago Press, 1938–44.

American Heritage Dictionary of the English Language, The. Edited by William Morris. New York: American Heritage Co.; Boston: Houghton Mifflin, 1969.

Funk & Wagnalls New Standard Dictionary of the English Language. Edited by I. K. Funk, Calvin Thomas, and F. H. Vizetelly. New York: Funk & Wagnalls, 1964.

Oxford English Dictionary. 13 vols. Oxford: Clarendon Press, 1933.

    A "corrected reissue, with an Introduction, Supplement, and Bibliography of *A New English Dictionary on Historical Principles* by Sir J. A. H. Murray et al."

    A *Supplement,* edited by R. W. Burchfield, to be published in three volumes, is in progress (Vol. 1, 1972).

Random House Dictionary of the English Language, The. Edited by Jess Stein. New York: Random House, 1966.

Webster's Third New International Dictionary of the English Language, Unabridged. Edited by Philip E. Gove et al. Springfield, Mass.: G. & C. Merriam, 1961.

Abridged

American College Dictionary. Edited by Clarence L. Barnhart et al. New York: Random House, 1962.

American Heritage Dictionary. New College Edition. Boston: Houghton Mifflin, 1975.

Chambers Twentieth Century Dictionary. Edited by A. M. Macdonald. Rev. ed. Edinburgh: W. & R. Chambers, 1973.

Concise Oxford Dictionary of Current English. Edited by H. W. Fowler and F. G. Fowler. 5th ed., revised by E. McIntosh. Oxford: Clarendon Press, 1964.

Funk & Wagnalls Standard College Dictionary. Text Edition. New York: Harcourt, Brace, 1963.

Random House Dictionary of the English Language. College Edition. Edited by Laurence Urdang and Stuart B. Flexner. New York: Random House, 1968.

Webster's New Collegiate Dictionary. 8th ed. Springfield, Mass.: G. & C. Merriam, 1974.

Webster's New World Dictionary of the American Language. 2d college ed. Edited by David B. Guralnik. New York: World Publishing Co., 1970.

Webster's New World Dictionary of the English Language. 2d college ed. New York: Prentice-Hall, 1973.

Specialized Dictionaries: Usage, Synonyms, etc.

Barnhart, Clarence L. *The Barnhart Dictionary of New English Since 1963.* New York: Harper & Row, 1973.

Follett, Wilson. *Modern American Usage: A Guide.* Edited and completed by Jacques Barzun et al. New York: Hill & Wang, 1966.

Fowler, H. W. *A Dictionary of Modern English Usage.* 2d ed., revised by Sir Ernest Gowers. Oxford: Clarendon Press, 1965.

Klein, Ernest. *A Comprehensive Etymological Dictionary of the English Language.* New York: Elsevier Publishing Co., 1971.

Mathews, Mitford M. *A Dictionary of Americanisms on Historical Principles.* Chicago: Univ. of Chicago Press, 1951.

    Deals exclusively with American contributions to the English language.

Mencken, H. L. *The American Language: An Enquiry into the Development of English in the United States.* 4th ed, and the two Supplements abridged, with annotations and new material by Raven I. McDavid. New York: Knopf, 1965.

    Not a dictionary, but filled with lexicographical information.

Nicholson, Margaret. *A Dictionary of American-English Usage, Based on Fowler's "Modern English Usage."* New York: Oxford Univ. Press, 1957.

Oxford Dictionary of English Etymology. Edited by C. T. Onions, with the Assistance of G. W. S. Friedrichsen and R. W. Burchfield. Oxford: Clarendon Press, 1966.

Partridge, Eric. *A Dictionary of Slang and Unconventional Usage.* 7th ed. 2 vols. in 1. New York: Macmillan, 1970.

Perrin, Porter G., and Ebbitt, Wilma R. *Writer's Guide and Index to English.* 5th ed. Glenview, Ill.: Scott, Foresman, 1972.

Roget, Peter Mark. *Roget's International Thesaurus.* 3d ed. New York: Crowell, 1962.

————.*The Original Roget's Thesaurus of English Words and Phrases.* New Edition, completely revised and modernized by Robert A. Dutch. New York: St. Martin's Press, 1965.

Wall, C. Edward, and Przeblenda, Edward. *Words and Phrase Index.* 4 vols. Ann Arbor, Mich.: Pierian Press, 1969–70.
    A guide to new words and meanings.

Webster's New Dictionary of Synonyms. 2d ed. Springfield, Mass.: G. & C. Merriam, 1968.

BOOKS OF QUOTATIONS AND PROVERBS

Bartlett, John. *Familiar Quotations.* 14th ed., revised and enlarged by Emily S. Beck. Boston: Little, Brown, 1968.

Benham, Sir Gurney. *Benham's Book of Quotations, Proverbs and Household Words.* Revised edition, with Supplement and with Full Indexes. London: Harrap, 1948.

Oxford Dictionary of English Proverbs. 3d ed., revised by F. P. Wilson. Oxford: Clarendon Press, 1970.

Oxford Dictionary of Quotations. 2d ed. London: Oxford Univ. Press, 1953.
    Classical sources are given in Greek and Latin, with translations.

Simpson, James B. *Contemporary Quotations.* New York: Crowell, 1964.

Stevenson, Burton E. *Home Book of Quotations, Classical and Modern.* 9th ed. New York: Dodd, Mead, 1964.

Taylor, Archer, and Whiting, Bartlett J. *A Dictionary of American*

Proverbs and Proverbial Phrases, 1820–1880. Cambridge, Mass.: Harvard Univ. Press, Belknap Press, 1958.

Tilley, Morris P. *A Dictionary of the Proverbs in England in the Sixteenth and Seventeenth Centuries.* Ann Arbor: Univ. of Michigan Press, 1950.

Tripp, Rhoda T. *The International Thesaurus of Quotations.* New York: Crowell, 1970; London: Allen & Unwin, 1973.

> Over a third of the quotations are from the twentieth century.

ATLASES AND GAZETTEERS

Columbia Lippincott Gazetteer of the World. Edited by Leon E. Seltzer, with the Geographical Research Staff of Columbia University and with the Cooperation of the American Geographical Society. New York: Columbia Univ. Press, 1962.

Encyclopaedia Britannica World Atlas. Chicago: Encyclopaedia Britannica, 1964.

> The maps in the latest edition of the *Britannica* are not published in a separate volume.

Goode's World Atlas. 12th ed. Edited by Edward B. Espenshade, Jr. Chicago: Rand, McNally, 1964.

> Formerly *Goode's School Atlas.* An excellent convenient small atlas.

Hammond's Contemporary World Atlas. 2d ed. New York: Doubleday, 1967.

National Geographic Atlas of the World. Rev. 3d ed. Washington, D.C.: National Geographic Society, 1970.

Rand, McNally & Co. *The International Atlas.* Chicago: Rand, McNally, 1969.

> Includes world, ocean, and continent maps, as well as those for particular countries. Metropolitan area maps are now grouped together, instead of being set within the maps of states. Many tables of climatic, economic, and political information, and an index of 170,000 names.

Stebbins, Richard P., and Amoia, Alba. *Political Handbook and Atlas of the World.* New York: Simon & Schuster for the Council on Foreign Relations, 1970.

> Continued by annual supplements (*The World This Year*).

Times Atlas of the World, The. Comprehensive edition. Edinburgh: Bartholomew; Boston: Houghton Mifflin, 1967.

Based on the five-volume mid-century *Times Atlas of the World.* An up-to-date atlas, with attention to space exploration, and an index-gazetteer of 200,000 place names.

U.S. Geological Survey. *The National Atlas of the United States of America.* Washington, D.C.: U.S. Geological Survey, 1970.

CURRENT NEWS MATERIAL

Canadian News Facts: The Indexed Digest of Canadian Current Events. Toronto: Marpep, 1967–. (Biweekly, with monthly indexes. Quarterly and annual cumulations.)

Christian Science Monitor Subject Index. Boston: Christian Science Publishing Society, 1960–. (Monthly, with semiannual and annual cumulations.)

Current Digest of the Soviet Press. New York: Joint Committee on Slavic Studies, 1949–. (Weekly, with quarterly indexes.)

Facts on File: Weekly World News Digest with Cumulative Index. 1940–. New York: Facts on File. 1940–. (Cumulative index every five years.)

Keesing's Contemporary Archives: Weekly Diary of World Events, with Index Continually Kept Up-to-Date. London: Keesing's, 1931–.
   Vol. 1 contains a "synopsis of Important Events" 1918–31.

New York Times Index. New York: New York Times, 1913–. (Semi-monthly, with annual cumulations.)
   Prior Series, to cover the period 1851–1912, published in book form. New York: R. R. Bowker, 1966–. In progress.

Times, The (London). *Official Index* London: The Times, 1906–. (Monthly, 1906–June 1914; quarterly, July 1914–1956; bi-monthly, 1957–.)

Vertical File Index. New York: H. W. Wilson, 1935–. (Monthly, except August, with annual cumulations.)
   An index to selected pamphlet material, arranged alphabetically by subject, with title index.

GOVERNMENT PUBLICATIONS

Boyd, Anne Morris. *United States Government Publications.* 3d ed., revised by Rae E. Rips. New York: H. W. Wilson, 1949.

Jackson, Ellen. *Subject Guide to Major United States Government Publications*. Chicago: American Library Assn., 1968.

Leidy, W. Philip. *A Popular Guide to Government Publications*. 3d ed. New York: Columbia Univ. Press, 1968.

Describes some 3,000 titles arranged by subject, with index.

Schmeckebier, Laurence F., and Eastin, Roy B. *Government Publications and Their Use*. 3d rev. ed. Washington, D.C.: Brookings Institution, 1969.

U.S. Government Manual, 1973/74. Washington, D.C.: Office of the Federal Register, National Archives and Records Service, General Services Administration, 1974.

The official handbook of the federal government. Former title: *Government Organization Manual*. Provides lists of senators and congressmen, officers of the government, agencies and personnel, etc. Revised annually.

U.S. Library of Congress, Processing Department. *Monthly Checklist of State Publications*. Washington, D.C.: U.S. Government Printing Office, 1910–.

U.S. Superintendent of Documents. *Monthly Catalogue of United States Government Publications*. Washington, D.C.: U.S. Government Printing Office, 1895–.

Various supplements. Decennial cumulative indexes.

Wilcox, Jerome K. *Bibliography of New Guides and Aids to Public Documents Use, 1953–1956*. New York: Special Libraries Assn., 1957.

———. *Manual on the Use of State Publications*. Chicago: American Library Assn., 1940.

YEARBOOKS AND HANDBOOKS OF MISCELLANEOUS INFORMATION

Americana Annual. New York: Americana Corp., 1923–.

Annual Register, The. London: Longmans, 1761–.

First edited by Edmund Burke. Now *The Annual Register of World Events*.

Britannia Book of the Year. Chicago: Encyclopaedia Britannica, 1938–.

Chambers's World Survey. London: George Newnes, 1960–.

Collier's Year Book. New York: Collier, 1938–.

Information Please Almanac, Atlas and Yearbook. New York: Information Please Almanac, 1947–.

International Year Book and Statesmen's Who's Who. London: Burke's Peerage, 1953–.
    Includes a biographical section on world leaders.

New International Year Book: A Compendium of the World's Affairs. New York: Funk & Wagnalls, 1908–.

New York Times Encyclopedic Almanac, The. Edited by Semour Kurtz. New York: New York Times, 1970.
    Continued as *The Official Associated Press Almanac* (Maplewood, N.J.: Hammond Almanac, 1972–).

Statesman's Year-Book, The. London: Macmillan, 1864–.
    Statistic and historical information about the governments of the world and international organizations such as NATO and the United Nations.

United Nations Statistical Yearbook. New York: U.N. Statistical Office, 1949–.

U.S. Bureau of the Census. *Statistical Abstract of the United States.* Washington, D.C.: Government Printing Office, 1879–.

World Almanac and Book of Facts. New York: Newspaper Enterprise Assn., 1868–.

Ackermann, Alfred S. E. *Popular Fallacies: A Book of Common Errors Explained and Corrected.* 4th ed. London: Old Westminster Press, 1950.

Benét, William Rose. *The Reader's Encyclopedia.* 2d ed. New York: Crowell, 1965.

Brewer, E. Cobham. *Brewer's Dictionary of Phrase and Fable.* Centenary Edition. Revised by Ivor H. Evans. London: Cassell; New York: Harper & Row, 1970.

Everyman's Dictionary of Dates. 5th ed., revised by Audrey Butler. London: Dent; New York: Dutton, 1967.

Kane, Joseph N. *Famous First Facts.* 3d ed. New York: H. W. Wilson, 1964.

Lingeman, Richard R. *Drugs from A to Z: A Dictionary.* New York: McGraw-Hill, 1969.

New Century Cyclopedia of Names. Edited by Clarence L. Barnhart, with the assistance of William D. Halsey et al. 3 vols. New York: Appleton, 1954.

Notes and Queries. London: Oxford Univ. Press, 1850–. A valuable source of out-of-the-way information in all fields. Originally published weekly, then fortnightly, now monthly.

Peyton, Geoffrey. *Peyton's Proper Names*. London: Warne, 1969.
 Published in the U.S. as *Webster's Dictionary of Proper Names* (Springfield, Mass.: G. & C. Merriam, 1970).

Public Affairs Information Service Bulletin. New York: Public Affairs Information Service, 1915–. (Weekly, with cumulations.)

Walsh, William S. *Handy Book of Curious Information*. Philadelphia: Lippincott, 1913.

Wheeler, William A. *Familiar Allusions: A Handbook of Miscellaneous Information*. 5th ed. Boston: Houghton Mifflin, 1890.

REFERENCE WORKS IN THE HUMANITIES

GENERAL

British Humanities Index. London: Library Assn., 1962. (Quarterly, with annual cumulations.)
 Covers "all material relating to the arts and politics."

Index to Book Reviews in the Humanities, An. Detroit: Philip Thomson, 1960–. (Quarterly.)
 Beginning with Vol. 12 (1971): *An Index to Book Reviews in Humanities Periodicals*.

Social Sciences and Humanities Index. See above p. 189.

LITERATURE

General Studies

Abrams, M. H. *A Glossary of Literary Terms*. 3d ed. New York: Holt, 1971.

Bateson, F. W. *A Guide to English Literature*. 2d ed. Chicago: Aldine Press; London: Longmans, 1967.

Baugh, Albert C., ed. *A Literary History of England*. 2d ed. 4 vols. Englewood Cliffs, N.J.: Prentice-Hall, 1967. (Published together as one volume and separately in paperback.)

> Vol. 1: *The Middle Ages (to 1500)*. By Kemp Malone and Albert C. Baugh.
> Vol. 2: *The Renaissance (1500–1660)*. By Tucker Brooke and Matthias A. Shaaber.
> Vol. 3: *The Restoration and Eighteenth Century (1660–1789)*. By George Sherburn and Donald F. Bond.
> Vol. 4: *The Nineteenth Century and After (1789–1939)*. By Samuel C. Chew and Richard D. Altick.

Berman, Ronald. *A Reader's Guide to Shakespeare's Plays: A Descriptive Bibliography*. Rev. ed. Glenview, Ill.: Scott, Foresman, 1973.

Bleznick, Donald W. *A Sourcebook for Hispanic Literature and Language*. Philadelphia: Temple Univ. Press, 1974.
> A selected annotated guide to Spanish and Spanish-American literature and language.

Bond, Donald F. *A Reader's Guide to English Studies*. 2d ed. Chicago: Univ. of Chicago Press, 1971.

Browning, D. C. *Everyman's Dictionary of Literary Biography, English and American*. 3d ed. London: Dent; New York: Dutton, 1962.

Campbell, Oscar J., ed. *The Reader's Encyclopedia of Shakespeare*. New York: Crowell, 1966.

Cassell's Encyclopaedia of World Literature. Edited by J. Buchanan-Brown. Rev. and enl. ed. 3 vols. London: Cassell; New York: Morrow, 1973.

Columbia Dictionary of Modern European Literature. Edited by Horatio Smith. New York: Columbia Univ. Press, 1947.

Encyclopedia of World Literature in the 20th Century. Edited by Wolfgang B. Fleischmann et al. 3 vols. New York: F. Ungar, 1969–71.

Gallagher, David P. *Modern Latin American Literature*. London: Oxford Univ. Press, 1973.

Gibian, George, et al. *Soviet Russian Literature in English: A Checklist Bibliography*. Ithaca, N.Y.: Center for International Studies, Cornell University, 1967.

Gohdes, Clarence. *Bibliographical Guide to the Study of the Literature of the U.S.A.* 3d ed., rev. and enl. Durham, N.C.: Duke Univ. Press, 1970.

Grigson, Geoffrey, ed. *The Concise Encyclopedia of World Literature*. 2d ed. New York: Hawthorn Books, 1971.

Hackett, Alice Payne. *70 Years of Best Sellers, 1895–1965*. New York: R. R. Bowker, 1967.

Halliday, Frank E. *A Shakespeare Companion, 1564–1964*. Rev. ed. New York: Schocken Books, 1964.

Hargreaves-Mawdsley, W. N. *Everyman's Dictionary of European Writers*. London: Dent; New York: Dutton, 1968.

Hart, James D. *The Oxford Companion to American Literature*. 4th ed. New York: Oxford Univ. Press, 1965.

Harvey, Sir Paul. *The Oxford Companion to Classical Literature*. Oxford: Clarendon Press, 1940.

―――――. *The Oxford Companion to English Literature*. 4th ed., revised by Dorothy Eagle. Oxford: Clarendon Press, 1967.

―――――, and Heseltine, J[anet] E. *The Oxford Companion to French Literature*. Oxford: Clarendon Press, 1959.
Reprinted with corrections, 1966.

Holman, C. Hugh. *A Handbook to Literature*. Indianapolis: Bobbs-Merrill, 1972.
A revision of the *Handbook* by William F. Thrall and Addison Hibbard.

Ivask, Ivar, and Wilpert, Gero von, eds. *World Literature since 1945: Critical Surveys of the Contemporary Literatures of Europe and the Americas*. New York: F. Ungar, 1973.

Jones, Howard Mumford, and Ludwig, Richard M. *Guide to American Literature and Its Backgrounds since 1890*. 4th ed., rev. and enl. Cambridge, Mass.: Harvard Univ. Press, 1973.

Klink, Carl F., ed. *Literary History of Canada: Canadian Literature in English*. Toronto: Univ. of Toronto Press, 1965.

Kunitz, Stanley J., and Colby, Vineta. *European Authors, 1000–1900: A Biographical Dictionary of European Literature*. New York: H. W. Wilson, 1967.

Kunitz, Stanley J., and Haycraft, Howard. *American Authors, 1600–1900*. New York: H. W. Wilson, 1936. *First Supplement,* 1955.

―――――. *British Authors before 1800*. New York: H. W. Wilson, 1952.

―――――. *British Authors of the Nineteenth Century*. New York: H. W. Wilson, 1936.

―――――. *The Junior Book of Authors*. 2d ed., rev. New York: H. W. Wilson, 1951.

A dictionary of writers for young people. See also *More Junior Authors,* by Muriel Fuller (New York: H. W. Wilson, 1967).

———. *Twentieth Century Authors: A Biographical Dictionary of Modern Literature.* New York: H. W. Wilson, 1942. *First Supplement* (by S. J. Kunitz and Vineta Colby), 1955.

Kunzle, David. *History of the Comic Strip.* Berkeley: Univ. of California Press, 1973.

Lanham, Richard A. *A Handlist of Rhetorical Terms: A Guide for Students of English Literature.* Berkeley: Univ. of California Press, 1968.

Liberman, Myron M., and Foster, Edward F. *A Modern Lexicon of Literary Terms.* Glenview, Ill.: Scott, Foresman, 1968.

Literary and Library Prizes. 8th ed., revised and edited by Jeanne J. Henderson and Brenda G. Piggins. New York: R. R. Bowker, 1973.
   Includes (1) International prizes; (2) American prizes; (3) British prizes; (4) Canadian prizes. Originally published as *Famous Literary Prizes and Their Winners,* by Bessie Graham (1935).

Literatures of the World in English Translation: A Bibliography. 3 vols. New York: F. Ungar, 1967–70.
   Vol. 1: *The Greek and Latin Literatures.* By George B. Parks and Ruth Z. Temple. 1968.
   Vol. 2: *The Slavic Literatures.* By Richard G. Lewalski. 1967.
   Vol. 3: *The Romance Literatures.* By George B. Parks and Ruth Z. Temple. 1970.

Long, Richard A., and Collier, Eugene W., eds. *Afro-American Writing: An Anthology of Prose and Poetry.* 2 vols. New York: New York Univ. Press, 1972.

McLeod, A. L. *The Commonwealth Pen: An Introduction to the Literature of the British Commonwealth.* Ithaca, N.Y.: Cornell Univ. Press, 1961.

Mahaffey, Denis. *A Concise Bibliography of French Literature.* London: Bowker Publishing Co., 1975.

MLA International Bibliography of Books and Articles on the Modern Languages and Literatures. Edited by Harrison T. Meserole et al. New York: Modern Language Assn., 1968–.
   Earlier annual issues (1921–67) were more limited in scope. Now published in three volumes: English and American Literature and Folklore; European and Other Literatures; Linguistics. A standard current bibliography.

Myers, Robin, ed. *A Dictionary of Literature in the English Language from Chaucer to 1940.* 2 vols. Oxford: Pergamon Press, 1970.

New Cambridge Bibliography of English Literature, The. Edited by George Watson and Ian Willison. Cambridge: Cambridge Univ. Press, 1969–.
    Vol. 1: *The Beginnings to 1660.*
    Vol. 2: *1660–1800.*
    Vol. 3: *The Nineteenth Century.*
    Vol. 4: *The Twentieth Century.*
    Vol. 5: *Index* (in press).
    The indispensable bibliography for research in all periods of English literature.

New Century Handbook of English Literature, The. Edited by Clarence L. Barnhart with the assistance of William D. Halsey. Rev. ed. New York: Appleton, 1967.

Osburn, Charles B. *Research and Reference Guide to French Studies.* Metuchen, N.J.: Scarecrow Press, 1968.
    Supplement, with Cumulative Index, 1972.

Oxford History of English Literature, The. Edited by Bonamy Dobrée and Norman Davis. Oxford: Clarendon Press, 1945–.
    Nine of the twelve projected volumes have been published.

Penguin Companion to Literature, The. 4 vols. London: Penguin Books, 1969–72.
    Vol. 1: *Britain and the Commonwealth.* Edited by David Daiches.
    Vol. 2: *European.* Edited by Anthony Thorlby.
    Vol. 3: *United States and Latin America.* Edited by Malcolm Bradley et al.
    Vol. 4: *Classical and Byzantine; Oriental and African.* Edited by D. R. Dudley and D. M. Lang.

Reader's Companion to World Literature. Edited by Lillian H. Hornstein and G. D. Percy. 2d ed., revised and updated by Lillian H. Hornstein, Leon Edel, and Horst Frenz. New York: New American Library, 1971.

Richardson, Kenneth R., ed. *Twentieth Century Writing: A Reader's Guide to Contemporary Literature.* London: Newnes, 1969.

Roach, Helen. *Spoken Records.* 3d ed. Metuchen, N.J.: Scarecrow Press, 1970.
    A survey of recordings of poetry, drama, etc.

Seymour-Smith, Martin, ed. *Funk & Wagnalls Guide to Modern World Literature.* New York: Funk & Wagnalls, 1973.

Spiller, Robert E., et al. *Literary History of the United States.* 4th ed., rev. 2 vols. New York: Macmillan, 1974.
   The standard history and bibliography of American literature.

Story, Norah. *The Oxford Companion to Canadian History and Literature.* Toronto: Oxford Univ. Press, 1967.
   Supplement, 1974.

Sutton, Roberta B. *Speech Index.* 4th ed., rev. and enl. New York: Scarecrow Press, 1966.
   An index to 259 collections of world-famous speeches.

Temple, Ruth Z., and Tucker, Martin. *Twentieth Century British Literature: A Reference Guide and Bibliography.* New York: F. Ungar, 1968.

Tezla, Albert. *Hungarian Authors: A Bibliographical Handbook.* Cambridge, Mass.: Harvard Univ. Press, Belknap Press, 1970.

U.S. Library of Congress, General Reference and Bibliography Division. *A Guide to the Study of the United States of America.* See under History (United States).

Wilkins, Ernest H. *A History of Italian Literature.* Revised by Thomas G. Bergin. Cambridge, Mass.: Harvard Univ. Press, 1974.

Zenkovsky, Serge A., and Armbruster, David L. *Guide to the Bibliographies of Russian Literature.* Nashville, Tenn.: Vanderbilt Univ. Press, 1970.

Drama

Adelman, Irving, and Dworkin, Rita. *Modern Drama: A Checklist of Critical Literature on 20th Century Plays.* Metuchen, N.J.: Scarecrow Press, 1967.

American Educational Theatre Association. *A Bibliography of Theatre Arts Publications in English.* Washington, D.C.: American Educational Theatre Assn., 1963–. (Annual.)

Baker, Blanch M. *Theatre and Allied Arts: A Guide to Books Dealing with the History, Criticism, and Technic of the Drama and Theatre and Allied Arts and Crafts.* New York: H. W. Wilson, 1952.

Bergquist, G. William, ed. *Three Centuries of English and American Plays: A Checklist.* New York and London: Hafner, 1963.
   English plays (1500–1800); United States plays (1714–1830).

Bowers, Faubion. *Theatre in the East: A Survey of Asian Dance and Drama*. New York: Nelson, 1956.

Breed, Paul F., and Sniderman, Florence M. *Dramatic Criticism Index: A Bibliography of Commentaries on Playwrights from Ibsen to the Avant-Garde*. Detroit: Gale Research Co., 1972.
    Indexes: by titles of plays, by critics, by titles of books.

Crowell's Handbook of Classical Drama. By Richard Y. Hathorn. New York: Crowell, 1967.

Crowell's Handbook of Contemporary Drama. By Michael Anderson et al. New York: Crowell, 1971.

Cumulated Dramatic Index, 1909–1940. A Cumulation of the F. W. Faxon Company's Dramatic Index. Edited by Frederick W. Faxon, Mary E. Bates, and Anne C. Sutherland. 2 vols. Boston: G. K. Hall, 1965.

Drury, Francis K. W. *Drury's Guide to Best Plays*. 2d ed. by James M. Salem. Metuchen, N.J.: Scarecrow Press, 1969.

Eslin, Martin. *The Theatre of the Absurd*. Rev. updated ed. Garden City, N.Y.: Doubleday (Anchor Books), 1969.

Gassner, John, and Quinn, Edward. *The Reader's Encyclopedia of World Drama*. New York: Crowell, 1969; London: Methuen, 1970.

Gohdes, Clarence. *Literature and Theater of the States and Regions of the U.S.A.: An Historical Bibliography*. Durham, N.C.: Duke Univ. Press, 1967.

Guernsey, Otis L. *Directory of the American Theater, 1894–1971*. New York: Dodd, Mead, 1971.

Guide to the Performing Arts, 1957–. Compiled by S. Yancey Belknap. New York: Scarecrow Press, 1960–. (Annual.)
    An author, title, and subject index to performances of dance, drama, and music. A separate section includes performances on television.

Hartnoll, Phyllis, ed. *The Oxford Companion to the Theatre*. 3d ed. London: Oxford Univ. Press, 1967.
    Pp. 1029–74: "Select List of Theatre Books," by D. M. Moore.

Index to Full Length Plays, 1895–1925. Edited by Ruth G. Thomson. Boston: F. W. Faxon, 1956.

Index to Full Length Plays, 1926–1944. Edited by Ruth G. Thomson. Boston: F. W. Faxon, 1946.

Index to Full Length Plays, 1944–1964. Edited by Norma O. Ireland. Boston: F. W. Faxon, 1965.

Index to One-Act Plays. Edited by Hannah Logasa and Winifred Ver Nooy. 5 vols. Boston: F. W. Faxon, 1924–58.
     Plays in English, or translated into English, since 1900.

Index to Plays, 1800–1926. Compiled by Ina Ten Eyck Firkins. New York: H. W. Wilson, 1927. *Supplement, 1927–34*. New York: H. W. Wilson, 1935.
     An author, title, and subject index of American plays and English translations of foreign plays.

Lumley, Frederick. *New Trends in 20th Century Drama: A Survey since Ibsen and Shaw*. 4th rev. ed. New York: Oxford Univ. Press, 1972.

Matlaw, Myron. *Modern World Drama: An Encyclopedia*. New York: Dutton, 1972.

Mikhail, E. H. *A Bibliography of Modern Irish Drama, 1899–1970*. London: Macmillan, 1972.

————. *Comedy and Tragedy: A Bibliography of Critical Studies*. Troy, N.Y.: Whitston Publishing Co., 1972.

New York Public Library: The Research Libraries. *Catalog of the Theatre and Drama Collections*. 21 vols. Boston: G. K. Hall, 1967.

New York Times Theater Reviews, 1920–1970, The. 10 vols. New York: New York Times and Arno Press, 1971.
     Photographic reproduction of reviews by Alexander Woollcott, Brooks Atkinson, Walter Kerr, Clive Barnes, and others. Vols. 9–10 = Index.

Nicoll, Allardyce. *A History of English Drama, 1660–1900*. Rev. ed. 6 vols. Cambridge: Cambridge Univ. Press, 1952–59.

————. *English Drama, 1900–1930: The Beginnings of the Modern Period*. Cambridge: Cambridge Univ. Press, 1973.

Ottemiller, John H. *Index to Plays in Collections: An Author and Title Index to Plays Appearing in Collections Published between 1900 and 1962*. 4th ed., rev. and enl. New York: Scarecrow Press, 1964.
     Includes plays from the earliest times to the present.

Palmer, Helen H., and Dyson, Anne J. *American Drama Criticism: Interpretations, 1890–1965 inclusive, of American Drama since*

the First Play Produced in America. Hamden, Conn.: Shoe String Press, 1967. *Supplement One,* 1970.
  Includes criticism in both books and periodicals.

—————. *European Drama Criticism.* Hamden, Conn.: Shoe String Press, 1968.

Play Index, 1949–52. An Index to 2,616 Plays in 1,138 Volumes. Compiled by Dorothy H. West and Dorothy M. Peake. New York: H. W. Wilson, 1953.

Play Index, 1953–60. An Index to 4,592 Plays in 1,735 Volumes. Compiled by Estelle A. Fidell and Dorothy M. Peake. New York: H. W. Wilson, 1963.

Play Index, 1961–67. An Index to 4,793 Plays. Compiled by Estelle A. Fidell. New York: H. W. Wilson, 1968.

Rigdon, Walter, ed. *The Biographical Encyclopaedia and Who's Who of the American Theatre.* New York: James H. Heineman, 1966.

Salem, James M. *A Guide to Critical Reviews.* 3 vols. New York: Scarecrow Press, 1966–68.
  Covers American drama since 1920; musicals; British and Continental drama, Ibsen to Pinter.

Schoolcraft, Ralph N. *Performing Arts/Books in Print: An Annotated Bibliography.* New York: Drama Book Specialists, 1973.
  A completely revised edition of A. E. Santaniello's *Theatre Books in Print* (New York: Drama Book Shop, 1963; 2d ed., 1965). Supplemented by the quarterly *Annotated Bibliography of New Publications in the Performing Arts.*

Sprinchorn, Evert. *20th-Century Plays in Synopsis.* New York: Crowell, 1966.
  Summaries by acts of 133 American, British, and Continental dramas from Strindberg to Albee.

Stratman, Carl J. *Bibliography of the American Theatre Excluding New York City.* Chicago: Loyola Univ. Press, 1965.

—————. *A Bibliography of English Printed Tragedy, 1565–1900.* Carbondale, Ill.: Southern Illinois Univ. Press, 1966.

—————. *A Bibliography of Medieval Drama.* Berkeley: Univ. of California Press, 1954.

Vinson, James. *Contemporary Dramatists.* London: St. James Press; New York: St. Martin's Press, 1973.

Who's Who in the Theatre. Edited by Freda Gaye. 14th ed. London: Pitman, 1967.

Young, William C. *American Theatrical Arts: A Guide to Manuscripts and Special Collections in the United States and Canada.* Chicago: American Library Assn., 1971.

Fiction

Adelman, Irving, and Dworkin, Rita. *The Contemporary Novel: A Checklist of Critical Literature on the British and American Novel since 1945.* Metuchen, N.J.: Scarecrow Press, 1972.

Author Bibliography of English Language Fiction in the Library of Congress through 1950. Compiled by R. Glenn Wright. 8 vols. Boston: G. K. Hall, 1973.

Baker, Ernest A. *The History of the English Novel.* 10 vols. London: R. F. & G. Witherby, 1924–39. Reprint: New York: Barnes & Noble, 1950. Supplement (forming Vol. 11): *Yesterday and After,* by Lionel Stevenson (New York: Barnes & Noble, 1967).

———, and Packman, James. *A Guide to the Best Fiction, English and American, Including Translations from Foreign Languages.* New and enl. ed. London: Routledge, 1932.

Bell, Inglis F., and Baird, Donald. *The English Novel, 1578–1956: A Checklist of Twentieth-Century Criticisms.* Denver: Alan Swallow, 1959.

Coan, Otis W., and Lillard, Richard G. *America in Fiction: An Annotated List of Novels That Interpret Aspects of Life in the United States, Canada and Mexico.* 5th ed. Palo Alto, Calif.: Pacific Books, 1967.

Fiction Catalog: Eighth Edition. Edited by Estelle A. Fidell. New York: H. W. Wilson, 1971.

Intended as a guide to the best fiction, past and recent. First published in 1908; annual supplements, cumulated periodically.

Freeman, William. *Everyman's Dictionary of Fictional Characters.* Revised by Fred Urquhart. London: Dent; New York: Dutton, 1973.

Gerstenberger, Donna L., and Hendrick, George. *The American Novel: A Checklist of Twentieth-Century Criticism on Novels Written since 1789.* 2 vols. Chicago: Swallow Press, 1961–70.

Hackett, Alice Payne. *70 Years of Best Sellers, 1895–1965.* New York: R. R. Bowker, 1967.

Hagen, Ordean A. *Who Done It? A Guide to Detective, Mystery, and Suspense Fiction.* New York: R. R. Bowker, 1969.

Logasa, Hannah. *Historical Fiction: Guide for Junior and Senior High Schools and Colleges.* 8th ed., rev. and enl. Philadelphia: McKinley Publishing Co., 1964.

McGarry, Daniel D., and White, Sarah H. *Historical Fiction Guide: Annotated Chronological, Geographical, and Topical List of Five Thousand Selected Historical Novels.* New York: Scarecrow Press, 1964.

Scholes, Percy. *The Elements of Fiction.* London: Oxford Univ. Press, 1968.

Short Story Index: An Index to 60,000 Stories in 4,320 Collections. Compiled by Dorothy E. Cook and Isabel S. Monro. New York: H. W. Wilson, 1953. Continued by Supplements.

VanDerhoof, Jack. *A Bibliography of Novels Related to American Frontier and Colonial History.* Troy, N.Y.: Whitston Publishing Co., 1971.

Vinson, James. *Contemporary Novelists.* London: St. James Press; New York: St. Martin's Press, 1972.

   Biographies of present-day novelists writing in English, with bibliographical information.

Poetry

Courthope, W. J. *History of English Poetry.* 6 vols. London: Macmillan, 1895–1910.

   The standard history, but comes up only to the nineteenth century.

Deutsch, Babette. *Poetry Handbook: A Dictionary of Terms.* 3d ed., rev. and enl. New York: Funk & Wagnalls, 1969.

Granger's Index to Poetry: Sixth Edition, Completely Revised and Enlarged, Indexing Anthologies Published up to December 31, 1970. Edited by William J. Smith. New York: Columbia Univ. Press, 1973.

   Title and first-line index, author index, and subject index, including such subjects as ecology, social protest, and women's liberation.

Hodgart, M. J. C. *The Ballads.* New York: Norton, 1962.

Kuntz, Joseph M. *Poetry Explication: A Checklist of Interpretation since 1925 of British and American Poems Past and Present.* Rev. ed. Denver: Alan Swallow, 1962.

Malkoff, Karl. *Crowell's Handbook of Contemporary American Poetry.* New York: Crowell, 1973.

Murphy, Rosalie. *Contemporary Poets.* London: St. James Press; New York: St. Martin's Press, 1970.
  Biographical and bibliographical information on 1,100 poets writing in English.

Nims, John Frederick. *Western Wind: An Introduction to Poetry.* Westminster, Md.: Random House, 1974.

Princeton Encyclopedia of Poetry and Poetics. Edited by Alex Preminger, Frank Warnke, and O. B. Hardison. Enl. ed. Princeton, N.J.: Princeton Univ. Press, 1974.

Spender, Stephen, and Hall, Donald. *The Concise Encyclopedia of English and American Poets and Poetry.* New York: Hawthorn Books, 1963.

Sutton, Walter. *American Free Verse: The Modern Revolution in Poetry.* New York: New Directions, 1973.

Thurley, Geoffrey. *The Ironic Harvest: English Poetry in the Twentieth Century.* New York: St. Martin's Press, 1974.

FILMS

De Nitto, Dennis, and Herman, William. *Film and the Critical Eye.* New York: Macmillan, 1975.

Dimmitt, Richard B. *An Actor Guide to the Talkies. A Comprehensive Listing of 8,000 Feature-Length Films from January, 1949, until December, 1964.* 2 vols. Metuchen, N.J.: Scarecrow Press, 1967.
  Vol. 2 = Index. Includes foreign and domestic films.

———. *A Title Guide to the Talkies. A Comprehensive Listing of 16,000 Feature-Length Films from October, 1927, until December, 1963.* 2 vols. New York and London: Scarecrow Press, 1965.

French, Philip. *Westerns.* New York: Viking Press, 1974.

Halliwell, Leslie. *The Filmgoer's Companion.* 4th ed., rev. and enl. London: Hart-Davis, 1974.
  This new edition is illustrated.

Harrington, John. *The Rhetoric of Film.* New York: Holt, 1973.
   On the elements of film composition.

Hochman, Stanley, ed. *American Film Directors.* New York: F. Ungar, 1974.

Michael, Paul. *The American Movies Reference Book: The Sound Era.* Englewood Cliffs, N.J.: Prentice-Hall, 1969.

New York Times Film Reviews, 1913–1968, The. 6 vols. New York: New York Times and Arno Press, 1970.
   Vol. 6 = Index. Photographically reproduced reviews from the pages of the *New York Times.*

Tudor, Andrew. *Theories of Film.* New York: Viking Press, 1974.

MUSIC

Apel, Willi. *Harvard Dictionary of Music.* 2d ed., rev. and enl. Cambridge, Mass.: Harvard Univ. Press, Belknap Press, 1969.

Baker, Theodore. *Biographical Dictionary of Musicians.* 5th ed., completely revised by Nicolas Slonimsky. New York: Schirmer, 1958.

Barlow, Harold, and Morgenstern, Sam. *A Dictionary of Musical Themes.* New York: Crown Publishers, 1948.

Belz, Carl. *The Story of Rock.* 2d ed. New York: Harper & Row, 1973.

Bronson, Bertrand H. *The Traditional Tunes of the Child Ballads with Their Texts According to the Extant Records of Great Britain and America.* 4 vols. Princeton, N.J.: Princeton Univ. Press, 1959–72.

Bull, Storm. *Index to Biographies of Contemporary Composers.* New York: Scarecrow Press, 1964.

Diehl, Katharine Smith. *Hymns and Tunes: An Index.* New York: Scarecrow Press, 1966.

Duckles, Vincent H. *Music Reference and Research Materials: An Annotated Bibliography.* 2d ed. New York: Free Press, 1967.
   Includes a subject index.

Ewen, David, ed. *American Popular Songs from the Revolutionary War to the Present.* New York: Random House, 1966.

———. *Complete Book of the American Musical Theater.* New York: Holt, 1958.

————. *Great Composers, 1800–1900: A Biographical and Critical Guide,* New York: H. W. Wilson, 1966. *Composers since 1900.* . . . New York: H. W. Wilson, 1969.

Feather, Leonard G. *Encyclopedia of Jazz.* New and enl. ed. New York: Horizon Press, 1960.

————. *The Encyclopedia of Jazz in the Sixties.* New York: Horizon Press, 1966.

Grout, Donald J. *A Short History of Opera.* 2d ed. New York: Columbia Univ. Press, 1965.

Begins with the Greek theater and comes down to modern times. Includes an extensive bibliography.

Grove's Dictionary of Music and Musicians. 5th ed., edited by Eric Blom. 9 vols. London: Macmillan; New York: St. Martin's Press, 1954.

Supplementary Volume (New York: St. Martin's Press, 1961). Eric Blom is also editor of an excellent *Everyman's Dictionary of Music* (4th ed., rev. by Jack Westrup): London: Dent; New York: Dutton, 1962.

Kobbé, Gustave. *Kobbé's Complete Opera Book.* Edited and revised by the Earl of Harewood. London and New York: Putnam, 1963.

Lawless, Ray McK. *Folksingers and Folksongs in America: A Handbook of Biography, Bibliography, and Discography.* New rev. ed. with Supplement. New York: Duell, 1965.

Lewine, Richard, and Struon, Alfred. *Songs of the American Theaters.* New York: Dodd, Mead, 1973.

Lists more than 12,000 songs, including selected titles from film and television productions.

Loewenberg, Alfred. *Annals of Opera, 1597–1940, Compiled from the Original Sources.* 2d ed., rev. 2 vols. Geneva: Societas Bibliographica, 1955.

A standard reference work.

Lubbock, Mark H. *The Complete Book of Light Opera. With an American Section by David Ewen.* New York: Appleton, 1963.

Includes "musicals."

Marcuse, Sibyl. *Musical Instruments: A Comprehensive Dictionary.* Garden City, N.Y.: Doubleday, 1964.

Music Index: The Key to Current Music Periodical Literature. Detroit: Information Service, 1949–. (Monthly, with annual cumulations.)

New Oxford History of Music, The. London: Oxford Univ. Press, 1954–. In progress.

Rosenthal, Harold, and Warrack, John. *Concise Oxford Dictionary of Opera.* London: Oxford Univ. Press, 1964.

Salzman, Eric. *Twentieth-Century Music: An Introduction.* 2d ed. Englewood Cliffs, N.J.: Prentice-Hall, 1974.

Schuler, Gunther. *Early Jazz: Its Roots and Musical Development.* New York: Oxford Univ. Press, 1968.

Song Index: An Index to More than 12,000 Songs in 177 Song Collections Comprising 262 Volumes. Edited by Minnie E. Sears and Phyllis Crawford. New York: H. W. Wilson, 1926.
    Supplement: An Index to More than 7,000 Songs . . . , 1934.

Stambler, Irwin. *Encyclopedia of Pop, Rock and Soul.* New York: St. Martin's Press, 1974.

————, and Landon, Grelun. *Encyclopedia of Folk, Country and Western Music.* New York: St. Martin's Press, 1969.

Thompson, Oscar, ed. *International Cyclopedia of Music and Musicians.* 9th ed., revised by Robert Sabin. New York: Dodd, Mead, 1964.

Van der Horst, Brian. *Rock Music.* New York: F. Watts, 1973.
    A history.

Vinton, John, ed. *Dictionary of Twentieth-Century Music.* London: Thames & Hudson, 1974.

Who's Who in Music and Musicians' International Directory. Edited by Peter Townsend and David Simmons. 5th ed. New York: Hafner, 1969.

DANCE

Balanchine, George. *Balanchine's New Complete Stories of the Great Ballets.* Edited by Francis Mason. Garden City, N.Y.: Doubleday, 1968.

Beaumont, Cyril W. *A Bibliography of Dancing.* New York: B. Blom, 1963.

Bowers, Faubion. *Theatre in the East: A Survey of Asian Dance and Drama.* New York: Nelson, 1956.

Chujoy, Anatole, and Manchester, P. W., eds. *The Dance Encyclopedia.* Rev. and enl. ed. New York: Simon & Schuster, 1967.

De Mille, Agnes. *The Book of the Dance*. New York: Golden Press, 1963.

> Traces the development of the dance, with examples from all periods and many countries; includes both classical ballet and modern dance.

Wilson, George B. *A Dictionary of Ballet*. London: Cassell, 1961.

RELIGION

Adams, Charles J., ed. *A Reader's Guide to the Great Religions*. New York: Free Press, 1965.

American Theological Library Association. *Index to Religious Periodical Literature, 1949/1952–*. Chicago: American Theological Library Assn., 1953–. (Annual.)

> Also indexes book reviews.

Attwater, Donald, ed. *A Catholic Dictionary*. 3d ed. New York: Macmillan, 1961.

———. *The Penguin Book of Saints*. Baltimore: Penguin Books, 1965.

Barrow, John G. *A Bibliography of Bibliographies of Religion*. Ann Arbor, Mich.: Edwards Bros., 1955.

Brandon, S. G. F., ed. *A Dictionary of Comparative Religion*. New York: Scribner, 1970.

Butler, Alban. *Lives of the Saints*. Complete edition revised and supplemented by Herbert Thurston and Donald Attwater. 4 vols. New York: P. J. Kenedy & Sons, 1956.

Cambridge History of the Bible. Edited by P. R. Ackroyd et al. 3 vols. Cambridge: Cambridge Univ. Press, 1963–70.

> Appendixes list aids to Bible study and commentaries. Includes bibliographies.

Catholic University of America. *The New Catholic Encyclopedia*. Edited by William J. McDonald et al. 15 vols. New York: McGraw-Hill, 1967. Vol. 15 = Index.

Deen, Edith. *All of the Women of the Bible*. New York: Harper, 1955.

Encyclopaedia Judaica. 16 vols. Jerusalem: Keter Publishing House; New York: Macmillan, 1971–72.

> *Encyclopaedia Judaica Year Book, 1973–*.

Gehman, Henry S., ed. *The New Westminster Dictionary of the Bible*. Philadelphia: Westminster, 1970.

Grollenberg, Luc H. *Atlas of the Bible*. Translated and edited by Joyce M. H. Reid and H. H. Rowley. New York: Nelson, 1956.

A scholarly work in which maps and illustrations are accompanied by narrative summarizing the course of biblical history, geography, and chronology.

Hastings, James, ed. *Dictionary of the Bible*. Revised edition by Frederick C. Grant and H. H. Rowley. New York: Scribner, 1963.

A thorough revision, made in the light of modern discoveries and scholarship, of the work of the same title by James Hastings and others published 1905–9.

————. *Encyclopaedia of Religion and Ethics*. 13 vols. New York: Scribner, 1908–27.

The standard encyclopedia. Treats of all religions and ethical systems; includes mythology, folklore, and philosophical concepts. Good bibliographies.

Interpreter's Dictionary of the Bible, The. Edited by George A. Buttrick. 4 vols. New York: Abingdon Press, 1962.

An important commentary.

Joy, Charles R. *Harper's Topical Concordance*. Rev. and enl. ed. New York: Harper, 1962.

A topical index of the King James Version.

Julian, John. *A Dictionary of Hymnology, Setting Forth the Origin and History of Christian Hymns of All Ages and Nations*. Rev. ed. with New Supplement. London: Murray; New York: Scribner, 1907.

Lockyer, Herbert. *All the Men of the Bible. A Portrait Gallery and Reference Library of More Than 3,000 Biblical Characters*. Grand Rapids, Mich.: Zandervan Publishing House, 1958.

Mayer, Frederick E., ed. *The Religious Bodies of America*. 2d ed. St. Louis: Concordia Publishing House, 1956.

Mead, Frank S. *Handbook of Denominations in the United States*. 5th ed. Nashville, Tenn.: Abingdon Press, 1970.

Miller, Madeleine S., and Miller, J. Lane. *Harper's Bible Dictionary*. 6th ed. New York: Harper, 1959.

Oxford Dictionary of the Christian Church, The. Edited by F. L. Cross. 2d ed., completely revised by F. L. Cross and E. A. Livingstone. London: Oxford Univ. Press, 1974.

Schaff, Philip. *The New Schaff-Herzog Encyclopedia of Religious*

Knowledge. Edited by Samuel M. Jackson et al. 12 vols. and Index. New York and London: Funk & Wagnalls, 1908–12.

    Supplement: *Twentieth Century Encyclopedia of Religious Knowledge.* Edited by Lefferts A. Loetscher. 2 vols. Grand Rapids, Mich.: Baker Book House, 1955.

Stevenson, Burton E. *The Home Book of Bible Quotations.* New York: Harper, 1949.

    Includes the Apocrypha.

Strong, James. *Exhaustive Concordance of the Bible.* London: Hodder & Stoughton, 1895; New York: Abingdon Press, 1963.

    The most complete concordance to the King James Version.

World Treasury of Religious Quotations. Compiled and edited by Ralph L. Woods. New York: Hawthorn Books, 1966.

    Does not include Bible quotations.

Young, Robert. *Young's Analytical Concordance to the Bible.* Revised edition by W. B. Stevenson. New York: Funk & Wagnalls, 1955,

Zaehner, Robert C., ed. *The Concise Encyclopedia of Living Faiths.* New York: Hawthorn Books, 1959.

PHILOSOPHY AND PSYCHOLOGY

Borchardt, Dietrich H. *How to Find Out in Philosophy and Psychology.* Oxford: Pergamon Press, 1968.

Contributions to Modern Psychology: Selected Readings in General Psychology. Edited by Don E. Dulany et al. 2d ed. New York: Oxford Univ. Press, 1963.

De George, Richard T. *A Guide to Philosophical Bibliography and Research.* New York: Appleton, 1971.

Dictionary of Philosophy and Psychology. Edited by James M. Baldwin et al. 3 vols. in 4. New York: Macmillan, 1901–5. Vol. 3: *Bibliography of Philosophy, Psychology and Cognate Subjects,* by Benjamin Rand.

    Out of date but still of considerable value.

Drever, James. *A Dictionary of Psychology.* Revised by Harvey Wallerstein. Rev. ed. Baltimore: Penguin Books, 1966.

Eidelberg, Ludwig, ed. *Encyclopedia of Psychoanalysis.* 2 vols. New York: Macmillan, 1968.

Encyclopedia of Philosophy, The. Editor-in-chief, Paul Edwards. 8 vols. New York: Macmillan; London: Collier-Macmillan, 1967.

Vol. 8 = Index. Covers all philosophy, discusses theories of authorities in other fields, both scientific and religious, where these have had an impact on philosophy. Extensive bibliographies.

English, Horace B., and English, Ava C. *A Comprehensive Dictionary of Psychological and Psychoanalytical Terms: A Guide to Usage.* New York: Longmans, 1958.

Goldenson, Robert N. *The Encyclopedia of Human Behavior: Psychology, Psychiatry, and Mental Health.* Garden City, N.Y.: Doubleday, 1970.

Harvard University. *The Harvard List of Books in Psychology.* Compiled and annotated by the psychologists in Harvard University. 4th ed. Cambridge, Mass.: Harvard Univ. Press, 1971.

International Encyclopedia of the Social Sciences. See p. 227.

Moore, G. E. *Ethics.* 2d ed. London: Oxford Univ. Press, 1966.

Morgan, Clifford T. *Introduction to Psychology.* 2d ed. New York: McGraw-Hill, 1967.

Philosopher's Index, The: An International Index to Philosophical Periodicals. Bowling Green, Ohio: Bowling Green University, 1967–. (Quarterly.)

Psychological Abstracts. Lancaster, Pa.: American Psychological Assn., 1927–. (Monthly.)

A subject bibliography of current books and articles, with abstracts of each item. See also the *Psychological Index,* Nos. 1–42 (1894–1935), published by Princeton Univ. Press (42 vols. in 40), later merged into *Psychological Abstracts.*

Roback, A. A. *A History of American Psychology.* 2d ed. New York: Collier, 1964.

Russell, Bertrand. *A History of Western Philosophy.* New York: Simon & Schuster, 1945.

————. *The Problems of Philosophy.* 2d ed. London: Oxford Univ. Press, 1967.

Schneider, Herbert W. *A History of American Philosophy.* 2d ed. New York: Columbia Univ. Press, 1963.

Thomas, Henry. *Biographical Encyclopedia of Philosophy.* Garden City, N.Y.: Doubleday, 1965.

Urmson, James O., ed. *The Concise Encyclopedia of Western Philosophy and Philosophers.* New York: Hawthorn Books, 1960.

From Abelard to the present. Bibliography, pp. 421–31.

U.S. Library of Congress, General Reference and Bibliography Division. *Philosophical Periodicals: An Annotated World List.* Compiled by David Baumgardt. Washington, D.C.: U.S. Government Printing Office, 1952.

Windelband, Wilhelm. *A History of Philosophy.* 2d ed. rev. and enl. New York: Macmillan, 1921. Also, translated by James H. Tufts, 2 vols. New York: Harper Torch Books, 1958.

PAINTING, SCULPTURE, AND ARCHITECTURE

American Art Directory. New York: R. R. Bowker, 1899–. Vols. 1–37 published as the *American Art Annual* (1899–1945).

Art Index: A Cumulative Author and Subject Index to a Selected List of Fine Art Periodicals. New York: H. W. Wilson, 1933–. (Quarterly, with biennial cumulations.)

Carrick, Neville. *How to Find Out about the Arts: A Guide to Sources of Information.* New York: Pergamon Press, 1965.

Chamberlin, Mary W. *Guide to Art Reference Books.* Chicago: American Library Assn., 1959.

Craven, Wayne. *Sculpture in America.* New York: Crowell, 1968.

Dictionary of Modern Painting. General editors, Carlton Lake and Robert Maillard. 3d ed., rev. and enl. New York: Tudor Publishing Co., 1964.

 Covers the period from the Impressionists to the Second World War.

Encyclopedia of Painting: Painters and Painting of the World from Prehistoric Times to the Present Day. Edited by Bernard S. Myers. New York: Crown Publishers, 1955.

Encyclopedia of World Art. 15 vols. New York: McGraw-Hill, 1959–68. Vol. 15 = Index.

 A monumental work of international scholarship, covering all aspects of the fine arts and profusely illustrated.

Gardner, Helen. *Art through the Ages.* 4th ed., rev. [under the editorship of Sumner McK. Crosby by the Department of the History of Art, Yale University.] New York: Harcourt, Brace, 1959.

 A popular and widely used brief survey.

Larkin, Oliver W. *Art and Life in America.* Rev. and enl. ed. New York: Holt, 1960.

Monro, Isabel S., and Monro, Kate M. *Index to Reproductions of American Paintings: A Guide to Pictures Occurring in More Than Eight Hundred Books.* New York: H. W. Wilson, 1948. Supplements, 1964–.

————. *Index to Reproductions of European Paintings.* New York: H. W. Wilson, 1956.

Murray, Peter, and Murray, Linda. *Dictionary of Arts and Artists.* Washington, D.C.: Praeger, 1965.

Myers, Bernard S., ed. *McGraw-Hill Dictionary of Art.* 5 vols. New York: McGraw-Hill, 1969.

Osborne, Harold, ed. *The Oxford Companion to Art.* London: Oxford Univ. Press, 1970.

    Covers art movements and biographies of artists of all ages and all countries. Does not include theater, cinema, dance, or practical arts and handicrafts. Excellent illustrations and a valuable bibliography (pp. 1231–77).

Rathbun, Mary C., and Hayes, Bartlett H., Jr. *Layman's Guide to Modern Art.* London: Oxford Univ. Press, 1964.

Reinach, S[alomon]. *Apollo: An Illustrated History of Art throughout the Ages.* Completely revised, with a new chapter by the author. New York: Scribner, 1935.

Upjohn, Everard M.; Wingert, Paul S.; and Mahler, Jane G. *History of World Art.* 2d ed., rev. and enl. New York: Oxford Univ. Press, 1958.

Who's Who in American Art. New York: R. R. Bowker, 1935–. (Biennial.)

MYTH, FOLKLORE, AND POPULAR CUSTOMS

Bonser, Wilfrid. *A Bibliography of Folklore.* London: Folk-Lore Society, 1961.

Brandon, Jan H. *The Study of American Folklore: An Introduction.* New York: Norton, 1968.

Briggs, Katharine M. *A Dictionary of British Folk-Tales in the English Language.* London: Routledge; Bloomington: Indiana Univ. Press, 1970–.

Bullfinch, Thomas. *Mythology: The Age of Fable, The Age of Chivalry, Legends of Charlemagne.* Rev. ed. New York: Crowell, 1970.

Chambers, Robert. *The Book of Days: A Miscellany of Popular Antiquities in Connection with the Calendar, Including Anecdote, Biography, and History, Curiosities of Literature and Oddities of Human Life and Character.* . . . 2 vols. Edinburgh: W. & R. Chambers, 1863–64; Philadelphia: Lippincott, 1899.

Diehl, Katharine S. *Religions, Mythologies, Folklore: An Annotated Bibliography.* 2d ed. New York: Scarecrow Press, 1962.

Dorson, Richard M. *Buying the Wind: Regional Folklore in the United States.* Chicago: Univ. of Chicago Press, 1964.

Douglas, George W. *The American Book of Days.* 2d ed. Revised by Helen Douglas Compton. New York: H. W. Wilson, 1948.
    Gives information about holidays, festivals, notable anniversaries, and Christian and Jewish holy days.

Everyman's Dictionary of Nonclassical Mythology. 2d ed. Revised by Egerton Sykes. London: Dent; New York: Dutton, 1961.

Frazer, James G. *The Golden Bough: A Study in Magic and Religion.* 3d ed. 12 vols. London: Macmillan, 1907–15.
    See also *Aftermath: A Supplement to "The Golden Bough"* (London: Macmillan, 1936) and an abridgment, bringing the work up to date, *The New Golden Bough,* edited by Theodor H. Gaster (New York: Criterion Books, 1959).

Funk & Wagnalls Standard Dictionary of Folklore, Mythology, and Legend. Edited by Maria Leach and Jerome Fried. 2 vols. New York: Funk & Wagnalls, 1949–50. Revised with minor corrections, 1972.

Gayley, Charles M. *Classic Myths in English Literature and in Art.* New ed., rev. and enl. Boston: Ginn, 1939.

Hamilton, Edith. *Mythology: Greek, Roman, and Norse Myths.* Boston: Little, Brown, 1942.

Hastings, James, ed. *Encyclopaedia of Religion and Ethics.* . . . 13 vols. New York: Scribner, 1908–27.
    Includes mythology and folklore.

Hazlitt, W. Carew. *Faiths and Folk Lore: A Dictionary of National Beliefs, Superstitions, and Popular Customs.* . . . 2 vols. London: Reeves, 1905.

Based on John Brand's *Observations on Popular Antiquities* (1777), revised by Henry Ellis (1813).

Jobes, Gertrude, and Jobes, James. *Outer Space: Myths, Name Meanings, Calendars, from the Emergence of History to the Present Day.* New York and London: Scarecrow Press, 1964.

Krappe, Alexander H. *The Science of Folk-Lore.* London: Methuen, 1930; New York: Norton, 1964.

Larousse Encyclopedia of Mythology. New York: Prometheus Press, 1959.

Meyer, Robert. *Festivals, U.S.A. and Canada.* New York: Washburn, 1967.

Mythology of All Races, Greek and Roman, The. 26th ed. Edited by Louis H. Gray et al. 13 vols. Boston: Marshall Jones, 1958.

Opie, Iona, and Opie, Peter. *The Lore and Language of Schoolchildren.* Oxford: Clarendon Press, 1959.

Radford, Edwin, and Radford, M. A. *Encyclopaedia of Superstitions.* Edited and revised by Christina Hole. Rev. and enl. ed. London: Hutchinson, 1966.

Robbins, Rossell H. *The Encyclopedia of Witchcraft and Demonology.* New York: Crown Publishers, 1959.

Spalding, Henry D. *Encyclopedia of Black Folklore and Humor.* Middle Village, N.Y.: Jonathan David, 1972.

Thompson, Stith. *Motif-Index of Folk Literature: A Classification of Narrative Elements in Folktales, Ballads, Myths, Fables, and Mediaeval Romances.* . . . Rev. and enl. ed. 6 vols. Bloomington: Indiana Univ. Press, 1955–58. Vol. 6 = Index.

Thorndike, Lynn. *A History of Magic and Experimental Science.* 8 vols. New York: Columbia Univ. Press, 1934–58.

Tripp, Edward, ed. *Crowell's Handbook of Classical Mythology.* New York: Crowell, 1970.

Ullom, Judith C., ed. *Folklore of the North American Indians: An Annotated Bibliography.* Washington, D.C.: Library of Congress, 1969.

Wright, A. R. *British Calendar Customs: England.* Edited by T. E. Lones. 3 vols. London: Folk-Lore Society, 1936–40.

Ziegler, Elsie B. *Folklore: An Annotated Bibliography and Index to Single Editions.* Westwood, Mass.: F. W. Faxon, 1973.

REFERENCE WORKS IN HISTORY

GENERAL STUDIES

American Historical Association. *Guide to Historical Literature.* Edited by George F. Howe et al. New York: Macmillan, 1961.
> A standard bibliography, covering all periods and all countries.

Calmann, John, ed. *Western Europe: A Handbook.* New York: Praeger, 1967.
> Gives basic information on each country and treats of Western integration, economic and social, and of contemporary arts.

Cambridge Ancient History, The. Edited by J. B. Bury et al. 12 vols. Cambridge: Cambridge Univ. Press; New York: Macmillan, 1923–39. 3d ed., 1970–, in progress.

Cambridge Medieval History, The. Edited by H. M. Gwatkin et al. 8 vols. Cambridge: Cambridge Univ. Press; New York: Macmillan, 1911–36. 2d ed., 1966–, in progress.

Cambridge Modern History, The. Edited by A. W. Ward et al. 13 vols. and atlas. Cambridge: Cambridge Univ. Press; New York: Macmillan, 1902–26.
> See also *The New Cambridge Modern History,* edited by G. R. Potter. 12 vols, 1957–68 (without the bibliographies).

Eggenberger, David. *A Dictionary of Battles.* New York: Crowell, 1967.
> Aims to provide "essential details of all the major battles in recorded history."

Heyden, A. A. M. van der, and Scullard, H. H. *Atlas of the Classical World.* New York: Thomas Nelson, 1959.
> Covers all historical aspects of Greece and Rome, with excellent maps and photographs.

Israel, Fred L., ed. *Major Peace Treaties of Modern History, 1648 to 1966.* 4 vols. New York: McGraw-Hill, 1967.

Langer, William L., ed. *An Encyclopedia of World History, Ancient, Medieval, and Modern, Chronologically Arranged.* 5th ed., rev. and enl., with Maps and Genealogical Tables. Boston: Houghton Mifflin, 1972.

Oxford Classical Dictionary. 2d ed. Edited by N. G. L. Hammond and H. H. Scullard. Oxford: Clarendon Press, 1970.

A standard reference work for all aspects of Greek and Roman culture.

Rand McNally Atlas of World History. Edited by R. R. Palmer. New York: Rand McNally, 1957.

Roach, John P. C., ed. *A Bibliography of Modern History*. Cambridge: Cambridge Univ. Press, 1968.

Shepherd, William R. *Historical Atlas*. 9th ed., rev. New York: Barnes & Noble, 1964.
From 1450 B.C. to A.D. 1964.

Steinberg, S. H. *Historical Tables, 58 B.C. – A.D. 1965*. 8th ed. London: Macmillan, 1966.

Thomson, J. Oliver. *Everyman's Classical Atlas*. 3d ed. London: Dent; New York: Dutton, 1966.

UNITED STATES

Articles in American Studies, 1954–1968. Edited by Hennig Cohen. 2 vols. Ann Arbor, Mich.: Pierian Press, 1972.
A cumulation of the annual bibliographies in *American Quarterly,* a journal (Philadelphia: Univ. of Pennsylvania Press, 1949–) which deals with the "culture of the United States, past and present."

Boutner, Mark M. *Encyclopedia of the American Revolution*. Rev. ed. New York: McKay, 1974.

Carruth, Gorgon, ed. *The Encyclopedia of American Facts and Dates*. 6th ed., with a Supplement of the 70s. New York: Crowell, 1972.

Commager, Henry S., ed. *Documents of American History*. 8th ed. New York: Appleton, 1968.

Dictionary of American History. Edited by James Truslow Adams, R. V. Coleman et al. 5 vols. New York: Scribner, 1940.
Articles by specialists in various fields of American history. Vol. 6 = *Supplement One,* 1961. Vol. 7 = Index Volume (revised to include *Supplement One*), 1963. See also the *Atlas of American History* (New York: Scribner, 1943), to accompany the *Dictionary*.

Documents on American Foreign Relations. Boston: World Peace Foundation, 1939.
Now published annually in New York by the Council on Foreign Relations.

Handlin, Oscar T. *The Americans: A New History of the People of the United States*. Boston: Little, Brown, 1963.

Harvard Guide to American History. Edited by Oscar Handlin et al. Cambridge, Mass.: Harvard Univ. Press, Belknap Press, 1954.
    A guide to study, with valuable bibliographies.

Johnson, Thomas H. *The Oxford Companion to American History.* New York: Oxford Univ. Press, 1966.

Lord, Clifford L., and Lord, Elizabeth H., eds. *Historical Atlas of the United States.* Rev. ed. New York: Holt, 1953.

Morison, Samuel Eliot. *The Oxford History of the American People.* New York: Oxford Univ. Press, 1965.

Morris, Richard B., ed. *Encyclopedia of American History.* Updated and rev. ed. New York: Harper & Row, 1970.

Nevins, Allan, and Commager, Henry S. *A Short History of the United States.* Rev. ed. New York: Knopf, 1966.

————; Robertson, James I., Jr.; and Wiley, Bell I., eds. *Civil War Books: A Critical Bibliography.* 2 vols. Baton Rouge: Louisiana State Univ. Press, 1967–69.

Notable Names in American History: A Tabulated Register. Third Edition of *White's Conspectus of American Biography.* Clifton, N.J.: James T. White & Co., 1973.

Paullin, Charles O. *Atlas of the Historical Geography of the United States.* Edited by John K. Wright. Washington, D.C.: Carnegie Institution; New York: American Geographical Society, 1932.

U.S. Library of Congress. General Reference and Bibliography Division. *A Guide to the Study of the United States of America: Representative Books Reflecting the Development of American Life and Thought.* Prepared under the Direction of Roy P. Basler, by Donald H. Mugridge and Blanche P. McCrum. Washington, D.C.: U.S. Government Printing Office, 1960.
    An excellent annotated bibliography.

Writings on American History. 1902/3–.
    The volume for 1902/3 was issued as Pubn. 38 of the Carnegie Institution of Washington. Subsequent volumes, except for 1904–5 and 1941–47, when no bibliographies were issued, have been published as part of the Annual Report of the American Historical Association, Washington, D.C.: U.S. Government Printing Office.

OTHER COUNTRIES

Association of Asian Studies. *Cumulative Bibliography of Asian Studies, 1941–1965.* 8 vols. Boston: G. K. Hall, 1969–70.

————. *Cumulative Bibliography of Asian Studies, 1966–1970.* 8 vols. Boston: G. K. Hall, 1972–73.

Lists books and articles (in European languages) on the Far East, Southeast Asia, and South Asia, covering philosophy, history, religion, economics, social science, education, language and literature, and political science.

Berton, Peter, and Wu, Eugene. *Contemporary China: A Research Guide.* Stanford, Calif.: Hoover Institution on War, Revolution, and Peace, 1967.

Catalog of the Oriental Institute Library, University of Chicago. 16 vols. Boston: G. K. Hall, 1970.

Dictionary Catalog of the Oriental Collection, The New York Public Library, Reference Department. 16 vols. Boston: G. K. Hall, 1960.

Encyclopaedia of Ireland. Edited by Victor Meally et al. Dublin: Allen Figgis, 1968.

Florinsky, Michael T. *The McGraw-Hill Encyclopedia of Russia and the Soviet Union.* New York: McGraw-Hill, 1961.

Hall, David E., ed. *Union Catalogue of Asian Publications 1965–1970.* 5 vols. London: Mansell, 1971.

Sponsored by and edited at the School of Oriental and African Studies, University of London.

Handbook of Latin-American Studies. Cambridge, Mass.: Harvard Univ. Press, 1936–.

An annual classified bibliography. Now published at Gainesville by the University of Florida Press and in two parts, Humanities and Social Sciences, published in alternate years.

Learmouth, Andrew T. A., and Learmouth, Agnes M. *Encyclopaedia of Australia.* New ed. London: Warne, 1974.

Legum, Colin, ed. *Africa: A Handbook to the Continent.* Rev. and enl. ed. New York: Praeger, 1966.

Martin, Michael R., and Lovett, Gabriel H. *Encyclopedia of Latin-American History.* Revised edition by L. Robert Hughes. Indianapolis: Bobbs-Merrill, 1968.

Oxford History of England, The. General Editor, Sir George Clark. 15 vols. Oxford: Clarendon Press, 1937–65.

Pasley, Malcolm. *Germany: A Companion to German Studies.* London: Methuen; New York: Harper & Row, 1972.

Steinberg's Dictionary of British History. Edited by S. H. Steinberg and I. H. Evans. 2d ed. London: Arnold; New York: St. Martin's Press, 1971.

Story, Norah, ed. *The Oxford Companion to Canadian History and Literature*. Toronto: Oxford Univ. Press, 1967.

Têng, Ssŭ-yü, and Biggerstaff, Knight. *An Annotated Bibliography of Selected Chinese Reference Works*. 3d ed. Cambridge, Mass.: Harvard Univ. Press, 1971.

Wint, Guy. *Asia: A Handbook*. New York: Praeger, 1966.

Zalewski, Wojciech. *Guide to Selected Reference Materials: Russia and East Europe*. Stanford, Calif.: Stanford Univ. Libraries, 1973.

REFERENCE WORKS IN THE SOCIAL SCIENCES

GENERAL

ABS Guide to Recent Publications in the Social and Behavioral Sciences, The. New York: American Behavioral Scientist, 1965. Supplements.

American Men of Science: A Biographical Dictionary. The Social and Behavioral Sciences. 11th ed. Edited by the Jaques Cattell Press. 2 vols. New York: R. R. Bowker, 1968.

Dictionary of the Social Sciences, A. Edited by Julius Gould and William L. Kolb. Compiled under the auspices of UNESCO. New York: Crowell-Collier, 1964.

Ernst, Morris L., and Posner, Judith A. *The Comparative International Almanac*. New York: Macmillan, 1967.
    Provides a quick glance at the vital statistics of 214 countries.

Hoselitz, Berthold F., ed. *A Reader's Guide to the Social Sciences*. Rev. ed. New York: Free Press, 1970.
    Pp. 419–25: Bibliography.

International Encyclopedia of the Social Sciences. Edited by David L. Sills. 17 vols. New York: Macmillan, 1968.
    Vol. 17 = Index. Substantial articles, with lengthy bibliographies. Designed to complement, not to supplant, its predecessor, the *Encyclopaedia of the Social Sciences,* edited by Edwin R. A. Seligman. 15 vols. New York: Macmillan, 1930–35.

Madge, John H. *The Tools of Social Science*. Garden City, N.Y.: Anchor Books, 1965.

Public Affairs Information Service. *Bulletin of the Public Affairs Information Service.* New York: P.A.I.S., 1915–. (Weekly, with five cumulations yearly.)

Social Sciences and Humanities Index. New York: H. W. Wilson, 1965– (Quarterly, with cumulated volumes.) Formerly the *International Index to Periodicals.*

Statistics Sources: A Subject Guide to Data on Industrial, Business, Social, Educational, Financial, and Other Topics for the United States and Selected Foreign Countries. 2d ed. Edited by Paul Wasserman, Charlotte Georgi, and Eleanor Allen. Detroit: Gale Research Co., 1966.

Vital Speeches of the Day. New York: City News Publishing Co., 1934–. (Monthly. A 25-year Index covers the period October 1934–October 1959.)

Prints the full text of important addresses of current leaders in the social sciences.

White, Carl M., and Associates. *Sources of Information in the Social Sciences: A Guide to the Literature.* Totowa, N.J.: Bedminster Press, 1964.

Includes an essay on the history and methodology of the discipline and annotated lists of reference works grouped by type.

Worldmark Encyclopedia of the Nations: A Practical Guide to the Geographical, Historical, Political, Social, and Economic Status of All the Nations, Their International Relations and the United Nations System. 3d ed. Edited by Mosha Y. Sachs. 5 vols. New York: Harper & Row, 1967.

Zadrozny, John T., ed. *Dictionary of Social Science.* Washington, D.C.: Public Affairs Press, 1959.

ECONOMICS

Alexander, Raphael, ed. *Business Pamphlets and Information Sources.* New York: Exceptional Books, 1967.

Alexander Hamilton Institute. *2001 Business Terms and What They Mean.* Garden City, N.Y.: Doubleday, 1962.

Bach, George L. *Economics: An Introduction to Analysis and Policy.* 8th ed. Englewood Cliffs, N.J.: Prentice-Hall, 1974.

Business Periodicals Index. New York: H. W. Wilson, 1958–. (Monthly, except July, with annual cumulations.)

Clark, Donald T., and Gottfried, Bert A. *Dictionary of Business and Finance.* New York: Crowell, 1957.

Coman, Edwin T., Jr. *Sources of Business Information.* 2d ed., rev. Berkeley: Univ. of California Press, 1964.

Directory of Business and Financial Services. Edited by Mary A. Mc-Nierney. 6th ed. New York: Special Libraries Assn., 1963.
    A selected list of business, economic, and financial publications. Supplements.

Economics Library Selections. New Books in Economics. New York: Gordon Breach Associates, 1964–. (Quarterly.)

Galbraith, John K. *The Affluent Society.* Rev. ed. Boston: Houghton Mifflin, 1969.

————. *The New Industrial State.* Boston: Houghton Mifflin, 1967.

Greenwald, Douglas, et al., eds. *McGraw-Hill Dictionary of Modern Economics: A Handbook of Terms and Organizations.* 2d ed. New York: McGraw-Hill, 1973.

Hanson, John L. *A Dictionary of Economics and Commerce.* 3d ed. London: Macdonald & Evans, 1969.

Manley, Marian C. *Business Information: How to Find and Use It.* New York: Harper, 1955.

Maynard, Harold B., et al., eds. *Handbook of Business Administration.* New York: McGraw-Hill, 1967.
    A comprehensive work, illustrated with tables and charts and including bibliographies.

Palgrave's Dictionary of Political Economy. Edited by Henry Higgs. 3 vols. London: Macmillan, 1923–26. Reprinted, New York: Augustus M. Kelley, 1963.
    The standard English work, by Sir Robert Palgrave, first published 1894–96. Signed articles by specialists and bibliographies.

Rand McNally Commercial Atlas and Marketing Guide. New York: Rand McNally, 1968.
    Issued annually, containing numerous statistical tables of agriculture, business and manufactures, population, etc.

Readings in Business Policy. Edited by Edmund R. Gray. New York: Appleton, 1968.

Sloan, Harold S., and Zurcher, Arnold J., eds. *A Dictionary of Economics.* 4th ed., rev. New York: Barnes & Noble, 1961.

Taylor, Philip A. S. *A New Dictionary of Economics*. London: Routledge; New York: Augustus M. Kelley, 1966.

United Nations. Department of Economic and Social Affairs. *World Economic Survey*. New York: United Nations, 1945/47–. (Annual.)

    A comprehensive survey of world economic conditions and trends. Supplements, 1948–.

EDUCATION

Burke, Arvid J., and Burke, Mary A. *Documentation in Education*. New York: Teachers College Press, Teachers College, Columbia University, 1967.

    A revision of *How to Locate Educational Information and Data,* by Carter Alexander and Arvid J. Burke (4th ed., 1958).

Education Index, January 1929–. New York: H. W. Wilson, 1932–. (Monthly, except July and August, with annual cumulations.)

    Covers the entire field and includes British publications.

Encyclopedia of Careers and Vocational Guidance, The. Edited by William E. Hopke et al. Rev. ed. 2 vols. Chicago: J. G. Ferguson Publishing Co. (distributed by Doubleday), 1972.

Encyclopedia of Education, The. Edited by Lee C. Deighton et al. 10 vols. New York: Macmillan and Free Press, 1971.

Encyclopedia of Educational Research: A Project of the American Educational Research Association. Edited by Robert L. Ebel et al. 4th ed. New York: Macmillan, 1969.

Good, Carter V., ed. *Dictionary of Education*. 2d ed. New York: McGraw-Hill, 1959.

Manheim, Theodore et al. *Sources in Educational Research: A Selected & Annotated Bibliography*. Detroit: Wayne State Univ. Press, 1969–. In progress.

Monroe, Paul, et al. *A Cyclopedia of Education*. 5 vols. New York: Macmillan, 1911–13.

    Still valuable for early history and philosophy of education.

U.S. Office of Education. *Education Directory*. Washington, D.C.: U.S. Government Printing Office, 1912–. (Annual.)

————. *Publications of the Office of Education*. Washington, D.C.: U.S. Government Printing Office, 1959–. (Annual.)

An annotated list of currently available publications arranged by subject with title-index.

SPORTS AND PASTIMES

Arlott, John, ed. *The Oxford Companion to Sports & Games.* London: Oxford Univ. Press, 1975.

Baseball Encyclopedia: The Complete and Official Record of Major League Baseball. New York: Macmillan, 1969.

Evans, Webster. *Encyclopedia of Golf.* 2d ed. New York: St. Martin's Press, 1973.

Gomme, Alice B. *Traditional Games of England, Scotland, and Ireland.* 2 vols. London: Nutt, 1894–98. Reprinted, New York: Dover, 1964.

Greenwood, Frances A. *Bibliography of Swimming.* New York: Wilson, 1940.

Hollander, Zander. *Great American Athletes of the 20th Century.* New York: Random House, 1972.
   Biographical sketches of fifty athletes in eleven different sports.

———, ed. *The Modern Encyclopedia of Basketball.* Rev. ed. New York: Four Winds Press, 1973.

Leckie, Robert. *The Story of Football.* New York: Random House, 1973.
   A history of the sport in America, from the first intercollegiate game in 1869.

Menke, Frank G. *The Encyclopedia of Sport.* 5th ed., revised by Roger Treat. South Brunswick, N.J.: A. S. Barnes, 1974.

Murdock, Joseph S. F. *The Library of Golf, 1743–1966: A Bibliography of Golf Books, Indexed Alphabetically, Chronologically, and by Subject Matter.* Detroit: Gale Research Co., 1968.

Pinkerton, James R., and Pinkerton, Marjorie J. *Outdoor Recreation and Leisure: A Reference Guide and Selected Bibliography.* Columbia, Mo.: Univ. of Missouri, Research Center, School of Business and Public Administration, 1969.

Quercetani, Roberto L. *A World History of Track and Field Athletics, 1864–1964.* New York: Oxford Univ. Press, 1964.

Reeves, Fred. *A Baseball Handbook.* New York: Heath Cote Publishing Co., 1973.

Robertson, Max, and Kramer, Jack. *Encyclopedia of Tennis: One Hundred Years of Great Players and Events.* New York: Viking Press, 1974.

Styer, Robert A. *Encyclopedia of Hockey.* Rev. ed. South Brunswick, N.J.: A. S. Barnes, 1973.

Treat, Roger, ed. *Encyclopedia of Football.* 12th ed., rev. South Brunswick, N.J.: A. S. Barnes, 1974.

GEOGRAPHY

(See also "Atlases and Gazetteers," p. 196.)

American Geographical Society, Library. *Research Catalogue.* 15 vols. and Map Supplement. Boston: G. K. Hall, 1962.

    See also *Current Geographical Publications: Additions to the Research Catalogue. . . .* New York: American Geographical Society, 1938–. (Monthly, except July and August.)

Brubaker, Sterling. *To Live on Earth: Man and His Environment in Perspective.* Baltimore: Johns Hopkins Univ. Press, 1972.

Colinvaux, Paul A. *Introduction to Ecology.* New York: Wiley, 1973. Pp. 580–600: Bibliography.

Falk, Richard A. *This Endangered Planet: Prospects and Proposals for Human Survival.* New York: Vintage Books, 1972.

Larousse Encyclopedia of World Geography. New York: Odyssey Press, 1964.

Lock, Clara B. M. *Geography: A Reference Handbook.* Hamden, Conn.: Archon Books, 1968.

Monkhouse, Francis J. *A Dictionary of Geography.* 2d ed. London: Arnold, 1970.

Schmieder, Allen A., et al. *Dictionary of Basic Geography.* Boston: Allyn & Bacon, 1970.

Southwick, Charles H. *Ecology and the Quality of Our Environment.* New York: Van Nostrand–Reinhold, 1972.

Webster's New Geographical Dictionary. Springfield, Mass.: G. & C. Merriam, 1972.

    Includes place names with geographical and historical information, not only of today, but of biblical and medieval times, and of ancient Greece and Rome.

White, William, Jr., and Little, Frank J., Jr. *North American Reference*

Encyclopedia of Ecology and Pollution. Philadelphia: North American Publishing Co., 1972.

Wright, John K., and Platt, Elizabeth T., eds. *Aids to Geographical Research.* 2d ed., completely rev. New York: Columbia Univ. Press for the American Geographical Society, 1947.

POLITICAL SCIENCE

Adams, A. John, and Burke, John M. *Civil Rights: A Current Guide to the People, Organizations, and Events.* (A CBS News Reference Book.) New York: R. R. Bowker, 1970.

Brock, Clifton. *The Literature of Political Science: A Guide for Students, Librarians, and Teachers.* New York: R. R. Bowker, 1969.

Brooks, Alexander S. *Civil Rights and Liberties in the United States: An Annotated Bibliography.* New York: Civil Liberties Educational Foundation, 1962.
    Includes selected fiction and audiovisual materials.

Carnell, Francis. *The Politics of the New Nations: A Select Annotated Bibliography with Special Reference to the Commonwealth.* London: Oxford Univ. Press, 1961.

Chandler, Robert. *Public Opinion: Changing Attitudes on Contemporary Political and Social Issues.* (A CBS News Reference Book.) New York: R. R. Bowker, 1972.
    Discussion of such subjects as the Bill of Rights, "Women's Lib," the Generation Gap, and use of marijuana, with the results of polls on these issues.

De Koster, Lester. *Vocabulary of Communism: Definitions of Key Terms, Summaries of Central Ideas, Short Biographies of Leading Figures, Descriptions of Significant Things and Events.* Grand Rapids, Mich.: William B. Ecrdmans Publishing Co., 1964.

Ernst, Morris L., and Posner, Judith A. *The Comparative International Almanac.* See p. 227.

Feuer, Lewis S. *The Conflict of Generations: The Character and Significance of Student Movements.* New York: Basic Books, 1969.

Harmon, Robert B. *Political Science: A Bibliographical Guide to the Literature.* Metuchen, N.J.: Scarecrow Press, 1965. Third Supplement, 1974.

Hyams, Edward. *A Dictionary of Modern Revolution.* New York: Taplinger Publishing Co., 1973.

Deals with such subjects as Action Française, African National Congress, Al-Fatah, Religion, Revisionism, Soledad Brothers, and George Sorel.

Kolarz, Walter. *Books on Communism: A Bibliography.* 2d ed. New York: Oxford Univ. Press, 1964.

Miller, Albert Jay. *Confrontation, Conflict, and Dissent: A Bibliography of a Decade of Controversy, 1960–1970.* Metuchen, N.J.: Scarecrow Press, 1972.

Morgenthau, Hans. *Politics among Nations: The Struggle for Power and Peace.* 5th ed., rev. New York: Knopf, 1973.
   Pp. 577–97 Bibliography.

Muller, Robert H., et al. *From Radical Left to Extreme Right.* See above, p. 192.

Patterns of Government: *The Major Political Systems of Europe.* Edited by Samuel H. Beer and Adam B. Ulam. New York: Random House, 1958.

Porter, Kirk H., and Johnson, Donald B. *National Party Platforms, 1840–1968.* 4th ed. Urbana: Univ. of Illinois Press, 1970.

Seidman, Joel, et al. *Communism in the United States—a Bibliography.* Ithaca: Cornell Univ. Press, 1969.

Smith, Edward C., and Zurcher, Arnold J. *Dictionary of American Politics.* 2d ed. New York: Barnes & Noble, 1968.

Sperber, Hans, and Trittschuch, Travis. *American Political Terms: An Historical Dictionary.* Detroit: Wayne State Univ. Press, 1962.

Staar, Richard F., ed. *Yearbook on International Communist Affairs, 1973.* Stanford: Hoover Institution Press, 1973.

Sworakowski, Witold, ed. *World Communism: A Handbook, 1918–1965.* Stanford: Hoover Institution Press, 1973.

Television News Index and Abstracts. A Guide to the Videotape Collection of the Network Evening News Programs in the Vanderbilt Television News Archive. Nashville, Tenn.: Joint University Libraries, 1972–. In progress.

A collection of evening news broadcasts of ABC, CBS, and NBC, beginning 5 August 1968; also various special news programs and presidential speeches, with accompanying comments. Includes complete coverage of the Democratic and Republican conventions of 1968.

University of California, Berkeley. *Subject Catalogue of the Institute of Governmental Studies Library*. 26 vols. Boston: G. K. Hall, 1970.

    Deals with such widely varied topics as Abandoned Vehicles, Abortion, Absentee Voting, Absenteeism, and Academic Freedom.

Wynar, Lubomyr R. *Guide to Reference Materials in Political Science: A Selective Bibliography*. 2 vols. Vol. 1. Denver: Colorado Bibliographic Institute, 1966. Vol. 2. Rochester, N.Y.: Libraries Unlimited, 1968.

Zawodny, Janusz. *Guide to the Study of International Relations*. San Francisco: Chandler, 1965.

SOCIOLOGY

General Studies

Hoult, Thomas F. *Dictionary of Modern Sociology*. Totowa, N. J.: Littlefield, Adams and Company, 1969.

International Bibliography of Sociology. Bibliographie internationale de Sociologie. London: Tavistock Publications; Chicago: Aldine, 1952–.

    An extensive listing of books, pamphlets, articles, and official publications in many languages, indexed by author and subject.

Merton, Robert K., et al., eds. *Sociology Today: Problems and Prospects*. 2 vols. New York: Basic Books, 1969.

Mitchell, G. Duncan, ed. *A Dictionary of Sociology*. Chicago: Aldine, 1968.

Theodorson, George A., and Theodorson, Achilles G. *A Modern Dictionary of Sociology*. New York: Crowell, 1969.

Special Topics

Marsden, Charles F., and Meyer, Gladys. *Minorities in American Society*. 4th ed. New York: Van Nostrand, 1973.

Simpson, George E., and Yinger, J. M. *Racial and Cultural Minorities*. 3d ed. New York: Harper & Row, 1965.

Bell, Barbara L. *Black Biographical Sources: An Annotated Bibliography*. New Haven, Conn.: Yale Univ. Library, 1970.

Bibliographic Survey: The Negro in Print. Washington, D.C.: Negro Bibliographic and Research Center, 1965–. (Bimonthly.)

Brink, William, and Harris, Louis. *Black and White: A Study of U.S. Racial Attitudes Today.* New York: Simon & Schuster, 1967.

Davis, John P., ed. *The American Negro Reference Book.* Englewood Cliffs, N.J.: Prentice-Hall, 1966.

Ebony. The Negro Handbook. Compiled by the Editors of *Ebony.* Chicago: Johnson Publishing Co., 1966.

Grant, Joanne, ed. *Black Protest: History, Documents, and Analysis, 1619 to the Present.* Greenwich, Conn.: Fawcett Pubns., 1968.

Howard University. *Dictionary Catalog of the Arthur B. Spingarn Collection of Negro Authors, Howard University Library, Washington, D.C.* 2 vols. Boston: G. K. Hall, 1970.

Index to Periodical Articles by and about Negroes. Compiled by the Staffs of the Hallie Q. Brown Memorial Library, Central State University, Wilberforce, Ohio, and the Schomburg Collection, New York Public Library. Boston: G. K. Hall, 1960–. (Annual.)

Miller, Elizabeth W. *The Negro in America: A Bibliography.* 2d ed., revised and enlarged by Mary L. Fisher. Cambridge, Mass.: Harvard Univ. Press, 1970.

Pioski, Harry A., and Brown, Horace C., Jr. *The Negro Almanac.* New York: Bellwether Publishing Co., 1967.
    Includes a wide range of topics, with sections on Africa and the Caribbean. Short biographies, charts and tables, and a bibliography.

Pollard, W. Robert. *Black Literature: A Classified Bibliography of Newspapers, Periodicals, and Books by and about the Negro in the D. H. Hill Library, North Carolina State University at Raleigh.* Raleigh: D. H. Hill Library, 1969. Supplement, 1970.

Porter, Dorothy B. *The Negro in the United States: A Selected Bibliography.* Washington, D.C.: Library of Congress, 1970.

Schatz, Walter. *Directory of Afro-American Resources.* New York: R. R. Bowker, 1970.

Sloan, Irving J. *Blacks in America, 1492–1970: A Chronology & Fact Book.* Dobbs Ferry, N.Y.: Oceana Publications, 1971.

Salk, Erwin A. *A Layman's Guide to Negro History.* New and enl. ed. New York: McGraw-Hill, 1967.

Turner, Darwin T. *A Convenient Guide to Drama, Fiction, and Poetry by Black Americans.* (Goldentree Bibliographies.) Northbrook, Ill.: AHM Publishing Corp., 1970.

Walton, Hanes, Jr. *The Study and Analysis of Black Politics: A Bibliography.* Metuchen, N.J.: Scarecrow Press, 1973.

Welsch, Erwin K. *The Negro in the United States: A Research Guide.* Bloomington: Indiana Univ. Press, 1965.

Work, Monroe N. *A Bibliography of the Negro in Africa and America.* New York: Octagon Books, 1958. (First published in 1928.)

American Indian Index. Chicago: J. A. Huebner, 1953–.
    Lists articles and books on all aspects of American Indians. Beginning in October 1962 issued by Russell L. Knor, River Grove, Illinois.

Index to Literature on the American Indian, 1970–. Edited by Jeannette Henry et al. San Francisco: Indian Historian Press, 1972–.

Prucha, Francis Paul. *A Bibliographical Guide to the History of Indian-White Relations in the United States.* Chicago: Univ. of Chicago Press, forthcoming (1977).

Swanton, John Reed. *The Indian Tribes of North America.* Washington, D.C.: U.S. Government Printing Office, 1952.

U.S. Department of the Interior, Library. *Biographical and Historical Index of American Indians and Persons Involved in Indian Affairs.* 5 vols. Boston: G. K. Hall, 1966.

Washburn, Wilcomb E. *The Indian in America.* New York: Harper & Row, 1975.
    Pp. 277–88: a valuable "Bibliographical Essay."

Barrios, Ernie, ed. *Bibliografía de Aztklán: An Annotated Chicano Bibliography.* San Diego, Calif.: Centro de Estudios Chicanos Publications, San Diego State College, 1971.

Moquin, Wayne, ed., with Charles Van Doren. *A Documentary History of the Mexican Americans.* New York: Praeger, 1971.
    A collection of 65 documents, from the early sixteenth century to 1970.

Navarro, E. G. *Annotated Bibliography of Materials on the Mexican-American.* Austin: Graduate School of Social Work, Univ. of Texas, 1969.

Steiner, Stan. *La Raza, the Mexican Americans.* New York: Harper & Row, 1970.

Adams, Mildred. *The Right to Be People: Woman's Struggle for Equality.* Philadelphia: Lippincott, 1966.

Friedan, Betty. *The Feminine Mystique.* New York: Norton, 1963.

Krichmar, Albert, et al. *The Women's Rights Movement in the United States, 1848–1970: A Bibliography and Source Book.* Metuchen, N.J.: Scarecrow Press, 1972.

Leonard, Eugenie A.; Drinker, Sophie H.; and Holden, Miriam Y. *The American Woman in Colonial and Revolutionary Times, 1565–1800: A Syllabus with Bibliography.* Philadelphia: Univ. of Pennsylvania Press, 1962.

Radcliffe College Library, Cambridge, Mass. *Arthur and Elizabeth Schlesinger Library on the History of Women in America: The Manuscript Inventories and the Catalogs of Manuscripts, Books and Pictures.* 3 vols. Boston: G. K. Hall, 1973.
    A combined author and subject catalog.

Wheeler, Helen. *Womanhood Media: Current Resources about Women.* Metuchen, N.J.: Scarecrow Press, 1972.

White, William, Jr. *North American Reference Encyclopedia of Women's Liberation.* Philadelphia: North American Publishing Co., 1972.
    Pp. 140–82: A Selected and Annotated Directory and Bibliography to Women's Liberation.

REFERENCE WORKS IN THE BIOLOGICAL AND PHYSICAL SCIENCES

GENERAL

AAAS Science Book List, The. A Selected and Annotated List of Science and Mathematics Books for Secondary School Students, College Undergraduates, and Nonspecialists. Compiled by Hilary J. Deason. 3d ed. Washington, D.C.: American Association for the Advancement of Science, 1970.

American Men of Science: A Biographical Directory. The Physical and Biological Sciences. 11th ed. Edited by the Jaques Cattell Press. 6 vols. New York: R. R. Bowker, 1965. Annual Supplements.

American Scientific Books. Edited by Phyllis B. Steckler. New York: R. R. Bowker, 1962–. (Annual.)

Applied Science and Technology Index. New York: H. W. Wilson, 1913–. (Monthly, except August.)
    From 1913 to 1957 entitled *Industrial Arts Index.*

Basic Dictionary of Science, The. Edited by Elsie C. Graham. New York: Macmillan, 1965.

Dictionary of Scientific Biography. Charles C. Gillespie, Editor-in-Chief. New York: Scribner, 1970–. In progress.
    Has reached Vol. 9. Covers a wide range; includes such figures as Abelard and Dr. John Arbuthnot.

Grogan, Denis J. *Science and Technology: An Introduction to the Literature.* Hamden, Conn.: Archon Books, 1970.

Harper Encyclopedia of Science, The. Edited by James R. Newman. Rev. ed. New York: Harper & Row, 1967.

McGraw-Hill Encyclopedia of Science and Technology, The: An International Reference Work. 3d ed. 15 vols. New York: McGraw-Hill, 1971.
    See also the *McGraw-Hill Yearbook of Science and Technology.* (Annual.)

Peterson Field Guide Series, The. Edited by Roger Tory Peterson. Boston: Houghton Mifflin, 1947–.
    Separate volumes treating such subjects as trees, shrubs, ferns, wild flowers, birds, insects, reptiles, amphibians, mammals, stars, and planets.

Putnam's Nature Field Books. New York: Putnam, 1928–.
    Separate volumes on such topics as wild flowers, trees and shrubs, insects, fishes, mammals, rocks, and minerals.

Sarton, George. *A Guide to the History of Science: A First Guide for the Study of the History of Science, with Introductory Essays on Science and Tradition.* Waltham, Mass.: Chronica Botanica Co., 1952.

Technical Book Review Index. New York: Special Libraries Assn., 1935–. (Monthly, except July and August.)

U.S. Library of Congress. National Referral Center for Science and Technology. *A Directory of Information Resources in the U.S.: Physical Sciences, Biological Sciences, and Engineering.* Washington, D.C.: U.S. Government Printing Office, 1965.

A Directory of Resources: Biological Sciences, updating and extending the 1965 Directory, was published in 1972.

————. *A Directory of Information Resources in the U.S.: Water.* Washington, D.C.: U.S. Government Printing Office, 1966.

Van Nostrand's Scientific Encyclopedia. 4th ed. Princeton, N.J.: Van Nostrand, 1968.

Van Royen, William, ed. *Atlas of the World's Resources.* Vol. 1: *The Agricultural Resources of the World.* Vol. 2: *The Mineral Resources of the World.* By William Van Royen and Oliver Bowles. Englewood Cliffs, N.J.: Prentice-Hall, for the University of Maryland, 1952–54.

Williams, Trevor I., ed. *A Biographical Dictionary of Scientists.* London: A. & C. Black, 1969.

Designed "for the general reader as well as for the serious student."

BIOLOGICAL SCIENCES

Altsheler, Brent. *Natural History Index Guide: An Index to 3,365 Books and Periodicals in Libraries: A Guide to Things Natural in the Field; Where and How to Find the Most Important Objects of Natural Interest in All Countries.* . . . 2d ed. New York: H. W. Wilson, 1940.

Biological & Agricultural Index: A Cumulative Subject Index to Periodicals in the Fields of Biology, Agriculture, and Related Sciences, 1964–. New York: H. W. Wilson, 1964–.

Formerly (vols. 1–49) *Agricultural Index.* Issued monthly, except September.

Blake, Sidney F. *Geographical Guide to Floras of the World: An Annotated List with Special Reference to Useful Plants and Common Plant Names.* 2 vols. Washington, D.C.: U.S. Government Printing Office, 1942–61.

Clark, Randolph L., and Cumley, Russell W., eds. *The Book of Health: A Medical Encyclopedia for Everyone.* 3d ed. New York: Van Nostrand–Reinhold, 1973.

Comstock, Anna B. *Handbook of Nature-Study.* 24th ed. New York: Comstock Publishing Co., 1939.

Pages 861–908 = Bibliography, by Eva L. Gordon.

Gleason, Henry A. *The New Britton and Brown Illustrated Flora of the Northeastern United States and Adjacent Canada*. 3 vols. New York: N.Y. Botanical Garden, 1952.
    Reprinted 1963 with slight revisions. First published 1896–98 by Nathaniel L. Britton and Addison Brown.

Gray, Peter, ed. *The Encyclopedia of the Biological Sciences*. 2d ed. New York: Van Nostrand–Reinhold, 1970.

————. *The Dictionary of the Biological Sciences*. New York: Reinhold Publishing Corp., 1967.

Handbooks of American Natural History. Edited by Albert H. Wright. Ithaca, N.Y.: Comstock Publishing Co., 1942–. In progress.
    A series of volumes on frogs and toads, salamanders, mosquitoes, lizards, spiders, turtles, snakes, etc.

Henderson, Isabella F., and Henderson, W. D. *A Dictionary of Biological Terms . . . in Biology, Botany, Zoology, Anatomy, Cytology, Genetics, Embryology, Physiology*. 8th ed. revised by J. H. Kenneth. Princeton, N.J.: Van Nostrand, 1963.

Jordan, Emil L., et al. *Hammond's Nature Atlas of America*. New York: C. S. Hammond, 1952.

Kerker, Ann E., and Murphy, Henry T. *Biological and Biomedical Resource Literature*. Lafayette, Ind.: Purdue University, 1968.
    With author-title index.

Palmer, E. Lawrence. *Fieldbook of Natural History*. Revised by H. S. Fowler. New York: McGraw-Hill, 1975.

Spector, William S. *Handbook of Biological Data*. Philadelphia: W. B. Saunders, 1956.

Stedman, Thomas L. *Medical Dictionary*. 21st ed. Baltimore: Williams & Wilkins, 1966.

U.S. Department of Agriculture. *Yearbook of Agriculture*. Washington, D.C.: U.S. Government Printing Office, 1894–.

Usher, George. *A Dictionary of Botany*. London: Constable, 1966.

Willis, John Christopher. *A Dictionary of the Flowering Plants and Ferns*. 8th ed., revised by H. K. Airy Shaw. Cambridge: Cambridge Univ. Press, 1973.
    See also Frank N. Howes, *A Dictionary of Useful and Everyday Plants and Their Common Names* (Cambridge, 1974), based on the 6th edition of Willis.

PHYSICAL SCIENCES

Advances in Space Science and Technology. New York: Academic Press, 1959–.

Published annually. Supplement (New York: Academic Press, 1963–).

American Institute of Physics. *American Institute of Physics Handbook*. Edited by Dwight E. Gray et al. 2d ed. New York: McGraw-Hill, 1963.

Annotated Bibliography of Economic Geology, 1928–. Urbana, Ill.: Economic Geology Publishing Co., 1929–. (Semiannual.)

Ballentyne, Denis W. G., and Lovett, D. R. *A Dictionary of Named Effects and Laws in Chemistry, Physics, and Mathematics*. 3d ed. London: Chapman & Hall, 1970.

Besançon, Robert M., ed. *The Encyclopedia of Physics*. 2d ed. New York: Van Nostrand–Reinhold, 1974.

Besserer, Carl W., and Besserer, Hazel C. *Guide to the Space Age*. Englewood Cliffs, N.J.: Prentice-Hall, 1959.

Braun, Wernher von, and Ordway, Frederick I. *History of Rocketry and Space Travel*. Rev. ed. New York: Crowell, 1969.

British Technology Index. London: Library Assn., 1962–.

Published quarterly. Subject and author indexes. Continues *The Subject Index to Periodicals* (1915–61).

Chambers's Technical Dictionary. Edited by C. F. Tweney and L. E. C. Hughes. 3d ed., rev., with Supplement. New York: Macmillan, 1958.

Reprinted 1962. Pp. 952–1028: Supplement (for more recent items).

Collocott, T. C., ed. *Dictionary of Science and Technology*. Edinburgh: W. & R. Chambers, 1971.

Condon, Edward U., and Odishaw, Hugh. *Handbook of Physics*. 2d ed., rev. New York: McGraw-Hill, 1967.

Emme, Eugene M., ed. *The History of Rocket Technology*. . . . Detroit: Wayne State Univ. Press, 1964.

Encyclopedia of Chemical Technology. Edited by Herman P. Mark et al. 2d ed., completely rev. 22 vols. New York: Inter-science Publishers, 1963–70.

Supplement, 1971. Index to Vols. 1–22 and Supp., 1972.

Encyclopaedic Dictionary of Physics: General, Nuclear, Solid State, Molecular, Chemical, Metal, and Vacuum Physics, Astronomy, Geophysics, Biophysics, and Related Subjects. Edited by J. Thewlis et al. 9 vols. London & New York: Pergamon Press, 1961–64. (Supplements.)

Glazebrook, Richard. *Dictionary of Applied Physics.* 5 vols. London: Macmillan, 1922–23.
  Still valuable for the historical aspects of physics.

Gray, H. J., et al. *Dictionary of Physics.* New York: Longmans, 1958.

Hempel, Clifford A., and Hawley, Gessner G. *The Encyclopedia of Chemistry.* 3d ed. New York: Van Nostrand–Reinhold, 1973.
  Earlier editions by George L. Clark et al.

Hix, C. F., Jr., and Alley, R. P. *Physical Laws and Effects.* New York: John Wiley & Sons, 1958.

Hogerton, John F., et al. *The Atomic Energy Deskbook.* New York: Reinhold Publishing Corp., 1963.

James & James Mathematics Dictionary. 3d ed. Multilingual Edition. [Edited by Robert C. James and E. F. Beckenbach.] Princeton, N.J.: Van Nostrand, 1968.
  Originally edited by Glenn James and Robert C. James.

Jordain, Philip B., and Breslau, Michael. *Condensed Computer Encyclopedia.* New York: McGraw-Hill, 1969.

Kemp, D. A. *Astronomy and Astrophysics: A Bibliographical Guide.* Hamden, Conn.: Shoe String Press, 1970.

Lange, Norbert A., and Parker, Gordon M. *Handbook of Chemistry.* Rev. 10th ed. New York: McGraw-Hill, 1967.
  "A reference volume for all requiring ready access to chemical and physical data used in laboratory work and manufacturing." (Subtitle.)

Marks, Robert W., ed. *New Dictionary and Handbook of Aerospace, with Special Sections on the Moon and Lunar Flight.* New York: Praeger, 1969.

Mellon, Melvin G. *Chemical Publications: Their Nature and Use.* 4th ed. New York: McGraw-Hill, 1965.
  Author, subject, and title indexes.

Muller, Paul. *Concise Encyclopedia of Astronomy.* London: Collins, 1968.

Parke, Nathan G. *Guide to the Literature of Mathematics and Physics, including Related Works on Engineering Sciences*. 2d ed., rev. New York: Dover Pubns., 1958.

Pemberton, John E. *How to Find Out in Mathematics: A Guide to Sources of Information*. 2d rev. ed. Oxford: Pergamon Press, 1969.

Pritchard, Alan. *A Guide to Computer Literature: An Introductory Survey of the Sources of Information*. London: Clive Bingley; Hamden, Conn.: Linnet Books, 1972.

Spencer-Jones, Harold, et al. *New Space Encyclopaedia: A Guide to Astronomy and Space Research*. 3d ed. Edited by M. T. Bizony. New York: E. P. Dutton, 1969.

Thorpe, Jocelyn F., and Whiteley, M. A. *Thorpe's Dictionary of Applied Chemistry*. 4th ed., rev. and enl. 12 vols. New York: Longmans, 1937–56. Vol. 12 = Index.

U.S. Bureau of Mines. *Mineral Resources of the United States, 1882/83–*. Washington, D.C.: Government Printing Office, 1883–1931. Continued annually by the *Minerals Yearbook,* 1933–.

Universal Encyclopedia of Mathematics, The. Foreword by James R. Newman. New York: Simon & Schuster, 1964.

Van Nostrand's Chemist's Dictionary, The. Edited by Jurgen M. Honig et al. New York: Van Nostrand, 1953.

Van Riper, Joseph E. *Man's Physical World*. 2d ed. New York: McGraw-Hill, 1971.

Whitford, Robert H. *Physics Literature: A Reference Manual*. 2d ed. Metuchen, N.J.: Scarecrow Press, 1968.

Index

A, an, beginning title, 3:56, 5:64,
  7:146–48
Abbreviations
  alphabetizing of, 3:4
  of books of Bible, 6:22
  capitalization of, 7:66
  capital letters as, 6:32, 6:122
  with company names, 6:33, 7:38
  with dates, 6:27, 6:29
  of degrees (academic), 6:16, 6:122
  division of, 6:122
  ed., comp., trans., 4:11–13, 7:30
  of edition number, 4:21–22, 4:35,
    7:32, 7:93, 7:120
  of geographic names, 6:23–26
  in legal references, 7:118
  listed, 7:68
  with measurements, 6:30, 6:66
  n.d., for date of publication, 7:41
  n.p., for place and publisher, 7:37,
    7:39–40
  on note cards, 4:58
  with numbers, 6:30, 6:66
  for organization names, 6:10, 6:32
  for parts of a book, 4:33, 6:31,
    7:18, 7:52–54, 7:64
  in periodical indexes, 3:27, 4:24
  periods with, 6:10, 6:129
  with personal names, 6:10, 6:14–21
  plurals of, 6:79
  of publisher's name, 7:38
  punctuation with, 6:10, 6:129
  of radio and television stations, 6:32,
    6:122
  of *Saint,* 6:20–21
  in scientific material, 6:30, 6:66,
    7:135
  in text, 6:13, 7:65
  of time designations, 6:27–29
  of titles of persons, 6:10, 6:14–21
  of titles of works, 7:135
  underlining of, 7:67

Accent marks
  diacritics, 6:8
  with syllabication, 6:109
Acknowledgments
  of aid received, 7:1
  of source of fact, 3:80, 4:59–60,
    4:64
Acronyms, 6:32, 6:122
Act and scene, 7:63–64, 7:122–23
Active voice, 5:23
Acts. *See* Statutory material
A.D., B.C., 6:29, 6:123
Addresses (street), 6:25–26, 6:65,
  6:67
Adjectives
  compound, 6:93, 6:95, 6:98
  proper, 6:105
Adverbs
  with adjective or participle, 6:91
  transitional, 6:150–51, 6:160
All-, compounds with, 6:94
Alphabetizing
  in bibliographies, 5:64, 7:73
  in card catalog, 3:4
  methods of, 3:4
A.M., P.M., 6:28, 6:56
Ampersand, 6:33, 7:38
And others, 7:24, 7:81
Anonymous works, 7:21, 7:82
Antonyms, 5:38, 5:41
Apostrophe, 6:79, 6:80–84
Appositives, punctuation with, 6:45
Arabic numerals. *See also* Numbers;
    Roman numerals
  in Bible references, 7:125
  in classical references, 7:121
  in enumerations, 6:71–73, 6:187
  for footnote numbers, 5:58–59, 7:2
  for measurements, 6:66
  in outlines, 6:73
  for parts of a work, 6:48–49, 6:65,
    6:67, 7:46, 7:63

Index

Research
background information for, 2:2, 3:7
meaning of, 1:2
techniques for, 1:2–6
uses of, 1:5–6
Research paper. *See* Paper, research
Residence, place of, 6:146–47. *See also* Addresses
Reverend, 6:19
Revised editions, 3:71, 4:22, 7:32
Roman numerals, 4:29. *See also* Arabic numerals; Numbers
with family names, 6:17, 6:61
with names of rulers, 6:60
in outlines, 4:49, 4:50, 6:73
for page numbers, 6:48–49
for volume numbers, 7:46
Rough draft, 5:7–49
Round numbers, 6:34, 6:40–41
Rule, typed, above footnotes, 5:63, 6:1
Rulers, names of, 6:60
Runover lines, 5:66, 6:6

Sacred writings, 6:22, 6:164, 7:58, 7:125
Saint, with names, 6:20, 6:21
Samples
of catalog card, 3:65
of note card, 4:65
of outline, 4:47, 4:53
of research paper, pp. 167–79
Science, encyclopedia of, 3:46
Scientific material
abbreviations in, 6:30, 6:66, 7:135
capitalization with, 4:19, 7:131, 7:135
citations in text, 7:132–34
references in, 7:130–35
Scripture references, 6:22, 6:164, 7:58, 7:125
Second, in family name, 6:17
Secondary sources, citation from, p. 5n, 7:129
Semicolon
with authors' names, 4:9, 7:80
in compound sentence, 6:128, 6:158–59, 6:162
with quotation marks, 6:183
in series, 6:142
with *yet,* etc., 6:160
Senior, abbreviation of, 6:17
"Sentence" style capitalization, 7:135
Sentences

arrangement of, 5:24–26
balanced, 5:22
compound, 6:128. 6:138
periodic, 5:21
topic, 5:9–13, 5:15, 5:16–19
types of, 5:20–22
Series of words or other elements, 6:139–42. *See also* Enumerations
Series titles, 7:8, 7:34, 7:58, 7:91
Sermons, titles of, 7:56, 7:57
Shortened references, in footnotes, 7:3, 7:136–53
Short stories, 3:22, 3:24, 3:30, 7:28
Sic, 4:69, 6:136, 7:67
Slang, 5:39
So, punctuation with, 6:160
Social sciences, encyclopedia of, 3:41
Sources. *See also* Reference works
acknowledgment of, 4:59–60, 6:1
citations of, 6:172
evaluation of, 3:64–81
types of, 2:4
Spacing
between lines, 5:53
in bibliographies, 5:66
of footnotes, 5:60, 5:62
of poetry, 6:6
with punctuation marks, 5:54
of quotations, 6:3, 6:6
in typing, 5:56, 5:62, 5:66
Spanish, capitalization in, 7:60
Spelling
authorities for, 6:74
of compound words, 6:85–103
of personal names, 6:21, 6:74
plurals, 6:75–79, 6:84
possessives, 6:80–84
in quotations, 4:69
of titles of works, 7:27
Split references, 7:155–56
Statutory material, 7:113
Streets
names of, 6:25
numbers with, 6:65, 6:67
Style
mechanics of, 6:1–188
writing, 5:1–43
Subheads, placement of, 5:55
Subject headings, in card catalog, 3:56, 3:59–63
Subject indexes, 3:20, 3:21
Subtitles, punctuation with, 7:29
Suffixes, word division with, 6:117
Summary, in notetaking, 4:61–62, 4:65

254

Kate L. Turabian

A Manual for Writers

of Term Papers, Theses, and Dissertations

Fourth Edition

A companion volume to the popular *Student's Guide for Writing College Papers,* Kate L. Turabian's *Manual* continues to be the definitive handbook for the preparation of formal papers in both scientific and nonscientific fields. Covering such subjects as how to divide the text of a paper, headings and subheadings, footnotes and bibliography, quotations and tables and illustrations, the volume is designed for the use of both writers and typists; in this new edition the material has been rearranged for easier reference.

1973   216 pages
Paper   P46   ISBN: 0-226-81621-4
Also in cloth   ISBN: 0-226-81620-6

The
University of
Chicago
PRESS

Chicago 60637